THE VILLAGE VOICE
GUIDE TO
MANHATTAN'S
HOTTEST
SHOPPING
NEIGHBORHOODS
■ ■ ■

An Insider's Guide
to the Best Fashion
and the Best Deals—from
East Village Storefronts
to Soho Boutiques
to Madison Avenue Salons

With contributions by
STEPHANIE CHERNIKOWSKI · LINDA DYETT
SUSAN FLINKER · DAVID KEEPS
ELAINE LOUIE · LYNN YAEGER

ILLUSTRATED BY JOHN HOWARD

the village VOICE

Guide to Manhattan's Hottest Shopping Neighborhoods

EDITED BY MARY PEACOCK

SARAH LAZIN BOOKS

VILLAGE VOICE BOOKS

FAWCETT COLUMBINE

New York

A Fawcett Columbine Book
Published by Ballantine Books
Copyright © 1987 by Sarah Lazin Books and The Village Voice

All rights reserved under International and Pan-American Copyright
Conventions. Published in the United States by Ballantine Books, a division of
Random House, Inc., New York, and simultaneously in Canada by Random
House of Canada Limited, Toronto.

Library of Congress Catalog Card Number: 86-91063
ISBN: 0-449-90206-4
Book design by Design and Printing Productions, New York City.
Manufactured in the United States of America
First Edition: May 1987
10 9 8 7 6 5 4 3 2 1

CONTENTS

Neighborhood maps follow pages 1, 15, 39, 75, 89, 128, 148, 155, 169, 193, 215, 247, and 315

ACKNOWLEDGMENTS

MANY hands helped make this book. Sarah Lazin, David Schneiderman of the *Voice*, and Joëlle Delbourgo of Ballantine brought it to life. Mary Peacock was the soul of the book, conceptualizing it, creating it, and refining it with her nonpareil team of gifted writers/shopping mavens; and Elisa Petrini helped develop and produce it. Ed Sturmer and Kathleen Westray of Design and Printing Productions provided their usual expert art direction and manufacturing advice, and more—some generous friendly support. John Howard created wonderful maps, unfazed by a tight schedule. Stephanie Franklin typed and trafficked and capably managed a myriad of details. Janis and Carol Bultman and Dana Nadel checked hundreds of facts, prices, addresses, and hours; while Donald Suggs bravely trekked the whole of Manhattan to chart store locations. Finally, Elizabeth Williams kindly opened her files to us; Carol Edwards gave the galleys a good eye at the right time; and the staff of Get Set, especially Jim Anderson and Audrey Berman, did their best to solve problems.

Each contributor would like to acknowledge the people who gave special help, time, or inspiration:

MARY PEACOCK: My thanks to the contributors— champion shoppers, astute judges of stores, and delightful writers—and to Elisa Petrini for all her help in getting the book together.

STEPHANIE CHERNIKOWSKI: To Mom, Mary, Mack, and everyone else whose name may or may not alliterate, but who participated in cross pollination: Thanks for being there. I will, too.

LINDA DYETT: Thanks to my husband John and my son Kim for their endless patience and good humor while I flitted about the shops and for trusting me (unjustifiably) not to wield my credit card. My thanks also go to Elisa Petrini for her sensitive editing; and to John Badum, Lyn Diamond, Kathy Crawford, Gwen and Ron Pardi, Bonnie Watts-Mason, Toni Wolfe, and Ann-Sargent Wooster for advice and assistance. Finally, to my mother and to Mary Peacock, I am grateful for supplying both a sense of style and prudence.

SUSAN FLINKER: Thanks to Sarah Lazin, Mary Peacock, and Elisa Petrini for their suggestions and enthusiasm; to Michael Shore for his late-night support; and to Iris Flinker for her invaluable input throughout the entire project.

DAVID KEEPS: I would like to thank my parents, who dressed me first; Katy and Jerry who dressed me next; Hugo Boss, who dresses me best; Sheryl, Henry, and Clark who made me a garmento; and Mary Peacock who made me write about it.

ELAINE LOUIE: I appreciate the advice and aid of my editors Mary Peacock and Elisa Petrini and of my agents Virginia Barber and Mary Evans.

LYNN YAEGER: For G.G., and for my parents, who took me shopping.

■   ■   ■

INTRODUCTION

By Mary Peacock

WHY YOU NEED THIS BOOK

Pretend you have a best friend in Manhattan who loves to shop—who knows the hottest new stores, gets the best bargains, and has figured out the best places to buy everything from the latest downtown fashions to classic cotton sweaters to the most gorgeous shoes in town. This person has just agreed to tell you everything. This book is that friend.

There are so many stores in New York, and the style and price options are so endless, that we could all use some insider information. Choices run from European couturiers' outpost salons on Madison Avenue to the storefronts of the East Village couturiers, who sew in the back and sell in the front. There are more fashion discounters, vintage clothing purveyors, one-of-a-kind artists, classic work clothes emporia—and every other clothing specialty under the sun—in

Manhattan than any other hunk of real estate on earth. There are guides to the discount outlets and to the most expensive shops, and guides that aim for exhaustive listings. *This* book, written by regular contributors to the *Village Voice*'s "Getting & Spending" shopping column, is a selective and opinionated guide to our favorite clothing and accessory shops—the most useful, the most fun, the most fashionable, and the most fairly priced. Chic with a bargain sense, and a sense of humor. Chic ranging from a little classic to a little crazy, something for everyone with a sense of style who isn't either concretely conservative or terminally trendy.

We define *chic* as personal style. Think about it: Who can remember you for your sense of style if it changes with every fad? And a few separates in your favorite colors and cuts combine into a lot more outfits than a closetful of unrelated items. Your personal style is the thread that should guide you through this book, and through the increasingly complex melodrama of New York shopping choices.

UNDERSTANDING SHOPPING

Shopping might seem simple: You spend, you get, you wear. But no. It is a tricky business because clothes are like high-class sandwich boards. We walk around advertising ourselves with what's on our backs. Just think about the popularity of fashion magazine makeovers—shopping for clothes can be a process of self-transformation that's no more expensive than therapy, but quicker.

Shopping is a necessity. Clothes not only have personalities, they have lifespans, as anyone starting the fall season with a drawer full of dead sweaters knows. But remember that you have to actually *wear* your clothes for hours on end. Even when you see the outfit you've been waiting for all your life, do not leave the dressing room before determining whether you can breathe, sit, eat a full dinner, descend a staircase, and withstand a gust of wind while wearing these clothes. Does this item call for underwear that pinches or high heels that would make your back ache? Is it one inch longer than your coat? Does it itch?

Shopping is, of course, fun, except for paying the bill. The problem of how much you should spend on a given garment may be clarified by considering how many times you are likely to wear it. Then you will see that $160 for a pair of perfectly cut plain black pants that you will wear to death is much cheaper than $60 for an on-sale trendy cocktail dress that you won't be able to stand the sight of after three outings.

Shopping can also be a comfort. Some days, it's the only thing standing between you and suicide. (If you kill yourself, no one will see you in your beautiful new jacket.) But you should shop seriously only when in a relatively good mood. Then you will have the confidence to resist improper purchases. If you're miserable and desperate for a treat, go to the nearest dimestore. Buy underpants. Buy stupid colors of nailpolish. Do not decide that this is the moment to spend your winter coat money on a lace evening dress, because when you realize that you have no place to wear it you will feel even worse.

Shopping can sometimes pass from the realm of diversion to the grip of compulsion. (Those of you who should be shipped off to Shoppers Anonymous, you know who you are.) But anyone can get obsessed with finding the perfect outfit to wear to a special event. Probably the largest number of things in closets that will never be worn again were bought at the last minute before some occasion. Don't panic. With sufficient aplomb, you can carry off wearing almost anything anywhere.

Shopping is a great common denominator. If you ask, "Where did you get that X?" most people will be glad to answer, in detail. The fact that shopping can establish a friendly basis of communication does not, however, make it a suitable activity for couples. You will be aghast at the unsuitable things your lover thinks you should try on, and immediately conclude that this person is obviously confusing your taste with that of a former paramour, upon whom he or she is clearly still fixated. It is a great idea, though, to take along a friend whose taste you admire. She or he can provide the objective view you might want when you're agonizing over a major purchase.

SHOPPING IN NEW YORK

Since New York is the shopping capital of the world, going shopping here ranks as entertainment, like going to the movies or the theater. There is not only a greater choice of styles available all at the same time than ever before, and at such a wide price range (the latest fashions are knocked off like lightning), but the nature of retailing in New York has changed. The great department stores are no longer your landmarks. Though good ones remain, many have closed or shrunk or lost their status as fashion leaders. The days of one-stop shopping are over, unless you want to abandon all hope and enter one of the nation's mega-malls. The biggest and best variety of midpriced clothing in New York now is scattered among increasing numbers of little shops. This is also an era of specialization: You'd be amazed at the number of stores in Manhattan devoted solely to men's underwear. And more and more of these new stores are not in the traditional midtown locations, but grouped together in residential neighborhoods all over the city. This is both the bad news—it sounds exhausting—and the good news. New York is a city of varied and colorful neighborhoods, and a city to walk in (plenty of street life, no hills to speak of). A lot of the fun of shopping in New York, especially for the nonresident, is in investigating the unique sensibility, architecture, restaurants, and street action of its different neighborhoods.

HOW TO USE THIS BOOK

Each chapter of this guide is an exploration of one of Manhattan's important shopping neighborhoods. There's an introduction to the area to give you a bit of its history, current ambiance, and shopping character, plus a few suggestions on where to eat (you must keep up your strength).

Maps in each chapter locate the stores reviewed so you can plan an educated wander through the neighborhood, picking up not only on our choices but on all the others in between. (If your favorite place isn't listed, well, we've probably missed a few gems, or their owners did not want to be included. And because of the book's organizational plan, we've skipped some stores that are geographically isolated.)

If you're looking for something specific, stores are indexed by category—women's shoes, vintage, children's clothing, jewelry, hats, discount, etc.—as well as by name.

You'll see that each writer has a personal viewpoint, but all have tried to evoke the spirit and essence (and price range) of the shops; specific items are described to give you a clear idea of the store's merchandise, but please remember that the time span between reporting and book publication means that you will *not* be seeing the exact same stock. This time gap also makes it inevitable that a few of the listed stores will have closed, especially on the rapidly gentrifying side streets of the East Village and Soho, where the real estate market is volatile, to say the least. But happily, new stores will have sprung up, and you'll have fun finding someplace new and special before the crowd.

■　　　■　　　■

THE VILLAGE VOICE
GUIDE TO
MANHATTAN'S
HOTTEST
SHOPPING
NEIGHBORHOODS

■ ■ ■

THE CENTRAL VILLAGE

INTRODUCTION BY
Stephanie Chernikowski

In 1916, artists John Sloan and Marcel Duchamp climbed to the top of the Washington Square Arch, armed with cap pistols and libations, to declare Greenwich Village a "Free Republic, Independent of Uptown." A statement of the obvious, it was a grand gesture, nonetheless. In the war between the north and south, or "uptown" and "downtown" as they are called in Manhattan, the Village has always been the American home of *la vie de Boheme*, with Washington Square Park the heart. Those who see it as an inferno of commies, beatniks, artistes, free-lovers, hippies, punks, junkies, intellectuals, and other ne'er-do-wells might deem another anatomical region a more apt metaphor, but it is the geographical center.

Be advised that the park is not for the frail of heart, no longer the study in elegance Henry James depicted, and considerably more chaotic than it appears in André Kertész's photos, shot from his window up above until his death in 1985. A typical

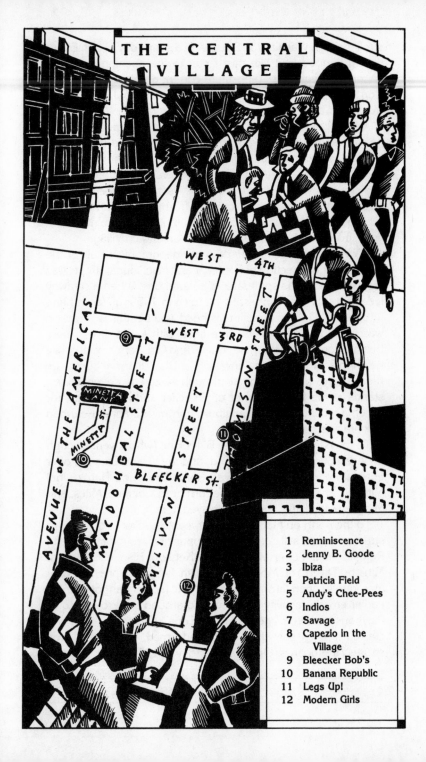

THE CENTRAL VILLAGE

1 Reminiscence
2 Jenny B. Goode
3 Ibiza
4 Patricia Field
5 Andy's Chee-Pees
6 Indios
7 Savage
8 Capezio in the
  Village
9 Bleecker Bob's
10 Banana Republic
11 Legs Up!
12 Modern Girls

stroll through Washington Square on a sunny day might, if your timing is good, run like this: Enter to the opening strains of "Absolute Beginners" (substitute current omnipresent pop hit) from blaster number one. Pause to hear an old coot with a guitar and amplifier crooning "Red River Valley." With the whir of wheels, a skateboard, semipro aboard, flies past you to a hard-core thrash coming from blaster number two. Move on to live steel drums crossed with reggae from blaster number three, carried by a dreamy-eyed man who offers in languorous drawl to sell you "smoke." Pass a trio of folkies trying to keep a tempo other than the dance beat coming from blaster number four. Exit to the closing strains of the guarantee, "I absolutely love you," from number five. Welcome to Greenwich Village.

If Washington Square Park is the geographical hub of the Village, the intersection of Bleecker and MacDougal streets was for many years the spiritual and cultural one. When a scrawny kid from Hibbing, Minnesota, hit town in 1959, guitar in hand and Woody Guthrie tunes in his head, you bet this is where he was heading. The streets were lined with low-lit dives where beatnik poets Kerouac, Ferlinghetti, and Ginsberg howled while neighbors lamented the invasion of the dharma bums. Le Figaro, one of the original (though restored) coffeehouses, stands at the famed corner of Bleecker and MacDougal, for which a recent compilation album commemorating the urban folk era was named.

To the east on Bleecker, the Bitter End (which went through an incarnation as the Other End) and the Village Gate still offer entertainment. From Dave van Ronk, Emmylou Harris, Joni Mitchell, and Neil Young at the former to Coltrane, Miles, and Mingus at the latter, they've all played here.

To the north on MacDougal between Bleecker and West 3rd streets, you can still get the best cappuccino around at the Caffe Reggio, have a beer at the murky Kettle of Fish, eat Italian at Minetta Tavern or Monte's, or shish kebab in pita bread at Mamoun's (open till 5 A.M.)—all historic hipster hangouts. In an earlier era, the activity was centered around the Provincetown Playhouse, where Eugene O'Neill, Edna St. Vincent Millay, and e.e. cummings saw their plays performed, and Bette Davis strutted the boards. On a winter's day in 1976, you could see

Patti Smith carrying her laundry down the block. Could she have been heading to Dylan's, where they could noodle around while they washed?

Clothes clean, Patti would wind up an evening at the Bottom Line, 15 West 4th at Mercer, where she would join Andy Warhol and Mick Jagger to hear Dolly Parton silence urbane slickers with an a cappella tearjerker about a dying orphan with a scruffy puppy. Lurking about in the shadows up at Fifth Avenue and 13th Street, Mick's bandmate was collecting honky-tonk tunes to keep him keening through his wasted nights in Toronto (please release them, Keith). There at the Lone Star Cafe Merle showed, and Willie once played all night for free. Meanwhile, back at Electric Ladyland at 52 West 8th Street, the psychedel-icized recording studio Jimi built, Doug Sahm was laying down a hell of a spell.

MacDougal Alley, the lovely little mews just below 8th Street, was the site of a studio opened by Gertrude Vanderbilt Whitney in 1908 with a showing of eight artists who were to become known as the "ashcan school" because their city grittiness offended the polite academic art establishment. From these boho beginnings would evolve the collection of the Whitney Museum. In the 1950s, notoriously physical in the controversies they generated, abstract expressionist artists Pollock, de Kooning, Rothko, Motherwell, Kline, and the guys, drawn to the area by cheap rents, would booze and brawl at their neighborhood bar, the Cedar Tavern at 82 University Place. It's still a good place for a burger and a beer.

The war between respectability and the underground has moved east, but traces of the Village's former beatnik glory still fight to survive, particularly in the face of New York University's expansion and increasing rents. At the vanguard of the struggle is Judson Memorial Baptist Church (campanile by Stanford White, who also designed the arch it faces, and stained glass by John La Farge), a nonsectarian center for experimental arts and lefty politics at 55 Washington Square South. As in so many places in the Village, everyone except George Washington slept here. Or married or showed or sang or danced. Among others, Lucinda Childs and Trisha Brown began as Judson dancers.

From its history as a breeding ground for the arts and as

home of NYU, you are safe in assuming that you'll find a more freewheeling spirit down here in the Village than you would at Brooks Brothers. Patricia Field offers originals that will inspire next year's ready-to-wear, which is discounted down the block at Bolton's. Both are on 8th Street, which is rapidly being revived into a strip of specialty shops: crisp Benetton (10 Fifth Avenue), trendy Urban Outfitters (20 University Place), Skin (55 East 8th Street) with its high-styled leathers. New stores seem to mushroom up daily. While the tendency is increasingly off-the-rack and middle-of-the-road, diehard individualists and disenfranchised youth can still find some great gear.

A spin through the Village might begin at Reminiscence at 74 Fifth Avenue just below 14th Street, head down University Place to 8th Street, west on 8th to MacDougal, down MacDougal to Bleecker, and east across Bleecker, with side street excursions along the way. Should food, shelter, and entertainment be added to your need to clothe, consider the following.

The 3rd Street Bazaar at number 125, near Avenue of the Americas, has good, cheap, basic home furnishings and accoutrements: tables, chairs, lamps, tablewear, filing cabinets. For expensive, sleek, and unique modern designs in furniture try Oops, 528 La Guardia Place, especially for memorable tables. Just down the street at 496 La Guardia is Jamie Canvas, an art supply store turned toy box. For film and camera supplies use Ben Ness, 114 University Place (next door to some of the best pizza in town), and Spectra at 510 La Guardia, just below Bleecker. B. Dalton, 396 Avenue of the Americas at 8th Street, has a good selection of books and a helpful information desk.

Should you find yourself in need of respite from the intense and chaotic street life, 1/5, at 1 Fifth Avenue, is elegant and atmospheric, but not cheap. Have a drink at the Deco bar, formerly the fittings of a luxury liner, or stay for a meal. In the dining room that looks out on Washington Mews, the light is lovely at lunch.

To reach the Central Village by subway: Take the IND B or F train to 14th Street; the BMT LL, N, R or the IRT 4, 5, 6 to Union Square. By bus: Take the M2, M3, M5 down Fifth Avenue to 14th Street; or the M14 crosstown to Fifth Avenue.

■   ■   ■

REMINISCENCE

REMINISCENCE is one-stop shopping for the young and hip who have more important things to do with their money than wear it. As the name implies, it specializes in modish 1950s repros and vintage items for men and women. Begun in 1975 by Stewart Richer, the shop started small, featuring army overalls dyed decadent pastels. From these humble beginnings on MacDougal Street, it has developed a line of nationally distributed casual wear that was described by one employee as "retro before it was called that."

Here, the floppy men's slacks in rayons, linens, and iridescents average $38 to $48 and are bebop cool enough for the youthful Elvis Presley. Rayon cowboy shirts at $26 are classic enough for Hank Williams and even available in black—the search has ended! Likewise, Reminiscence produces that rare Hawaiian shirt that does justice to the original. T-shirts begin at $8. Vintage trenchcoats and rayon robes are $28 to $38. For women, there are remakes, too—nice straight skirts with kick pleats or bustles—and rows of vintage party frocks and blouses.

No need to go elsewhere for accessories. Jewelry runs from $2 for fun stuff to $200 for antiques and local artisans' one-of-a-kind pieces, with some real gems around $50. From socks to shades, you can wardrobe yourself here for not much over $100 if you try. Even though most items are selling at their wholesale prices, Reminiscence does have semiannual sales. — S.C.

Reminiscence, 74 Fifth Avenue, 243-2292. Open Monday to Saturday, noon to 8 P.M.; Sunday, 1 P.M. to 6 P.M. AE, MC, V, checks.

JENNY B. GOODE
11 East 10th Street, 505-7666. See index for main listing.

IBIZA

Y O U are in Stevie Nicks country here. Ibiza is a luxurious little island retreat for women whose tastes run toward magical and mysterious feminine finery in florals and lace; whose notions of "classic" lean more toward neat little antique-styled rayon dresses and separates than toward Chanel; who don't feel that what you buy this month should be replaced the next by some new trend. Ibiza is pricier than most of the downtown dens, and co-owner John Husiak points out that its exclusive top-of-the-line clothing is imported from the island of the same name. Often running up to $250 per item, it never goes on sale. But unlike its antique counterparts, it will not disintegrate on first wearing.

Ibiza manages to walk the line between timeless and contemporary. More practical seasonal items include oversized cotton sweaters priced around $40, and circle skirts, slacks, and tops that often push $100. These are sometimes marked down.

Don't miss the jewelry at Ibiza, most of which is by such contemporary artisans as Richard Minadeo (jewelry's answer to Antonio Gaudi) and Gaetano Fazio. It is frequently more visionary than what sells as art a few block south. Prices from $24 to $550.

Ibiza has opened a tiny annex two doors south, Ibiza Home, where antique curtains and fabrics (again, lots of lace and florals) are available, some made into pillows and hatboxes.   — S.C.

Ibiza, 46 University Place, 533-4614. Open Monday to Saturday, 11:30 A.M. to 8 P.M.; Sunday, 12:30 P.M. to 6 P.M. AE, MC, V, checks.

PATRICIA FIELD

PATRICIA Field runs her shop rather the way Robert Altman runs a film set: Get a bunch of gifted people together and improvise. She will deny being its guiding light. Blending art, fashion, music, and politics, she describes her store as an "open forum" for associates to collaborate in creating one environment where customers may come "just for the experience." It comes off.

One Saturday in spring the shop is jammed with people. In the window are skateboards and surfing clothes being sold as streetwear. "What's that?" one customer asks. "A bicycle seat," someone behind a counter answers, "but I don't work here." A woman is having her makeup done at the cosmetic counter, which sells exclusive French, British, and German imports. A second woman is rummaging through the $5 sale baskets, while a third is trying on a $1,500 Andre Walker evening dress. Kinky rubber surfwear from California hangs on one rack; elegant little wool or gabardine separates by the East Village design house Ganzo are opposite. So are Pilar Limosners and Carmel Johnsons, works from two of the best downtown pop couturiers. Patricia, her formerly black hair and eyebrows flaming scarlet today, is helping coordinate jewelry, hosiery, gloves, and diaphanous robes into a shoot for *Playboy.* This place is varied and unpredictable.

Theme and stock change regularly: Field's "Dump Reagan" campaign got her advertising banned from *Vogue,* and her antiapartheid window featured a mural by graffiti artist Keith Haring, whose T-shirts are sold in the rear. Having opened her first store in 1966, and in her present location since 1972, Patricia Field sets the pace for downtown inventiveness and provides an outlet for young talent. Don't miss this place.

— S.C.

Patricia Field, 10 East 8th Street, 254-1699. Open daily, noon to 8 P.M. AE, MC, V, checks.

ANDY'S CHEE-PEES

16 West 8th Street, 460-8488. See index for main listing.

INDIOS

26 West 8th Street, 505-6065. See index for main listing.

SAVAGE

59 West 8th Street, 473-8171. See index for main listing.

CAPEZIO
IN THE VILLAGE

S O M E people are more comfortable shopping with the tuneful chiming of early R.E.M. played at a moderate volume than with a loud disco thumpthumppounding. A nice soft jazz oxford will do for a shoe. "Current" appeals to them more than "flashy"—not everyone dresses to be stared at. They shop at Capezio. Okay, it's a franchise. This branch is intelligently stocked with casuals for men and women who have an eye for a good fabric and cut. Its specialty is still shoes and dancewear.

The shoes here will appeal to men and women who still let their feet do the walking. Simple little house-brand skimmers and pumps for the girls, Keds, espadrilles, and rubber-soled jazz oxfords are priced from $12 to around $50. Pricier Jan Jansen's high-style designs from Amsterdam put women in sturdy if eccentric oxfords, and men in sleek, pointy slippers ($110 to $120). Check out the dance shoes, many of which have been soled for the street. If you can dance in it, you can sure walk in it. Some of the dance clothing is street-wearable as well: jersey skirts, warm-up sweaters and jackets, leg and ankle warmers. A markdown rack starts at $5.

MacDougal Alley is a department featuring a house line of inexpensive sportswear in cotton knits, $12 to $28. Better womenswear is on the ground floor. Upstairs, the men's department shines if you like beautifully textured fabrics. Moderately priced with ongoing sales. A wide range of accessories for men and women includes sunglasses, jewelry, bags, and hats.

— S.C.

Capezio in the Village, 177 MacDougal Street, 477-5643. Open Monday to Friday, noon to 8 P.M.; Saturday, 11:30 A.M. to 8 P.M.; Sunday, 1 P.M. to 6 P.M. AE, MC, V, checks.
   Other branches: Capezio Dance-Theatre Shop (featuring dance wear and shoes only), 755 Seventh Avenue, 245-2130. Open daily, 9:30 A.M. to 5 P.M.; Thursday till 7:30 P.M.

BLEECKER BOB'S

B L E E C K E R Bob's, actually a record store famous for its rare and imported records, houses in its rear two little clothing outlets: Hot Clothing, featuring rare and imported T-shirts, and 'Amma, which specializes in military clothing and accessories, also often rare and imported.

Hot Clothing's T-shirts, mostly from England, are underground artifacts for the antisocial. Silk-screened with your fave punk, new-wave, and hard-core heroes from the Cramps to Ian Curtis to the Meatmen to the Replacements, this joint caters to a specialized taste, but within that taste offers the most innovative merchandise available. The best stuff is done by a line called Artistique et Sentimental. The designer wishes to remain anonymous, but deserves better for his (her?) striking designs and intense colors. Prices are $10 to $20, with a $5 sale bin (for idols fallen from favor?). Punk amulet jewelry—crosses abound— is $4 to $40.

'Amma is similarly specialized, carrying men's and women's military wear at army surplus prices—$1 for ribbons to $100 for leathers and flight suits. You can pick up a pair of slacks for around $15. Some wares are domestics, lots are imported from Europe and Canada, and all are drabs, camouflage, or black-dyed. Styles are hip and prices cool.   — S.C.

Bleecker Bob's, 118 West 3rd Street, 475-9017. Open daily, noon to 1 A.M.; Friday and Saturday till 3 A.M.

BANANA REPUBLIC

S U B T L E T Y is requisite in the stalking of prey, whether the jungle in question is tropical or concrete. Clothing must blend into the environment or, like a loud noise or sudden movement, it will alert the game and scare it away. Banana Republic may describe its wares as clothing for travel and safari, but you should interpret it loosely and hit the streets in them, too. For men and women, fabrics are real, styles traditional, and stock international. Clothing is "travel tested" and should last for years. Colors will match your pet ocelot, not outshine it.

Do not be put off by the hordes of pale people who flock to this atmospheric outpost on weekends. The venerable beat poet Lawrence Ferlinghetti not only endorses but rhapsodizes over the hairsheep leather "On The Road" jacket, $239 (see the catalogue—many items are tested by world-traveling writers). An all-night flight suit is made of comfy cotton fleece ($56) and is chic enough for border crossings. Good T-shirts and rafters of hats are priced from $10 to considerably more. Bogie-style trenchcoats and a wonderful assortment of durable duffels and other bags are made for those whose sense of style comes more from old flicks than from fashion rags.

If your hands are full carrying that leg of lamb home to Elsa, take a catalogue and order by phone or mail.   — S.C.

Banana Republic, 205 Bleecker Street, 473-9570. Open Monday to Saturday, 10 A.M. to 9 P.M.; Sunday, noon to 6 P.M. AE, MC, V, checks.

Other branches: 2376 Broadway, 874-3500. Open Sunday till 5 P.M. 130 East 59th Street, 751-5570. Open the same hours. Pier 17 Pavilion, South Street Seaport, 732-3090. Open Sunday till 7 P.M.

LEGS UP!

L E G S Up! clothing is painless to wear—no corsets, no bras, no waist cinchers. Maybe no shoes—depends on where you are going. Dresses are simple oversized flounced shifts, with or without sleeves, with or without belting sashes (waist where and if you will), in natural fabrics. The chef d'oeuvre is the crumpled silk. Flowing and romantic, it seems to need nothing more than a strong wind as an accessory. Wash it. No ironing necessary.

These dresses, along with the similarly simple separates, are designed by co-owner Fia Cappello, whom you can usually find behind the counter. While, strictly speaking, this is womenswear, if you've seen a Tina Turner video or live performance, you've probably seen Fia's husband, Timmy, the Conan look-alike on sax and keyboards, wearing her pants . . . literally. Since he is usually shirtless, you will have to go to the store to see the tops. Between the cottons and the silks, this stuff will go anywhere, from a walk on the beach to dinner at the Rainbow Room. Top it all off with a coarse-textured cape to keep the chill away.

Dresses are about $45 for cotton, $89 for silk. Tops $10 to $35. Oversized pants $35 to $60. Capes $110.   — S.C.

Legs Up!, 215 Thompson Street, 254-7315. Open Tuesday to Sunday, 1 P.M. to 8 P.M. AE, checks.

MODERN GIRLS

M O D E R N Girls, like so many of the downtown boutiques, is a tiny storefront enterprise. It is owned and operated by young designers Susan Balcunas and Dana Fraiser. On a Sunday afternoon one can wander in to find Susan sitting on the floor stamping paper bags with their logo, wearing one of their peace symbol T-shirts and "love" earrings while a customer browses through their next wave postcards, many created by Dana's husband, Tom. Costume clothing and jewelry, mostly for modern girls (with some for guys) changes regularly and radically. One season it's fuzzy stuffed-animal fake-fur coats in day-glow colors, the next it's slinky, stretchy, and sexy basic black tube dresses with padded bra tops. In the spirit of her garb, Susan comments on store organization, "We all kinda do our own thing."

That "thing" also includes carrying other locals' wares. Today there is a wall of bolo ties, the most striking of which is a bejeweled scorpion that goes for the throat—just to make sure you don't get too blissed out staring into the eyes of the bright yellow vinyl happy-face purses.

Postcards are 50¢, and jewelry is $10 to $30. Clothing starts at $5 in the sale basket; T-shirts are $14 to $22, dresses $35 to $90.

— S.C.

Modern Girls, 169 Thompson Street, 533-1022. Open Tuesday to Sunday, 1:30 A.M. to 7 P.M.; Saturday till 8 P.M. AE.

THE WEST VILLAGE

INTRODUCTION BY
David Keeps

It's a place to have brunch, to cruise, to find that special record, book, movie, or play, and to wander hopelessly lost through winding streets that criss and cross, changing names, numbers, and directions as they go. It's the melting pot of 1970s gay liberation culture and what's left of the beatniks, folkies, and hippies, with just a splash of yuppieism. It's the West Village, a bohemian paradise lost to staggering rents and hordes of late-night and weekend tourists.

Trendsetters may flit from theme restaurants to concept clubs in Soho and the East Village, but everyone can party around what New Yorkers refer to as Sheridan Square, the locus of West Village life at the intersection of Seventh Avenue South and Washington, Waverly, Christopher, Grove, and West 4th streets. (Practically no one knows that the tiny park there with its statue of General Sheridan is actually named Christopher Park, and that the real "Sheridan Square" is a concrete triangle

THE WEST VILLAGE

1   Peanutbutter & Jane
2   Panache
3   Army Navy Stores
4   Chameleon
5   Agiba
6   Indios
7   The Loft
8   Dorothy's Closet
9   L'Uomo
10 La Provence de Pierre Deux
11 Constantine & Knight

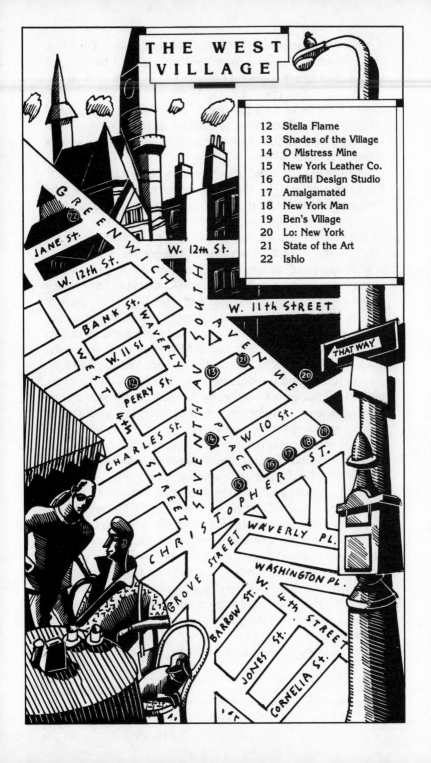

a couple of blocks farther south.) This is the site of the Gay Pride parade that trucks down the boutique- and bar-studded Christopher Street, drawing fun-lovers of all ages and ethnic, sexual, and fashion persuasions. All cultures and colors—from campy queens and leathermen to suburbanites and streetsy Jersey kids who flock in to see cult movies at the Waverly Twin Theatre's and Eighth Street Playhouse's late shows—mix relatively peaceably here.

The Village spirit is laid back, with a fashion outlook to match. It's jeans territory—be they corduroy scruffy and collegiate, designer and down-for-the-day, or skin-tight and sexual—with no compelling motive to come any other way than as you are. Sportswear is the unofficial uniform, and most shops cater to a young, slightly trendy unisex market; the gay influence ensures a wide range of denim, leather, and workout wear. Indian merchants on Greenwich Avenue and Christopher Street stock popular designs by Matinique and Ton Sur Ton, often at substantial savings. Vintage and ethnic clothing abounds, and the most notable shops (those selected here) serve as outlets for private-label goods and one-of-a-kinds by local designers, bucking the trend of weekend chic with imaginative variations on sportswear and the classically elegant. Prices, in the main, tend to be moderate to expensive, but since many stores carry the same lines of merchandise, brand-name buyers should comparison-shop for the best values.

The West Village is comprised of bustling commercial strips (Christopher and Hudson streets, Greenwich Avenue, Avenue of the Americas, and Seventh Avenue South) and quiet residential blocks lined with trees and beautifully tended brownstones. Gentrification has not ravaged the area architecturally; tall luxury apartment buildings are largely prewar beauties; there are splendid examples of Federal period row houses, and many shops maintain their original tin ceilings. Unlike plasticized Columbus Avenue, most storefronts and local merchants hold on to an almost quaint village individuality, and each street—from the antique row on Hudson to Bleecker Street's line of record stores and bakeries—has an ambience of its own.

This diversity appeals to the Villager, who can by no other

means be classed as typical. Long regarded as the intellectual and artistic enclave of the East Coast, the Village endows its residents with the geographical privilege of peculiarity. No matter who they are—an Italian immigrant living above an espresso house, a preppy stockbroker who digs the location and the restaurants, or a dignified matron living in a splendid parlored duplex near the Hudson River—their life-styles have a place in the West Village. It is a community, more than just a neighborhood, with a rhythm all its own.

It wasn't always so, of course. In the 1630s, the Dutch governor, Van Twiller, planted a large tobacco farm in the wilds above the original Wall Street settlements, building a home at the foot of the present Charlton Street. Wealthy landowners followed his lead, mainly driven north by a series of smallpox and yellow fever epidemics. In 1822, the worst outbreak displaced even the businesses of Wall Street, who settled temporarily on what is still called Bank Street. By the turn of the century, the middle-class residents of what was once called New York's American Ward were outnumbered by a wave of black, Italian, and Irish immigrants. Slowly the affordable rents and bonhomie began to attract struggling artists—among them future literary giants like Poe, Walt Whitman, Mark Twain, and Henry James—who made homes in the Village. Coffeehouses, places to discuss art, politics, and philosophy until the wee hours, sprang up. Theater made radical turns in the Village with the formation of the Provincetown Players (including Eugene O'Neill and Edna St. Vincent Millay) and Eve La Gallienne's Civic Repertory Theatre on West 14th Street.

Today the artistic tradition continues, albeit in a more commercialized atmosphere. The West Village is home to such groundbreaking Off-Broadway theaters as Circle Repertory and the Ridiculous Theatrical Company, the highly recommended troupe of America's premier farceur, Charles Ludlam. Music lovers flock to clubs like the Village Vanguard, one of the most celebrated jazz rooms in the world, and cabaret/piano bars like The Duplex, where Joan Rivers and Dick Cavett began their careers. Record buyers have their choice of such specialist stores as the Record Runner (new wave and imports) at 5 Cornelia Street; Vinyl Mania (disco) at 52 Carmine; and Golden

Disc (oldies and jazz) at 239 Bleecker. Bibliophiles can browse at a host of newsstands, magazine stores, and book shops, including Foul Play at 20 Eighth Avenue for murder mysteries and the Science Fiction Shop up the street at number 56. Antiques fanciers can prowl through an assortment of Victoriana, classic Americana and Art Deco at numerous stores, as well as the fabulous clutter of Atomic Age kitsch at Beige, 119 Greenwich Avenue, a personal favorite.

The West Village is an afternoons-and-weekends shopping experience, one that should be planned for with a good pair of walking shoes and a street map or the willingness to ask strangers for directions. Most stores are open from noon until eight o'clock (later in summer), with shorter hours on Sunday (usually 1 P.M. to 6 P.M.). There's no single perfect route, but here's one suggestion for a Sunday stroll. You might begin with brunch at The Cottonwood Cafe (415 Bleecker between Bank and West 11th), famed for its hearty Texas cuisine (as well as long lines, made bearable by killer Bloody Marys and frozen margaritas). Circle down Hudson Street to Grove and then head back up Bleecker to Perry and Seventh Avenue South. Take a breather at one of the glass-front and outdoor cafés to the north and south on Seventh Avenue, then weave through Christopher to wind up at the top of Greenwich Avenue. Or you can start at the other end, with espresso and pastry or a light salad and sandwich on crunchy Italian bread at Caffe Lucca (Bleecker and Sixth Avenue) and wend your way northward. But above all, be spontaneous—after all, this is the Village!

To reach the West Village by subway: Take the IND A, B, C, D, E, F, or K to West Fourth Street (A, C, E, or K to 14th Street if you are planning brunch at The Cottonwood Cafe); or the IRT 1 to Christopher Street/Sheridan Square. By bus: Take the M10 south on Seventh Avenue or the M13 crosstown to Sheridan Square; or the M6 north on Sixth Avenue to Bleecker.

■   ■   ■

PEANUTBUTTER & JANE

YOU'VE come a long way, baby! No longer must you contend with icky synthetic rompers in infantile pastels. And if you like the swinging styles at this comfortably crowded browse-house, you can find fashions and toys that will fit you until you hit your teens!

Peanutbutter & Jane carries "high-tech sportswear for high-energy kids" from newborn to size 14 (with some groovy message T-shirts for mom and pop, too) specializing in one-of-a-kind cotton designs from around the world. French and Italian designers like Petit Boy, Scubidu, Enfantillage, and Chicco offer hip variations of current fashion trends in a price range of $13 to $26 for camp shirts and $20 to $45 for unisex pants. Sweaters include hand-loomed cotton checkerboard pastels ($46) and locally produced hand-knits for up to $100. Winter warmups come from major domestic suppliers like OshKosh, with snowpants and snowsuits running from $35 to $110. On the wackier side, there are two-piece bathing suits with two Oreos for a bra and a cotton jersey one-piece zip tuxedo romper complete with tails ($34), a PB & J exclusive.

Fabulous shoes, from under-$10 jellies to $25 leopard sandals and cowboy boots to $38 multi-patterned high top sneakers, await trendy tootsies. Charm jewelry—including globe bead necklaces and gummi bear earrings—exudes just that. On a less whimsical note, there's a full stock of Snuglis, diaper bags, babysitter chairs, bassinettes, crib sheets, receiving blankets, quilts, and knockout Babar the Elephant comforters and robot sleeping bags (to $110).

Major sales are held here in January and July, with 20% to 50% markdowns. — D.K.

Peanutbutter & Jane, 617 Hudson Street, 620-7952. Open Monday to Saturday, 11 A.M. to 7:30 P.M.; Sunday, noon to 6 P.M. AE, MC, V, checks.

PANACHE

VISITORS to Hudson Street's row of excellent antique stores shouldn't overlook this jewel box of fine vintage clothing, located just up the block from the famed Statue of Liberty gallery. Here you'll find the kind of 1940s cocktail dresses and full-length gowns that would do a screen goddess proud, an impeccable choice of silk lingerie and rayon and satin dressing gowns that could easily double as eveningwear, and a respectable selection of classic menswear.

And, if they're not in nearly perfect shape, they'll probably be on the year-round sale rack. "I'm very, very fussy about condition," owner Ann Saposnick declares. "I want it to be like a new piece of clothing, so you don't put it on and it self-destructs in a restaurant." For this you'll pay $65 to $265 for evening gowns (maybe a worth-every-penny $200 for a cascading silk velvet torch singer dress) and somewhere between $35 and $135 for a seasonless stock of beaded sweaters, most from the pre-Kennedy era. Men can drop from $38 for a basic gabardine shirt to $45 to $150 for an authentic rayon Hawaiian shirt, and choose from swanky Deco brocade and Beacon brand blanket robes in the hundred bucks neighborhood. In winter there are impressive hand-knit, letter, and reindeer sweaters, as well as ever-popular tweed overcoats, for $50 and up.

Panache sells stylish silk and rayon scarves all year, along with hats, beaded evening bags, and Bakelite and celluloid jewelry. Also notable is a collection of World War II drapery fabrics, chenille bedspreads, and handmade patchwork quilts.

— D.K.

Panache, 525 Hudson Street, 242-5115. Open daily, noon to 7 P.M. AE, MC, V.

ARMY NAVY STORES
328 Bleecker, 242-6665. See index for main listing.

CHAMELEON

S O M E things never change with this Chameleon. They're always well stocked with 1940s, 1950s, and 1960s clothing (a whole lot of which seems to be on sale at any given moment), including classics like authentic rayon Hawaiian shirts ($45 and up), tweedy-to-cashmere overcoats (from $10 to $125), and a large collection of World War II flight jackets ($125 and up). Then there are constant discoveries like French shirting cotton nightshirts ($15 to $55); wonderfully muted blue, gray, and brown men's kimonos from Japan ($20 to $40); wool-lined leather Dutch motorcycle-cop overalls ($125); and worn and unworn shoes for men (1920s and 1930s, $55 and up) and for women (1940s, $19 and up).

Wool sweaters run an incredible $19 to $30, and there's always a fine selection of silk ties for under ten bucks. Women can get terribly nostalgic with smart little suits, tailored wool coats, and floral bubble gowns from an array of dresses in a

$45-to-$150 price scale. The selection is quite large (and generally unsullied) without being overwhelming, laid out as it is under green-glass shaded hanging lamps, amid displays that were once part of steamer trunks.

In addition, Chameleon produces tie-dyed white dinner jackets ($49) and jean jackets with fake-fur appliqué inserts ($45) exclusively for the store. Jewelry, apart from the usual tie and cuff paraphernalia, takes a decided ethnic twist, with hand-painted Indonesian and Bali shell earrings and beautifully rococo ear bobs made from antique Czechoslovakian glass in reproduction settings.

— D.K.

Chameleon, 270 Bleecker Street, 924-8574. Open Monday to Friday, noon to 8 P.M.; Saturday and Sunday, 11 A.M. to 11 P.M. MC, V, checks.

AGIBA

A G I B A means "something strange or miraculous" in Arabic, and here it definitely means both. Painted palm trees adorn the wall and an Egyptian good-luck eye symbol hangs above the arched entry to the dressing room. Agiba is a showcase for very individual couturiers, most notably owner Katrina Vrebalovich, who paints silks and rayons, sews her own designs, and willingly takes her friends' creations on consignment.

Typical one-of-a-kinds might include bustiers and matching skirts in embossed leather or lamé (up to $375) and hand-painted T-shirt dresses ($50) that can pair with billowing silk harem pants in neon colors, one of the few staple items at $75. Kilsy, a designer for Albert Nipon, provides architectural variations on the pillbox hat and giant brocade tams (around $32) in a mélange of fabrics, some with holes in the top for ventilation or creative coifing. A pal named Tina paints beautiful silk scarves (around $60) and evening bags ($40), and even Katrina's mom, a painter living in Egypt, gets in on the act with wild and woolly bulky multifiber and multistitch hand-knit sweaters (from $400).

Agiba's jewelry emphasizes the North African connection, with heavy nickel-silver belts, Bedouin ankle bracelets, brass rings from Ghana ($10), and Ethiopian fertility necklaces of silver and turquoise ($100). Best of all are hand-strung brass and ancient bead necklaces, some made with precious stones that date to 2000 B.C. ($300 and up). Whether it's mystical exotica from long ago and far away or avant-garde fashions that would hold their own tomorrow in Soho, Agiba is unexpectedly wonderful.   — D.K.

Agiba, 49A Grove Street, 206-9326. Open daily except Tuesday, 12:30 P.M. to 8 P.M. AE, Discover, MC, V.

INDIOS

I F you change your look as often as you change your mind, this is one store to keep an eye on. Indios stocks new items every week, emphasizing one-size and unisex sportswear in traditional shapes and up-to-date colors and patterns that are hip, but not so trendy you won't want to wear them next year and the year after that. It's one of the few spots in the West Village where women can find the ever-popular long-tailed shirts, colorful knit tops, flannel drawstring trousers, and slouchy, figure-flattering dresses for under $50, and men can choose from a zippy collection of printed shirts, shorts, and around-town trousers in a $20-to-$65 price range. After ten years in a tiny, corridorlike space, Indios is still flourishing in a fickle market and an area that's hardly a fashion mecca, so it must be doing something right.

One thing Indios does flawlessly is sweaters. The house line, Luna d'Oro, features handmade summer cotton sweaters from Mexico and Peru in full contemporary cuts and vibrant colors from a mere $40 to $100. In winter, fancy woolen hand-knits appear in fiesta colors and patterns, along with solid classic pullovers, a steal at $40 to $140. To complement, there are espadrilles from Spain and a complete line of vivid South American wovens, including sashes, obis, and tiny purses from $8 to $15. — D.K.

Indios, 88 Christopher Street, 989-4488. Open Monday and Tuesday, 1 P.M. to 8 P.M.; Wednesday to Saturday, noon to 9 P.M.; Sunday, 1 P.M. to 9 P.M. AE, Discover, MC, V.

Other branches: 26 West 8th Street, 505-6065. Open Monday to Saturday, noon to 9 P.M.; Sunday, 1 P.M. to 9 P.M.

THE LOFT

89 Christopher Street, 691-2334. See index for main listing.

DOROTHY'S CLOSET

"THIS doesn't smell like New York," the Sunday-casuals gent sniffed. Indeed not—for Dorothy Tyler, the proprietor of this cozy Closet, keeps a bottle of hyacinth oil open to sweeten the air and the disposition. Not that there's anything remotely musty in her collection of sensibly priced antique clothing. With an integrity that most thrift shop owners could learn from, Dorothy personally inspects and repairs the rips, tears, and stains other stores would simply let slide and also does tailoring on the premises.

Sound a bit sweet and old-fashioned? Think again. "I like the hot, sexy clothes from every era," Dorothy demurs, "especially for women." Lingerie is a specialty and there're always lots of little black dresses, many for under $50. Skirts in a wild variety of prints, shapes, and lengths generally cost below $25. Values can be exceptional: An exquisite Roaring Twenties ladies' coat in wool and mink, for instance, bore a $300 tag last spring, and full-length sequined sheaths ran even less. Men fare equally well with classic 1950s and 1960s shirts in cotton, rayon, and acetate ($10 to $25); jazzy jackets and sober suits ($30 to $75); and a large selection of leathers for fall.

Vintage hatboxes, a lived-in straw armchair, and a *Wizard of Oz* poster (all not for sale, unfortunately) add to the homey atmosphere here. One wall enshrines a distinctive array of vampy hats. Dorothy's selection varies "according to my mood," which tends toward the funky and flamboyant in the spring and summer and outdoorsy in fall, but there's never a shortage of interesting and inexpensive treasures on hand.

Look for sales here around New Year's and toward the end of the summer, with markdowns from 30% to 50%.   — D.K.

Dorothy's Closet, 335 Bleecker Street, 206-6414. Open daily, 2 P.M. to 8 P.M. during the winter; till 9 P.M. during the summer. AE, MC, V.

L'UOMO

T H E name alone speaks volumes of pretension, but inside the goods are certainly in vogue. Using the same interior decorations as Constantine & Knight (black tin ceiling and terra-cotta floors) in a smaller, somehow less-inviting space, this store is not for the easily intimidated. Prince and Bryan Ferry croon loudly through a tape deck as perma-tanned moneyed dudes bat not an eyelash at high-altitude price tags that seem impossible to locate without help from a clerk. You have entered serious fashion territory, the one place in the West Village to look for European men's suits and sportswear, heavy on leather and wool for the fall and big on cotton, linen, and trendy synthetics for spring.

The accessories here, Vittorio Ricci shoes aside, aren't a big deal. Instead, the front of the store is dedicated to sport and dress shirts and slacks and the rear is devoted to jackets and suits. L'Uomo is where you'll find magnificent shirts in bold patterns and unthought-of color combinations by a West German line called Haupt, the exquisitely tailored suits of Hugo Boss and Valentino, and nifty neon tops by Jeff Sayre. It's also where you'll find price tags from $50 to $150 for shirts and up to $1,000 for suits, often with an attitude to match. It's hard to imagine being a regular customer at L'Uomo, but it's certainly worth a look come the sales in January and July.   — D.K.

L'Uomo, 353 Bleecker Street, 206-1844. Open Monday to Saturday, noon to 7:30 P.M.; Sunday till 6 P.M. AE, MC, V.

LA PROVENCE
DE PIERRE DEUX
381 Bleecker, 675-4054. See index for main listing.

CONSTANTINE & KNIGHT

C O U L D your preppy be more peppy? Constantine & Knight could be the answer. It is a handsomely appointed gentleman's clothier where you just might find a button-down shirt with *turquoise* pinstripes or a golfing cardigan in cool pastel cotton. Better yet, it's a relaxing place to shop, free from the hubbub of Madison Avenue and major department stores. The open, airy, yet firmly masculine interior and sensible displays encourage browsing, and there never seems to be a shortage of attentive and knowledgeable staff.

Classy silk ties and jazzy socks fit neatly between a fine

selection of dress shirts and suits, while the rear of the store is devoted to outerwear from M. Julian and contemporary rainwear. At the sales counter, a case displays fine jewelry, handkerchiefs, bow ties, and slightly flashy cotton tartan boxer shorts that are certainly tempting at $10.

"We're more forward than Brooks Brothers," Mr. Knight reveals, "but classic in design." And he should know, as a good half of the store's merchandise is designed by him and domestically produced for the store's own label. C & K's best buys include Sea Island cotton shirts (around $80), linen trousers (in the $100 range), and colorful, adventuresome sweaters in spring cottons and fall wools ($55 and up). The look blends easily with their large selection of shirts and suits by Alexander Julian. So, who says gray flannel has to be boring?

Sales are held here in February and July. — D.K.

Constantine & Knight, 383 Bleecker Street, 741-8030. Open Monday to Friday, noon to 7:30 P.M.; Saturday, 11 A.M. to 6 P.M.; Sunday, noon to 6 P.M. AE, MC, V, checks.

STELLA FLAME

T H E legend on the window reads "Contemporary Style in a Classic Setting." "That," owner-designer Stella Flame explains, "means the clothes are new, but the building is old." Old, maybe, but also severely classy. Inside this "wholesale-to-retail-priced" outlet for Flame's famed sweater and clothing line, there are checkerboard tile floors, whitewashed brick, and display cases made from barococo picture frames.

Then there are the clothes! Updated dressy items for men and women that serve equally well in a boardroom or a ballroom; everything in natural fibers (especially fine-patterned Solbiatti linens from Italy); and cut, sewn, and finished by hand. Men's suits work perfectly as separates, with innovative saddle-cut shoulders on jackets and eternally graceful pleated trousers that run from $85 in cotton to $175 for wool and cashmere. Ladies can choose from simple but sophisticated shirtdresses, boldly patterned skirts, and a variety of cleverly fashioned blouses. Hand-knit and hand-loomed sweaters designed by Stella herself are a specialty, typically jacquards of complex geometrics or witty renderings of animals and people. Styles include the usual crew and V-necks, cardigans, vests, and a roomy, long-sleeved variation on a polo shirt done up in two-toned patterns and dubbed "The Eddie Haskell," with price tags from $80 to $500.

Incredible antique jewelry, dazzling antique watches ($145 and up), and unique contemporary pieces (including plastic jewelry and scarves made from silk and latex) round out the merchandise, and there's a small, interesting selection of picture frames, marbleized pottery, and Italian modern tableware. Prices on these unique items aren't as generous as the savings on Stella Flame's line, which often costs double in pricey department stores, but you can always look for a break during January and July and the special sales before Mother's Day and Father's Day. — D.K.

Stella Flame, 41 Perry Street, 675-1237. Open Tuesday to Saturday, 12:30 P.M. to 7 P.M.; Sunday, 11 A.M. to 7 P.M. AE, MC, V, checks.

Other branches: 476 Columbus Avenue, 874-5262. Open Monday to Saturday, noon to 9 P.M.; Sunday till 6 P.M.

SHADES OF THE VILLAGE

"O V E R 1,000 styles," the sign on the door of this sunglasses sanctuary boasts, "from $3-$180." Sure enough, there's a long shelf covered with nasty neon and op art frames, Goodyear-framed cheaters bearing the legend "Tired Eyes," wraparounds, and garage-sale specials for less than a fiver. But the $180 sterling-silverplated Guccis trimmed in 22K gold are kept in the display case behind the counter along with the Ray•Bans, the

Vuarnets, the Persols, the L.A. Eyeworks, the Nikons, and the Laura Biagiottis.

Budget-minded shady operators will appreciate Shades's extensive range of spirited designer-type glasses, and embellishing types will flip over the variety of leashes that includes cartoon cloth, day-glow beads, and sproingy telephone cord ($1 to $4). For the hopelessly nostalgic there's an ever-changing supply of vintage French and Italian specs from the 1950s and 1960s (maxing out, pricewise, at $25).

Sunglasses aren't the only good-looking buys; one display case arranges funky earrings by price categories, and others show cigarette cases, driving gloves, brooches, watches, and bracelets. Available air space is devoted to a beautiful range of bolo ties (from $4-tacky to $52 for handmade rhinestone numbers) and silk and wool scarves for under $40. Finicky accessorizers and eyewear fetishists should certainly find their way (not to mention Wayfarers) here.   — D.K.

Shades of the Village, 167 Seventh Avenue South, 255-7767. Open Sunday to Thursday, 11 A.M. to 9 P.M.; Friday and Saturday till midnight. AE, Discover.

O MISTRESS MINE

O vintage clothes! They're either crushed onto racks—stains and horrible colors intact—or else pampered and priced at an outrageous fortune. Wanda Hanlon, this store's headmistress, knows it, and being in this location since 1968 makes her one of the few veterans in a tough market. "The public has become a lot smarter about what they're buying," she contends correctly, which is why she handpicks, cleans (and repairs, if necessary) classic styles from the 1930s to the 1960s with some 1920s and Victoriana "when I can find it."

Salvaged fabrics from otherwise unwearable garments often find their way into lovely originals designed by Hanlon. Denim skirts ($24) are constructed from blue jeans with the original labels and pockets; silk scarves become kimonos ($48); and three different dress fabrics combine with deft scissorwork to create wrap blouses ($75) that can be worn a variety of ways.

O Mistress Mine emphasizes ladies' dresses, particularly draped 1940s numbers from $18 crepes to $250 floral silks, with striking hats and shoes to mix and match ($25 to $65). Men can choose from a good selection of tweed jackets ($25 to $50), suits (around $125), and trousers ($25). In winter there's usually a supply of fox-fur hats for men and women for less than $40. Late hours are maintained to lure after-dinner shoppers, who'll find that merchandise is rotated and marked down on a monthly basis and that a good attitude about any flaws or imperfections may net additional reductions.

Sales are held here in January and August, with 20% to 50% markdowns.   — D.K.

O Mistress Mine, 143 Seventh Avenue South, 691-4327. Open Monday to Saturday, 1 P.M. to 10 P.M.; Sunday till 9 P.M. AE, CB, MC, V, checks.

NEW YORK LEATHER CO.

F R O M the serious hardware and kink of The Leather Man in the clone zone of Christopher Street to a handful of repair/ design shops offering belts, bags, jackets, and even custom-made chain mail minidresses, the West Village is a leather lover's paradise. And the attractively appointed New York Leather Co. does a year-round business in exquisitely cut high-fashion leathers you're not likely to find elsewhere.

Crave a mint-green blazer with matching skirt? Or natural skin trousers embossed with Floridian froufrou? Look here in spring, when vibrant colors dominate women's separates and men's classic suede baseball jackets. In winter the emphasis is on basics in traditional browns and blacks, ranging from simple bomber and biker jackets (from $175) to full-length shearling coats with cowl hoods ($2,000). Made-on-premises belts and bags are seasonless and beautifully designed in a cost spread of $20 to $250, including durably chic backpacks. To complete a look there's always a small selection of shirts and sweaters in cotton, wool, linen, and viscose that are slightly pricey, but consistently tasteful.

January is sale time here. — D.K.

New York Leather Co., 33 Christopher Street, 243-2710. Open Monday to Thursday, 11 A.M. to 7:45 P.M.; Friday and Saturday, noon to 8:45 P.M.; Sunday, 1 P.M. to 5:45 P.M. AE, MC, V, checks.

GRAFFITI DESIGN STUDIO

HAND-PAINTED clothing, it comes as no surprise, is Graffiti's signature. And the small store is crammed with unique, contemporary men's and women's clothing that's as individual and lively as the squiggles that cover the subways. Prints range from Jackson Pollock-like freakouts to patterned figurative imagery, including portraits of dollar-bill presidents, adding texture and color to plain cotton T-shirts and short- and long-sleeved button-downs in a price spread from $20 to $65.

One-of-a-kindism is the guiding principle that distinguishes Graffiti from the trendy sportswear pack. Its own clothing line, which leans toward denims and knits in varying weights year-round, can be customized to your measurements or your selection from their fabrics. Chanel-inspired collarless blazers, two-tone baseball jackets, and fall/winter coats ($75 to $250) pair well with coordinated trousers and skirts ($30 to $65) in sturdy fabrics and basic colors (black, blue, white), neatly achieving the house goal of creating "perfect shapes with a little bit of dynamics." Short- and long-sleeved shirts ($38 to $75) mix and match patterns, prints, and vivid hues with wild abandon and generous one-size cutting. Basic shapes and novelty pieces in a reasonable cost category from hip lines like Kikit and Body

Map help fill up the well-worth-pawing-through racks, and there always seems to be something on sale.

Naturally, there's a diverse selection of hats and belts from young, innovative designers that runs the gamut from functional to fun to fashion victim, and a small, but no less impressive, array of jewelry made from chains, enameled pieces, wire, glass, and mirrors ($15 to $75).

Sales are held here around New Year's and the Fourth of July. — D.K.

Graffiti Design Studio, 19 Christopher Street, 206-0954. Open Monday to Thursday, noon to 9 P.M.; Friday and Saturday till 11 P.M.; Sunday, 1 P.M. to 7 P.M. AE, MC, V.

AMALGAMATED

THIS comfortably browsy emporium of "simple clothes," accessories, jewelry, stationery, and not-just-for-kids toys is small but well done. The accent is on basic clothing from popular designers like Basco and Creeks, but eccentric accessories reinforce the whimsical, eclectic range of the store, with a variety of pricey but precious socks from Shady Character and Format (who have new sleepwear and clothing lines), underwear by Joe Boxer and Tous Le Caleçons, and wacky scarves for winter.

Tongue-in-chic paraphernalia is also amalgamated into the let's-make-shopping-fun atmosphere, with shelves of postmodern and "new wave" pencils, pens, and pads as well as such strange treasures as a Godzilla cigarette lighter and a New York City pigeon bottle opener. Only a humorless Scrooge could deny that this is one of the very best places to shop for The Man Who's Got Everything. — D.K.

Amalgamated, 19 Christopher Street, 691-8695. Open daily, 11 A.M. to 9 P.M.; noon to 8 P.M. during the winter. AE, MC, V, checks.

NEW YORK MAN

O N the quiet strip of Christopher Street between Avenue of the Americas and Seventh Avenue, a short flight of stairs leads up to a small enclosure decorated with corrugated aluminum and black trimmings, resembling a high-tech cocktail lounge in a construction site. A butch setting, to be sure, but certainly not men's-only, as there's a generous selection of sporty tops that will appeal to women as well.

The best of these are designed by New York Man's Robert D'Antonio, who cuts mammoth tank tops in richly striped cotton for $24 and oversized short-sleeved camp shirts in fancy jewel-toned silk prints, Italian linen ($64), and wowsome cotton prints for $50. In the fall these tops grow long sleeves and tails ($64) and pair with handsomely slouchy cardigans in cotton knit ($64) and fancy wools and linen ($125). Spandex knee-length bicycle shorts ($40), like the above, come in wild prints and stripes and are never cut in quantities of more than a dozen per print to help spare you the nightmare of seeing somebody else in your outfit.

Current is the word D'Antonio uses to describe the rest of New York Man's contemporary sportswear, featuring predominantly natural fabrics. New York Man is one of the few non-department store outlets for Generra, a stylish purveyor of inexpensive shirts and trousers ($26 to $32), as well as other hip labels, with shirts in a $30-to-$50 range and trousers for up to $75 in wool, silk, and linen. Accessories are flashy but basic: a rainbow of E.G. Smith's bulky cotton socks, Shady Character sunglasses, and the occasional shoes by Zodiac. Christmas brings out the truly imaginative accents: Last year $100 bought hand-beaded-bow-tie-and-cumberbund sets and an Elmer Fudd cap in wool, leather, and velvet, with ranch mink earflaps.

Many items go on sale in late January and late August, at one-third off the regular price. — D.K.

New York Man, 13 Christopher Street, 255-2809. Open daily, noon to 7 P.M. AE, MC, V.

Other branches: 222 Eighth Avenue, 645-5441. Open daily, noon to 7:30 P.M.

BEN'S VILLAGE

7 Greenwich Avenue, 924-8145. See index for main listing.

LO: NEW YORK

E N T E R Lo and behold a world of delicate, romantic fantasy. English garden benches sit on deeply stained wood planks that converge in a sunburst design at the center of the store, while the white-planked walls are lined with mirrors set into large Norman-styled arches—creating the illusion that you've discovered a favorite auntie's attic from the turn of the century.

"We are a design house, actually," says the droll proprietor, known as Murphy. "We are couturiers of hand-crocheted design, the only one in existence!" All of the work is done in England from cotton, silk, and flax, custom-dyed to order, with custom variations available to their huge range of airy, delicately woven, Victorian-styled blouses, dresses, and bridal wear that costs from $100 to $1,000. "You can choose from 547 designs," Murphy declares, "as of yesterday."

Lo sells duplicates of its wondrously lacy creations off the rack, but most of the customers over the last seven years have been happy to wait three months for a special order that might also include coordinating gloves, hats, and veils ($30 to $100). The store works closely with customers, doing final fittings till they are satisfied. Lo also offers one shoe style per season, and the design is remarkably consistent with the soft English beauty of the innocent-looking-but-sexy garments.

They're also happy to part with their elegant hatboxes for a mere $2 and occasionally have antique chests that decorate the store for sale.   — D.K.

Lo: New York, 22 Greenwich Avenue, 741-9285. Open Monday to Saturday, noon to 8 P.M. AE, MC, V, checks.

STATE OF THE ART

A prismatic rainbow arches across a whitewashed brick wall, and they sell the waffley plastic Dri-dek that covers the shop's floor for $5 a square foot. State of the Art is everything the name implies, proprietor Russ Lackey explains. "The Village is very craftsy and we want to offer it a place to buy high design that has style, form, and function, whether it's a Porsche pipe or a typewriter or dinnerware."

This is the place to find matte black accessories, such as a contact lenses case, ID bracelet, money clip, or cuff links ($10 to $25) to match the black plastic pocket calculator, countertops, and minimalist alarm clock in your high-tech hacienda. Amid the dinnerware, small electrical appliances, suede-to-the-touch rubber briefcases ($30 to $80), and Miami-colored postmodern woodworking tools, you'll discover bold, streamlined versions of personal grooming items and fashion-meets-function eye- and wristwear. Porsche electric razors feature clean-cut lines for clean-cut guys; and the shieldlike Porsche driving shades are the sunglasses that made Yoko Ono famous (or is that the other way around?).

Watches range from the sporty $40 Casio Analog model to Georg Jensen's less-is-more-and-costs-it dress ticker, which is bettered by the stark elegance of S.O.T.A.'s private-label quartz timepiece in gray and black at $150.   — D.K.

State of the Art, 47 Greenwich Avenue, 924-8973. Open Tuesday to Sunday, 1 P.M. to 8 P.M. AE, MC, V, checks.

ISHIO

THIS is the place for lace. Ishio has filled his store with romantic yet sophisticated women's clothing (sizes 2 to 12) of his own design, heavy on beautiful silks and new and antique lace. The charming, parlorlike decor reflects the quiet glamour of this boutique; soft floral curtains and rugs, pink walls, and antique furniture may fool a casual passerby (as it did me) into thinking that this is a particularly frilly vintagerie.

Indeed, Ishio's blouses and camisoles made of antique linens (tablecloths, doilies, and cocktail napkins) are a specialty. But you'll also find sleek Chanelesque skirts in silk and French wool crepe ($85) and cleverly pleated walking shorts with an elastic waist in the back in crisp linen for $60. Each is cut and sewn by Ishio as a one-of-a-kind classic and typifies his strong eye for the fabrics and the shapes that appeal to youngish professionals. Formal and bridal wear is Ishio's stock-in-trade, with fine vintage lace worked into new Victorian-to-1940s-styled gowns ($350 to $1,350); most are designed as two-piece ensembles that offer hope for posthoneymoon wear of a decidedly elegant nature. Custom designing for any type of garment is also a specialty here.

Lace collars and scarves to embellish simple necklines are plentiful, and prices vary from $25 for new lace to $125 for beautiful antiques. Silk scarves are lavish in bright crumply solids, florals, and embroidered metallic thread designs. There is also a collection of handbags, including shoulder bags sporting the classic opulence of 1940s drapery, tapestry, and upholstery fabrics. Best, by far, are lacy clutches with wooden clasps, handmade and individually dyed in Japan.

Look for sales here in January and July, with 20% to 50% markdowns. — D.K.

Ishio, 117 Greenwich Avenue, 243-5015. Open Monday to Saturday, noon to 8 P.M.; Sundays in December. AE, MC, V.

THE EAST VILLAGE

INTRODUCTION BY
Linda Dyett

Discerning foreigners taxi down here directly from the airport. Yuppies with punkoid fantasies get their haircuts here, and seekers of the relentlessly chic prowl the streets, the dozens of art galleries, and the after-hours clubs that drip with attitude. The East Village has been discovered by everybody.

The draw is its tumultuous street life, a cross between MTV, *Birth of a Nation*, and an avant-garde fashion show, which goes on twenty-four hours a day. The streets are an endless parade of extreme looks, the latest and the most outrageous—America's cauldron of style.

Here reside the remnants of the neighborhood's Jewish, Ukrainian, and Italian immigrants; office clerks who attach their ear cuffs and lacquer their hair into spikes at night; and an impressive number of artists, craftsmen, and designers who like to work close together and could hardly afford any other

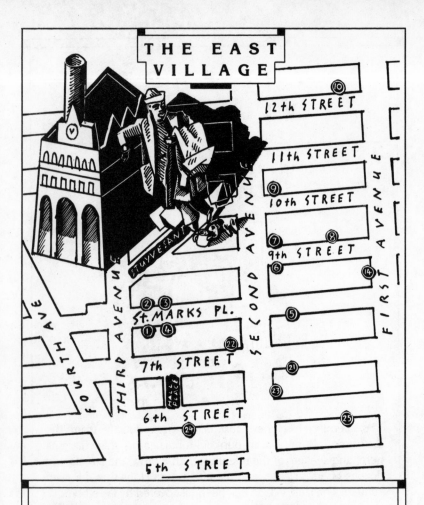

THE EAST VILLAGE

1   Trash and Vaudeville
2   Enz
3   Eleven Saint Marks Place
4   Andy's Chee-Pees
5   Phenomena
6   Dinosaur Hill
7   Tribe
8   Fetisch or Die
9   Bogies Antique Clothing and Furs
10   000 Evolutionary General Store
11   Gabay's
12   Keni Valenti
13   Batislavia
14   Everything in the Store Is Made
of 100% Cotton

15   109
16   A Repeat Performance
17   Nasty Habits
18   Clear Metals
19   Lilla Lova
20   Einstein's
21   Enelra
22   Love Saves the Day
23   Men-za Men-za
24   99X
25   Yuzen
26   Ona
27   Landeaux Studio X
28   Shrimpton & Gilligan
29   Design East

neighborhood in Manhattan. The latter set their own style, no longer recognizably punk, but closer to the cutting edge than anywhere else in America. You'll spot them sweating in their all-rubber outfits or in tight, ribbed ankle-length skirts worn under trapeze shirts and over sockless men's oxfords. They're the ones with the best Louise Brooks bobs and deceptively angelic faces to match. They charge up the scenery by restlessly creating new looks. That's the difference between East Village style and the careful trend-following you find in Soho and on Columbus Avenue—anything goes here. In spirit, this neighborhood is closer to London and advanced sectors of Paris than any other part of Manhattan.

The ground floors of the tenements have recently begun filling with boutiques. They can't have huge inventories—there's neither the room nor the financial wherewithal. Instead, the stock in trade is often risky stuff. The latest in London dry goods is imported to Trash & Vaudeville and other trendsetting stores on St. Marks Place. Seventh Street between Second Avenue and Avenue A has turned into a miniature fashion mall, with stores that sell urban primitive jewelry and killer sophisticate dresses you can wear with assurance at Palladium's Mike Todd Room.

The most interesting new clothes shops to look for are on the side streets and the alphabet avenues. They're run by dress-maker/designers with their sewing machines in the back, where they often do private-label lines for uptown department stores. Up front, in their tiny retail areas, they offer the locals and adventurous uptowners limited-edition clothes, mostly of the postpunk variety, but sometimes elegant and classic. Their businesses have turned into a thriving storefront couture, written up in every self-respecting European fashion magazine.

Not that all East Village boutique clothes are great discoveries: The workmanship and fabrics can be shoddy, and the styles can be predictable or downright ugly. On the up side, prices are relatively inexpensive, and a number of the designers, such as the ones with shops reviewed here, are truly inventive and talented. But there's a fast turnover at these new East Village boutiques. Even some of the best of these stores tend to have short and volatile life spans. This guide will concentrate on the most stable ones.

For the seasoned department store or uptown boutique shopper who's used to viewing wide arrays of clothes divided into neat categories according to designer or color group, these little storefront shops can be unsettling. They require a different approach. Keep in mind that they're not being stocked by wholesalers and their wares are invariably limited, often only to samples. And these places don't have the glass showcases and fluorescent lights that characterize most stores. They're make-shift arenas, storehouses of unusual finds displayed in settings that run the gamut from tenement-humble to zany.

Ethnic boutiques, left over from the hippie days, are on side streets from 5th through 9th. Here you can buy the latest from Guatemala, the Himalayas, Afghanistan, and Japan. Scattered among these shops are the Ukrainian retailers, with embroidered blouses, suede slippers, and painted Easter eggs any time of the year. On First Avenue are a couple of emporiums stocked with cardboard boxes bursting with hankies, undershirts, overalls, even nylon stockings that haven't moved for decades. Here, too, are the junk and used-clothing stores that the designers sift through for inspiration. Bogies, on 9th Street, with its mountains of 1950s and 1960s clothes, is a virtual library of modernist fashion. Gabay's, on First Avenue, is a repository of today's surplus—the goods that were scorned at the department stores but here are readily put to good use. Almost any sort of wardrobe can be had in the East Village, from sturdy and sensible to outrageous. The only things you won't find are clothes to appease the mass market.

You will find other small shops with unusual wares. Kiehl's Pharmacy at 109 Third Avenue has its own line of skin-care products and cosmetics. Meadowsweet Herbal Apothecary, 77 East 4th Street, sells a wide variety of herbs. O-Zora, 238 East 6th Street, imports Japanese tools and work clothes. Clodagh• Ross•Williams, at 122 St. Marks Place, seeks out new-line home furnishings, lighting, and jewelry. House Party, 151 Avenue A, has vintage homewares. The Five & Dime at 341 East 9th Street sells oddball home-decor items. Little Rickie, 72 East 1st

Street, offers "novelties, notions, and nonsense"—old and new toys and whimsies, plus the best photo booth in the city (four crisp black and white shots for $1). Finger Fortunes, 155 2nd Avenue, sells exquisite antique furniture and objets d'art, especially from the Arts and Crafts movement. Finyl Vinyl, at 89 Second Avenue, specializes in vintage rock-and-roll and rhythm-and-blues records. And there are several booksellers, including the St. Mark's Bookshop at 13 St. Marks Place—possibly the best in the city.

The East Village is also topheavy with dozens of art galleries. It was here that the now-passé polyglot graffiti-art movement got its start. As opposed to the warehouse-sized Soho galleries of the 1970s, they're distinctly 1980s phenomena, showing small-scale works for small storefront spaces. The paintings and prints, by and large expressionist in the past, have recently been turning toward abstractionism. Several prime galleries are Bridgewater, Greathouse, Poemaster, Ellen Sragow, International with Monument, Pat Hearn, and Gracie Mansion.

Twenty years ago, neither the galleries nor the East Village existed. The neighborhood name was invented by real estate brokers to lend bohemian allure to the tightly packed grid of streets east of the Bowery and Third Avenue, north of Houston Street, and south of 14th Street. An extension of the Lower East Side, it's served as a portal for immigrants and not-yet-fashionable artists and the dispossessed (the area still has more men's and women's shelters than any other part of the city). It's been a refuge for those living en route to, or from, the mainstream, and they've given the neighborhood its authenticity and astonishing diversity. Where else—even in Manhattan—can you find a combination as bizarre as the 10th Street Turkish Baths (which also serves caviar and borscht), the Hebrew Actors Union, La Mama Experimental Theater, McSorley's Ale House, the Hell's Angels' East Coast headquarters, the Ukrainian Liberation Front, Slavic furriers, and Italian pasticcerias with marble-topped tables and amber-tinted lights?

The Lower East Side was a thriving, bustling neighborhood until shortly after the Second World War, when many of its upwardly mobile residents relocated to the suburbs and the drug dealers and shooting galleries moved in. By the 1960s, it was in serious decline. Then the Fillmore East and the Electric Circus made the East Village a hippie cultural center. But that world was distinctly dead by the mid-1970s, and so was the East Village—nearly.

Meanwhile, the neighborhood was exuding just the right degree of unfashionableness and authenticity for the pioneer punks, who found the low rents desirable; and the East Village began picking up by the early 1980s.

Architecturally, the area is undistinguished except for the Federal style and Greek Revival townhouses on St. Marks Place, a couple of Italian Renaissance mansions (now the Stuyvesant Polyclinic and the Ottendorfer Branch of the New York Public Library) on Second Avenue, elegant rowhouses bordering Tompkins Square Park, and St. Mark's in-the-Bouwerie, a Dutch church that was begun in 1795, when the East Village was farmland. Despite renovations, it still looks like a country chapel—an incongruity surrounded by a couple of 1920s high rises and squat old tenements with narrow hallways and almost equally narrow railroad flats.

The best time to explore the clothing stores is during the afternoon late in the week (many are closed Mondays and Tuesdays and open at noon or later during the rest of the week). To keep up your strength as you scour the streets, try mid-morning cappuccino and cakes at De Robertis Pasticceria, 176 First Avenue near 11th Street, or at Veniero's, 342 East 11th Street just off First Avenue; have an impeccable corned beef sandwich for lunch at the Second Avenue Kosher Delicatessen and Restaurant (number 156, corner of 10th Street); a tea-time egg cream at the Gem Spa, on the corner of Second Avenue and St. Marks Place; take-out coffee and refined French pastries at Encore Patisserie, 141 Second Avenue; or a beer at McSorley's, at 15 East 7th Street.

There are numerous restaurants to choose from for dinner. If you're on a budget, try Leshko's at 111 Avenue A or the Veselka, 144 Second Avenue at 9th Street, for Ukrainian fare; or one of the many Indian restaurants on 6th Street between Second and First avenues. If you can't decide which one, try Mitali, with a particularly broad menu—and don't let the blender drinks dissuade you. If you care to splurge East Village-style, try the Mogador at 101 St. Marks Place for cous cous and other North African specialties; or Sugar Reef, the crowded Pan-Caribbean hothouse at 93 Second Avenue. If you want to spend even bigger bucks but in a decidedly unpretentious atmosphere, try Hawaii 5-0 at 121 Avenue A for nouvelle California grills.

The local café society nighttime hangouts are the Pyramid Bar on Avenue A and Limbo Lounge on Seventh Street. And don't forget CBGB on the Bowery for nonstop rock and roll. Or if you like your drinks in an old-fashioned bar, check out the Grass Roots on St. Marks Place.

To reach the East Village by subway: Take the BMT R to 8th Street or the IRT 6 to Astor Place and head due east. By bus: Take the M1 up Bowery or down Park Avenue South; the M3 or M5 down Fifth Avenue; the M101 or 102 up or down Third Avenue; or the M13 crosstown to Astor Place. As soon as you pass Cooper Union (one of the country's great art and engineering colleges), you'll be on St. Marks Place, where the shopping commences.

■　　■　　■

TRASH AND VAUDEVILLE

O N E of the original punk/new wave emporiums, Trash and Vaudeville has grown from one small room featuring vintage and surplus clothing for hungry East Villagers to a full two floors of trendy fashion for men and women, including accessories and shoes. Downstairs, where you are likely to be met by a mannequin wearing a black leather studded bra, the stock is kinkier. Their infamous shoe collection, mostly flash English two-toned, needle-toed jivecoverings for his tootsies, is in the rear; average prices are $50 to $100, with snakeskin boots about $170, and a sale rack of markdowns to $20. There's also a large collection of leathers, especially jackets, most reasonably priced with a high end of $450. Womenswear, some imported from England, some from the house line, Tripp, tends toward trendy with class: One season's stretchy tube dresses and separates were cut in simple, elegant lines, using fabrics that were silky, not sleazy, priced under $80. A good collection of accessories featured Western-wear bolos, metal collar tips, and belts—before they were trendy. There is jewelry, too, at $10 to $65, most new, some vintage.

Upstairs, the vintage clothing—a small, judiciously selected section at excellent prices—is in the back room with sale racks offering steals. In the front is current sportswear, with men's slacks priced $15 to $100 and shirts $15 to $80. — S.C.

Trash and Vaudeville, 4 St. Marks Place, 982-3590. Open Monday to Friday, noon to 8 P.M.; Saturday, 11:30 A.M. to 8 P.M.; Sunday, 1 P.M. to 7:30 P.M. AE, MC, V.

ENZ

"E V E R Y T H I N G is black and sexy," says designer Mariann Marlowe. Before it was Enz it was Ian's in the West Village. Mariann can't remember exactly when she opened it—other than "around the time of the New York Dolls." Starting to get the picture? Looking for a "prom dress" made of body hugging plastic and tulle? Or one of those form-fitting numbers Marilyn might have worn in *Gentlemen Prefer Blondes*, but in a slippery-eel stretchy shirred black?.

This is fetish country. Want a studded black leather bra or maybe one fringed for tougher-than-gingham punk cowgirls? Enz has 'em. The "basics" here are stretch separates and dresses with flesh-revealing laced slits for seams. The hard-core set comes in for the loose-weave mohair sweaters. Most of the stock is Mariann's, but she also imports from England: black on black jeans silk-screened with rubber can be bought with matching waist-length tux jackets.

There're accessories here, too: claw rings, bat earrings, belts, gloves, and a wall of wigs. Lots of pointy shoes from England. Heeled ankle-high granny boots have skull buckles. Prices run from $2 for a trinket to $350 for special designerwear, but clothing averages $25 to $100.   — S.C.

Enz, 5 St. Marks Place, 420-1857. Open daily, 11:30 A.M. to 8 P.M. AE, MC, V.
Other branches: Ian's Uptown, 1151 Second Avenue, 838-3969. Open Monday to Saturday, 11 A.M. to 7 P.M.

ELEVEN SAINT MARKS PLACE

E D D I E will probably greet you at the door with a murmured, "Make yourself at home. Let me know if you need help." Several customers do. One asks the price of a black wool and leather Claude Montana. It's $90. Clothing dates from the 1920s to recycled current designers, and is clearly hand picked. Another woman swirls in wanting eveningwear for a black-and-white ball down South. He offers up a Victorian-styled wedding dress for $75. A third is trying to find vintage dresses she can wear to work at Tiffany's where, she snickers, convention-bound customers frequently ask when buying baby gifts if the silver spoons are for boys or girls. She pulls out very few duds—lots of blacks, rayons, silks, no polys. Then comes the prize—a pair of over-the-elbow black snakeskin and kid gloves that Eddie calls "the best I ever had . . . no, ever saw." Yes!

Eddie has good menswear and jewelry as well. The smoking jackets with brocade roses are $60, far less than in larger stores. Shirts, $8 to $25, are cotton or silk—no synthetics. A matching silver necklace, bracelet, and earrings set from Denmark runs $110, as does the 14K white gold Elgin ladies watch from the 1950s. New merchandise arrives daily, with everything in the store available for rental. Recommended by musician Alex Chilton.   — S.C.

Eleven Saint Marks Place, 11 St. Marks Place, upstairs, no phone. Open daily, noon to 10:30 P.M.

ANDY'S CHEE-PEES

S O you want a white wedding, but all that virgin garb just lacks the edge so inevitable in modern love. Maybe the answer is Andy's Chee-Pees, where second-time-around gowns in just-off white, trains a tad tattered, can lend authenticity to that ceremonial glide down the aisle. Register your crystal with Dixie Cups.

Andy's Chee-Pees, now having overflowed from its original location on St. Marks to a second outlet on 8th, always calls to mind the Britishism, "jumble sale." Both stores are stuffed full of vintage clothing unceremoniously displayed. It bulges from racks; it hangs from rafters. Don't go in for a hit-and-run purchase. These stores are for browsers, rooters, and discerning eyes. Their atmosphere is as effusive as Andy, who today is speaking lovingly of "the kids," his customers, as he marks a new shipment of elephant-leg trousers.

Furs heaped near the door are marked down, prices beginning at $45, to make way for the seersucker jackets and cotton dresses being brought in for the spring. From casual to cocktail, Andy has it. There are ties at $5, silk scarves around $15. Cowboy shirts sell for $30. Men's jackets are $12 to $24. Hanging from the ceiling is the better stuff: antique beaded dresses, some not for sale, and the wedding gowns, $75 to $125.   — S.C.

Andy's Chee-Pees, 14 St. Marks Place, 674-9248. Open Monday to Saturday, noon to 9 P.M.; Sunday, noon to 7 P.M. AE, MC, V, or layaway.
 Other branches: 16 West 8th Street, 460-8488. Open the same hours.

PHENOMENA

PHENOMENA'S forte is fabric. One of the first designer-run boutiques in the neighborhood, it features designs for men and women by David Francis and Michael Wennerlund, with select pieces by other young designers. They stick to clean, contemporary cuts—oversized blazers, tux jackets, pleated pants, sarong skirts—kept current with mostly natural fabrics, such as silks, cottons, wools, and the occasional synthetic when it strikes them.

David and Michael clearly love texture, whether it's the sleek black and white or green and purple of woven sharkskin or the crumple of unpressed rayon satin. From the latter they have made a wraparound dress ($85) and a flamboyant free-form trenchcoat ($235), also available in raw silk ($600). Suits in cotton or sharkskin run $124 to $240.

An excellent selection of accessories includes Jack Spectrum's semiprecious stone and metal pins and earrings ($39 to $89), as well as a caseful of other pieces by young jewelers, many one of a kind. There are good bags, belts, and socks— Phenomena introduced Hue hosiery and bags made of rubber to the neighborhood. It also carries a reasonably priced line of fragrance-free, hypo-allergenic cosmetics in snazzy colors.

Sales are held in January and July, with markdowns of 20% to 70%.   — S.C.

Phenomena, 40½ St. Marks Place, 674-3067. Open Tuesday to Sunday, 1 P.M. to 9 P.M. AE, DC, MC, V.

DINOSAUR HILL

T H E R E are no Cabbage Patch dolls or Garbage Pail Kids' trading cards here. Dinosaur Hill's toys are the old-fashioned variety: glass marbles, tiny plastic figures stored in fishbowls, and Chinese and Russian windup animals. The only concession to modernity is the day-glow Silly Putty. These goods intrigue the kids and a lot of adults. This is one of the few shops in New York where it's possible to make multiple purchases for under a buck.

You can also buy unusual kids' clothing, almost all of it cottage-industry wares sized from six months to six years. There are assortments of brightly colored Chinese appliqué vests for $30 to $35, and Guatemalan striped handwovens—mostly *huipiles* (rectangular-cut shirts) and skirts, $10 to $20. From local artisans, you can find separates in stark, squiggly Memphis prints for under $15. Or if you're looking for something demure, the shop keeps a supply of traditional Mexican angel pinafores and honeymoon-style cotton shifts with embroidered floral designs, all under $25.

Also on hand are silk-screened East Village T-shirts and handmade sweaters from Ecuador and Peru, none priced over $35.

This place is a lot of fun on Saturdays and Sundays, when the marble browsers congregate.

Sales are held here in January and July or August.   — L.D.

Dinosaur Hill, 302 East 9th Street, 473-5850. Open Monday to Friday, 1 P.M. to 7 P.M.; Saturday, noon to 7 P.M.; Sunday hours are irregular. AE.

TRIBE

T R I B E is a clan gathering of East Village designers and their kin from London, Canada, and Los Angeles. The goods in this long, narrow, below-street-level shop reflect the changing local fashion. When Tribe opened in 1984, it was devoutly high punk. Since then, its horizons have expanded. You'll still find true-blue postpunks here, but also a smattering of worldy and sophisticated designers.

One of them is Eugenia, a Russian émigré who does sleek, flapper-inspired separates and coats for women. Her details and trim say stylized Chanel or Rykiel, but the price tags read $50 to $300.

Other Tribe members include Isaia, who's known for his slinky, mostly jersey eveningwear, $30 to $100; and Lari Shox, who does hand-painted vintage business suits and jackets, $80 to $250, and one-of-a-kind fezzes and beanies, $15 to $50.

Among the out-of-towners are Body Map, from London, with its nontraditional jersey print sportswear, $25 to $500; Tony Vermillion, a Canadian menswear designer who works in outré fabrics and cuts, $50 to $200; and Dosa, low-priced activewear from California.

The young owners, Jerome Darby and Richard Stout, design

most of the jewelry—unfussy bangles and earrings in gold and silver plate and gunmetal brass, bargains at $6 to $40. They sell it to other shops, too.   — L.D.

Tribe, 309 East 9th Street, 674-6990. Open daily, 1 P.M. to 8 P.M. AE, MC, V, checks.

FETISCH OR DIE

T H E decor consists of a whip, barbed wire, and a hatchet planted in the wall, dripping with day-glow blood. The merchandise includes nail-studded rubber shifts and Charles Manson T-shirts. Many assume Fetisch or Die is a bondage supply house. Completely wrong. It sells nonserious bondage parodies. There's a difference. Even those who are extremely old-fashioned about clothes have been known to think highly of this little shop.

All the goods come directly from London. Fetisch, the mother-shop there, supplies the rubber items—tight skirts in various lengths (the midcalf version looks like an Azzedine), corselettes, and other tops, stockings, tights, and cocktail dresses. They come in basic Michelin black and lush solids and animal prints, some decorated with netting or buckles. Most are cotton-backed and surprisingly comfortable. They make the thin look voluptuous and give a smooth, trim look to the heavyset. Best of all, these rubber goods never need washing or dry cleaning. All you do is spray them with Windex or, if you want them to shine, with Pledge. To repair rips, just dab on some mending fluid. Of course, if you get overheated, you may smell like a highway accident, but that's the only disadvantage of wearing rubber.

The cottons, from Artificial Eye in Kensington Market, include such hard-to-find items as SS-guard-style dresses, T-shirts depicting twentieth-century murderers, and buckle-covered shirt jackets.

Everything's reasonably priced, from about $10 for the T-shirts to $50 to $60 for the skirts and tops, and about $100 for the fancy rubber dresses.   — L.D.

Fetisch or Die, 333 East 9th Street, no phone. Open Thursday to Saturday, 1 P.M. to 8 P.M.

BOGIES ANTIQUE CLOTHING AND FURS

N O T H I N G ' S folded or hung or stored away neatly at Bogies. The normal state in this used and vintage clothing shop is terminal disarray—nearly as messy as a teen bedroom. There's a huge mound of lingerie and evening sweaters against the right window, while day dresses are heaped against the left. Yank a few, and you risk an avalanche. Coats, suits, and jackets of various eras and sizes are hung from wire dry cleaners' hangers on groaning racks, while blouses and scarves are strewn in large bins. The regulars wouldn't have it any other way. Without the jumble, there'd be no thrill of discovery.

Martin Bodenstein started Bogies and its low-price policy in 1967. His little shop not only kept a poor neighborhood clothed but helped initiate the era of vintage fashion, which led to designer retro knockoffs and possibly aided in the formation of postmodernism. The store has become an institution. After Bodenstein's death in 1980, his wife, Esther, took over and has continued bringing biweekly supplies from mysterious sources. She's also maintained the low prices—$5 to $50, maybe a little more for a good fur coat.

There's no telling what will turn up. Pre-1950s is doubtful. But Bogies always has some beautiful early 1950s New Look women's suit jackets and gorgeous lingerie. With luck, you might find a $7 bias-cut, gardenia-colored satin nightgown there that friends will beg you to leave them in your will.

The men's selections are limited but usually include varsity and bowling jackets, Hawaiian shirts, and jewel-toned rayon dressing gowns.

If you want to rummage through the large sizes, ask. Esther keeps them in pillowcases. If you want to try something on, tunnel your way to the back. Privacy is assured behind the bundles and mounds. This place is so intriguing that you could spend a day and build up a sizable wardrobe for under $100. And if you can't afford to pay for it all at once, Bogies will hold your goods on its one-month layaway plan. If you want to avoid large, friendly, enthusiastic crowds, stay away on Saturdays.

— L.D.

Bogies Antique Clothing and Furs, 201 East 10th Street, 260-1199. Open Monday to Thursday, 12:30 P.M. to 5:30 P.M.; Friday and Saturday till 6 P.M. Closed Saturday during July and August. Checks.

OOO EVOLUTIONARY GENERAL STORE

E V E N for the East Village, OOO (pronounced Oooooh, not Zero, Zero, Zero) is spacy. The proprietors, Peggy and David Vigon, are Aquarians seeking new styles and new materials. Their specialties are wearable accoutrements for the 1990s spiritual revival, which is certain to precede the Millennium.

They concoct large, plumed drum majorette and mad hatter hats from military caps covered with acrylic pile fur. They squeeze rubber silicon into icicle patterns on sunglass frames and oxford shoes. The rubber is then encrusted with jewels. These items look barnacled or like they'd been through radiation melt.

Peggy and David's designs are your basic postapocalypse Mad Max clothes for women—rubber triangle tops to go with unitards and electronic belts (with battery-operated lights), and Clorox-painted cotton net shifts.

They paint, too. David takes T-shirts, or better yet old leather, tweed, or Yves Saint Laurent jackets—men's and women's —and covers them with layers of absorbent acrylic paint. Favored colors are bright orange, blue, and yellow; phosphorescents; and gold. His swirling panoramic style evokes Bosch, Dali, Gerhard Richter, and Klimt. His motifs: Christ (sometimes depicted on the back of a bomber jacket), zodiac signs, fertility symbols, the psychic realm, clowns, cockroaches, and praying mantises. The jackets are oddly beautiful.

Prices range from $10 for minimally decorated sunglasses to $50 for the hats to $250 for a painted Saint Laurent jacket. If you supply the garment, David will paint a motif of your choice for $25 to $100.

If the clothes are too advanced for you, Peggy, who was an oracle in one of her former incarnations, will review your past life regressions or give you a Tarot reading for $10 to $20.

Sales are held at the end of the summer and before Halloween.   — L.D.

OOO Evolutionary General Store, 347 East 12th Street, 475-6928. Open daily, noon to 10 P.M. MC, V, checks.

GABAY'S

GABAY'S has been a neighborhood mainstay since 1926, when it began carting distressed merchandise over from the original John Wanamaker department store on nearby Astor Place. Wanamaker's has gone, but Gabay's remains in its third generation as one of the best department store undertakers in the city. Every day of the week, it trucks in the overstock and detritus from several high-ticket uptown emporiums.

Some of the goods are damaged beyond repair, some torn where the labels were removed, while others are merely soiled, and a few are in perfect condition. If you search carefully, you may luck into a flawless Bottega Veneta bag for $75, a pair of Maud Frizon shoes for $45, or a Polo Ralph Lauren all-cotton business shirt for $10. Mixed in with the Bistro flatware, I've found $5 Italian lace bras that couldn't sell uptown for $50 the week before. And nestled under a cache of singing copper teakettles with spouts sometimes intact, I've uncovered $15 Girbaud baggy pants. Prize items, like the occasional $45 Yves Saint Laurent gown—maybe in a garish style, but the genuine article nonetheless—and $75 pristine condition pin-striped banker's suits are ceremoniously displayed up front near the cash register.

Neighborhood regulars say the jackpot pieces seem to surface on Saturdays, when the crowds descend. Prices are somewhat negotiable, but generally men's shirts are $5 to $10, sports jackets $25 to $50, and suits up to $75. Most women's and children's clothes go for $5 to $15, and shoes are $15 to $40. There's an actual dressing room at the back. Gabay's gift certificates are ardently welcomed by local residents.   — L.D.

Gabay's, 225 First Avenue, 254-3180. Open Monday to Friday, 9 A.M. to 5:30 P.M.; Saturday till 5 P.M.; Sunday, 10 A.M. to 4 P.M. MC, V, checks.

KENI VALENTI

K E N I Valenti has the distinction of being the first couturier to descend on Avenue B. Yet despite the Badlands location, a past history of creating wacky cocktail hats for Betsey Johnson, and his current line of outré clothes for men, Valenti concocts mostly uptown ladies' fare with a lingering Japanese esthetic. His look is spare and elongated. His signature—a wrapped, draped, comfortable line with no zippers or other hardware—is best displayed in tie or high-rise pants, done in wool for winter, cotton and linen for summer.

For stellar clients like Grace Jones, Valenti musters up body-hugging panne velvet or silk lamé eveningwear. For risqué men, he offers high-rise maillot swimsuits, bolero jackets, and wool jersey underwear pants. But his major output is redefined classic women's day gear, like jackets pleated on one side and denim dresses with a wide A-line (the 1950s reinterpreted by the 1980s), exaggerated cowl necks, and overlong push-up sleeves. Sometimes he designs matching square berets and double-brim sun hats.

You won't see clothes like these everywhere. Production is extremely limited, and the look is singular, which may help to justify the price range. Dresses are usually no less than $200; pants cost $80 to $200; shirts start at $60 and go to $450 for silk chiffon; coats are $250 to $800; and hats are $40 to $300.

The decor is tenement storefront black-paint chic, with a wallful of long, skinny-making mirrors placed between purposely exposed beams.   — L.D.

Keni Valenti, 170 Avenue B, 420-8260. Open Wednesday to Sunday, 1 P.M. to 6 P.M.; maybe till 7 P.M. on weekends. MC, V, checks.

BATISLAVIA

B E W A R E clothing stores with decor that's meant to lure. Fake marble Greco-postmodern columns against peach walls often mask dull products. But the interior of Batislavia, a cross between tropical and baroque with post-high tech thrown in—there's a pink pineapple-style chandelier, a mirror with a model airplane attached to its rococo frieze, a fake fireplace, and a functioning oversized desk shaped like a mutant parallelo-gram—is the background for two of the area's most talented storefront couturiers.

Like the ambience, the clothes designed by Pilar Limosner and Carmel Johnson are witty but practical and well made. You can take them almost anywhere, and prices range from $30 for little tops to $300 for novelty coats. Johnson specializes in elegant-looking clothes that transform themselves by means of strategically placed rows of buttons and buttonholes. Undo the buttons on her dresses, for example, turn them sideways, and they become skirts or pants. Fabrics change with the season and tend toward the avant-garde (she was cutting brocades pre-Gaultier).

Limosner's clothes are inspired by cultural myths: from Gandhi to Liberace to "Star Trek." For example, one line featured a high-collared damask patterned tunic, $90, with a practical weatherproofed silver lamé lining: "Mr. Spock imitating Elvis Presley while visiting Liberace at home," she suggests.

Though the store is small, Limosner and Johnson would never omit accessories. There are Limosner's revamped sailor hats, $40 to $60, and primitive-looking jewelry from local artists, $15 to $60.

Sales are held at the end of each season, with markdowns from 25% to cost. — L.D.

Batislavia, 151 Avenue A, 982-1959. Open Wednesday to Saturday, 1 P.M. to 8 P.M. Checks.

EVERYTHING IN THE STORE IS MADE OF 100% COTTON

IN 1979, Roberta Davis opened the only specialty lingerie shop between East Houston and East 14th streets. Her customers kept asking for pure cotton underwear. She listened and dropped the polyester Christian Diors, but she couldn't find any manufacturers of inexpensive all-cotton bikinis and bras. So, working with small local contractors, she produced them herself and changed the name of her shop from Lingerie for Less to Everything in the Store Is Made of 100% Cotton—surely the longest store name in retail history.

Except for a small percentage of Lycra in the pantyhose, Davis's claim is absolutely true. Most of the goods are basics at ultralow prices, $3 to $15. Many of the customers buy a year's supply at a time. The stock includes various panty styles and basic but charming slips, bras, tank tops, teddies, fabulous G-strings (they don't leave lines under tight pants), and anklets. A lot of items come in wovens *and* jerseys, some of them in a wide range of colors. Favorites here are the old-fashioned jersey tap pants, garter belts, and stockings, in black and white only.

Lately, Davis has expanded into loungewear and street clothes—oversized heavy cotton jersey shirts, long cardigan jackets, shifts, pull-on elastic-waist skirts, and pants. Nothing's over $35. She's also added a children's line of colorful jersey shirts, pants, and T-shirt dresses, sizes 2 to 10, all under $20.

Though the shop occupies one of those narrow Lower East Side tenement storefront spaces, Davis has carved out a dressing niche at the back.   — L.D.

Everything in the Store Is Made of 100% Cotton, 143 First Avenue, no phone. Open Monday to Friday, 1 P.M. to 6 P.M.; Saturday, 11 A.M. to 6 P.M. AE.

---

1 0 9

S C O T T Gibson, the designer often holding down the shop at 109, refers to Eva Goodman's piece he's modeling as "the black hole." Worn as a dress, jacket, or pants, the black jersey garment with foam tubing hoops looks like Fellini does Wonderland in Tokyo. Goodman's raincoats drip with worms or explode in profusions of psychedelic colors and plastic flowers.

She creates some of the more radical fashions carried at this store that describes itself as "a cooperative of new designers." Similarly strong are Dinosaur Counter Couture's wearable political statements: A dollar bill stenciled on an oversized T-shirt features Nancy Reagan's mug and the motto, *Why change the world when you can change your clothes?* Authentic maid and waitress uniforms bear images of women whose work is never done.

Many pieces are one of a kind, but these days 109 is anchoring avant-garde wares with more accessible basics. The less flamboyant can try the dresses by England's Body Map, Louis Ho's jerseys and linens in clean, simple lines, or Scott's "gentrified" denim trenchcoat. Add flash with Sonda Weber's loomed chenille black cutaway tux or her coat of many colors. Top it all off with a dyed bunny fur and leather hat by Linda Geraci or bottom out with plastic fish sandals. Finishing touches come from unique pieces by local jewelers. One of the original East Village boutiques, 109 will amuse as it clads, whatever the season or sex. Prices average $25 to $200. — S.C.

109, 109 St. Marks Place, 260-2622. Open daily, 1 P.M. to 7 P.M.; 2 P.M. to 11 P.M. during the summer. AE, MC, V.

A REPEAT PERFORMANCE

B E V E R L Y Bronson is unpacking a care package full of men's travel kits and cigarette cases sent from England by Mum and Dad, whom she has trained to scour jumble sales to supplement her stock at A Repeat Performance. She left a successful career in journalism to mind what she dismisses as her "junk" shop, along with her partner, J. Lee Smith, a former emergency-room nurse. Indeed, she doesn't tack extravagant prices on her vintage clothing and collectibles. Merchandise is varied: "Anything I like, I put in." Since she can buy cheap, she sells cheap, catering to a neighborhood clientele. Having "starved" herself for years, she's struggling to survive upcoming rent increases without capitulating to inflating her own prices. More power to her.

Beverly feels her forte is menswear. A lot of guys come in for her vintage shoes, which begin around $20 and run to $35 for hand-stitched English imports, and for her cuff links, usually about $8. Jackets are around $18, suits, $35. Women's dresses can be as inexpensive as $5 or $10, or as much as $50 for finely finished party clothes. She also carries interesting odds and ends of furniture, luggage, cutlery, lamp shades, curtains, hats, eyeglasses, bags. Be sure to check out the adjoining shop, an atmospheric herbalist called Penny's General Store.   — S.C.

A Repeat Performance, 126 St. Marks Place, 529-0832. Open Monday and Wednesday, noon to 6:30 P.M.; Thursday till 9 P.M.; Friday and Saturday till 10 P.M.; Sunday, 1 P.M. to 8:30 P.M. Checks.

NASTY HABITS

N A S T Y Habits is not a clothier for punk nuns, but that notion might provide an insight into its predominantly black (some white, some red, sometimes) line of clothing for men and women drawn to the darker persuasions. There's every variation of the black basics, often featuring less-than-decent exposures. On stretchy pants, a clear vinyl strip runs from ankle to waist. Kinky hot pants connect with fake garters to built-in stockings. House designers Giancarlo, Alberto, and Kimberly cut jersey and vinyl into designs that polite society probably wouldn't greet with open arms. While there are some fairly discreet little black dresses, a keyhole or two is usually removed to show some skin; and though the vinyl tux might manage to make it into an urban ball, it would stop traffic at a small-town mall.

Nasty Habits is the outlet for a wholesale line, but it does stay irreverent and tend toward tartery: kinky clothes for him or her at reasonable prices, usually $18 to $50, with one-of-a-kind pieces running $100 to $200. Black turtleneck tees feature huge shoulder pads. The rayon skirt that puns off tux pants has an irregular hem, and a black skirt that looks polite from the front is a little more than a bun warmer from arrears. Accessorize with their mirror-shard jewelry. Oddly enough, the atmosphere here is homey. Don't be surprised to see one of the guys ironing up front, or to hear the roar of Kimberly at the sewing machine come from the back room.

Sales are held in January, April (when winter merchandise may be marked down by 50% to 75%), and midsummer.

— S.C.

Nasty Habits, 102 St. Marks Place, 673-5516. Open daily, noon to 8 P.M. AE.

CLEAR METALS

T H I S ain't the place to come with a tour bus full of people. It's minuscule and crammed with accessories: jewelry, hats, belts by Barbara Klar and Tamera Lyndsay, who run the joint. Barbara does the mostly-leather-and-metal belts and gauntlets and a lot of the jewelry; Tamera, the hats and wraparound wrist wallets. The back room is the workshop where it's all wrought.

Barbara's jewels are usually semiprecious stones and metal. A series called "Hearts in Bondage" dangles crystal hearts tangled in delicate barbed wire from bracelets, earrings, and necklaces, $50 to $75. Don't miss her large brass and acrylic mirror neo-Egyptian-eye necklaces and fur-trimmed hat pins. Her belts often have hidden pockets, and while her gauntlets may appeal to bikers, they are as well suited to accompany sleek, sexy eveningwear.

Tamera's hats are mutable shapes in leather, canvas, velvet ribbon, or combinations thereof, one of the better styles being an exaggerated newsboy's cap. Her pocketed wrist wallets in a variety of fabrics and leathers, including manta ray, hide whatever secret you wish to stash, leaving hands free for higher callings.

Of the outside designers, Janet Stein's Eastern European-influenced winter hats with earflaps are about the most stylish protection from the elements a girl could hope to find. On the lighter side are Carrie Hollister's White Sugar earrings—fantastical and beautifully colored trinkets. Prices begin at $10 and rarely exceed $75, with a $5 sale basket.   — S.C.

Clear Metals, 117 East 7th Street, 598-1102. Open Wednesday to Sunday, 1 P.M. to 7 P.M. AE, checks.

LILLA LOVA

W I T H a name like Lilla Lova she's got to be elusive, elegant and very European. She is. She won't commit herself to whether she will be here in a year. Her lease is in order. She is just a bit the child of the changing winds. If it's a rainy day she may not feel like opening. Don't be put off. She's also warm and earthy and will set up private appointments if her erratic hours aren't to your convenience.

Lilla's salon specializes in old-school elegance in dress clothing. Casuals don't interest her. Pure fabrics, particularly silks and wools, are crafted into carefully finished classic lines. Raglan-sleeved, shawl-collared cruise coats reminiscent of the

1930s come in wool ($300) or linen ($200). A walking suit with a three-quarter-length jacket is wool tweed ($275). The silk taffeta (one of her favorite fabrics) dinner suit is made with a skirt or slacks. For after dark a black silk organza dress with a diagonal dropped waist and pussy cat bow could crash a Jay Gatsby party. It's been marked down to $150. Everything seems timeless, alluding to the past, flirting with the glamour of old films, but constructed to be worn for the next twenty years. Lilla Lova will also custom-tailor to suit your taste. Sophie Pujebet contributes her jewelry.

Sales are held in January and mid-June and, in December, holiday clothes are marked down as much as 50%.　— S.C.

Lilla Lova, 117 East 7th Street, 505-9653. Open Wednesday to Sunday, 2 P.M. to 8 P.M.; or by appointment. AE, checks.

EINSTEIN'S

T H E R E' S more to this than meets the skin. Julia Morton might be called the Marcel Duchamp of fashion, and her partner, Paul Monroe, the Fabergé of the Lower East Side. With Greer Lankton, who makes the dolls on display, they have created Einstein's, an "experimental lab" where they've cooked up the definitive East Village boutique—not because it is the most typical, but because it best incorporates the imaginative pioneer spirit that put this neighborhood on the map for its music, art, and fashion. Iggy Pop and Lauren Hutton shop here.

Julia names the highly conceptual visions she translates into fabrics. "The Backyard I Never Had" has a flowing green grasslike jacket. "All About Suburbia" is a linen pun of a dress—Jackie O on LSD. "Drag Race" is a basic black sheath with toy cars that roll down the front on ribbon strips. A hat featuring a smashed watch, her answer to Swatch, was part of an ensemble called "My, How the Time Flies." Her now-notorious dresses for men are more conservatively styled, the concept alone being a courageous enough statement for any man to make, she feels.

Paul's pièces des résistance are his found-object jewelry, though his clothes hold their own. Plastic toys, cherubs, nails, little mermaids from the edges of margaritas served at a local restaurant—anything he finds lying around is alchemically transformed into objects of delight and desire. Other gems are jewel-encrusted.

Einstein's prices are up since it opened down the block in 1981, rents having tripled. Paul's jewelry runs from $36 to $425, but averages $68 to $120. Julia's dresses begin under $50 and can go for as much as $130, but usually don't exceed $100. A wool flannel trenchcoat in an optical illusion design and lined in velvet was $400. Novelty hats begin at $4.99 for a folded Weekly World News (read it) or a "TV antenna," but average $34.

Storewide sales are held from January 18 to February 18 and from July 18 to August 18.   — S.C.

Einstein's, 96 East 7th Street, 598-9748. Open 2 P.M. to 8 P.M.; closed Tuesday. AE, MC, V, checks.

ENELRA

A R L E N E, who owns the place, refers to her intimate apparel for women as "transitional . . . from sheets to streets." She also stresses that it is sexy. By and large it is. If you are looking to lose your revolutionary credentials, just touch the silk lingerie and nighties, shiver, and capitulate.

Streetwear is well represented here—stretchy little black dresses by Sally Beers and Body Map will carry you through dinner at L'Acajou and over to the Palladium. Stirrup pants and imported Italian swimsuits are comfortable activewear. But it's the lingerie that's the real draw. The array of bras, many with matching undies, ranges from sports supports to bustiers, includes many with pushups and padding for aspiring Dianne Brills. Yes, she shops here. Slips are feminine, form-fitting stretch lace and delicate silk charmeuse, with teddies and nightgowns in the latter, too. There are innocent white cottons as well—just to keep up the variety. Sexy G-strings are clearly a house specialty.

When you must hit the street (as alas one must at some point), do it in her wonderful accessories: Stylish socks, ladylike modish gloves, hosiery. A plush chenille robe will ease the . . . transition.

Prices are as low as $4 for a pair of gloves to $250 for a street ensemble, with bras $7.50 to $52, silk teddies and slips $60 to $89, swimwear around $50.   — S.C.

Enelra, 48½ East 7th Street, 473-2454. Open Monday to Wednesday, noon to 9 P.M.; Thursday and Friday till 11 P.M.; Saturday and Sunday till 7:30 P.M. AE, MC, V, checks.

LOVE SAVES THE DAY

W H A T you probably won't find here is the jacket that a desperately sought Susan claimed was worn by Jimi Hendrix. What you will find is a room full of vintage clothes, jewelry, bric-a-brac, jokes, toys, and costumes. For Halloween they bring in masks and witches' hats at disposable prices. There are wonderful windows, too—red and white hearts and lace for Valentine's Day, or animal skin prints celebrating the savage fecundity of spring. Look up when you walk in. Evening gowns from the 1920s and 1930s, usually $100 to $200 but running to $700, hang from the ceiling. Skirts are on sale for $5 at the door, and flannel shirts are $2.50 to $4. Dresses are moderately priced at $12 to $30 (half what they are marked), and goofy old hats are $8 to $30. Men's tweed jackets are often on sale for $9.95. For the home, crochet throws, lace curtains, and chenille bedspreads are reasonably priced and worth a rummage. Several cases display jewelry—vintage and current, including a large selection of turquoise, as well as 1950s sunglasses and old fur pieces. — S.C.

Love Saves the Day, 119 Second Avenue, 228-3802. Open Monday to Friday, 1 P.M. to 9 P.M.; Saturday and Sunday till midnight; 2 P.M. to midnight during the summer. AE, MC, V.

MEN-ZA MEN-ZA

W H E N you wake up in the morning with hangover-hypersensitive skin that feels as if it has undergone penetration by poisoned quills, there is only one fabric with which to balm it—silk charmeuse, the fabric that feels like rose petals. Amazing stuff. Men-za Men-za specializes in teaching the oft-benighted sex about the pleasures of this breath of a fabric against flesh with robes, pajamas, and undies for him. They're expensive—boxers begin at $40, robes and pajamas may run $200—but what a way to go. The more compulsively butch may prefer the sumptuous "Rocky" robe, which features a built-in neck towel/hood, $109.

Clothing in this shop is body-conscious—intimate apparel and sportswear intended to show off bulges, acquired or innate. There is a wide selection of jockeys and boxers, swimwear, bicycle pants, and T-shirts, much of which is imported. From Calvin jockeys to Playboy bunny socks to Tous les Caleçons French T-shirts to hand-painted silk ties with matching handkerchiefs, merchandise is well displayed in the swank stone-gray setting that generated more than a few cries of "there goes the neighborhood." As in its sister store, Enelra, Men-za Men-za's best stock is for the boudoir.   — S.C.

Men-za Men-za, 104 Second Avenue, 477-3661. Open Monday to Wednesday, noon to 8:30 P.M.; Thursday to Saturday till 11 P.M.; Sunday till 7:30 P.M. AE, MC, V, checks.

9 9 X

9 9 X maintains an irrevocable link with rock and roll. Previously the other half of 99 Records on MacDougal, it now adjoins Some Records, a tiny store specializing in "hard-core" music. Duane comes in from next door to announce to the young woman carefully applying purple and gold vertical stripes to her eyelids that the Butthole Surfers have just settled into their motel in New Jersey. A couple of guys are trying to decide between a pair of thick-soled British brothel creepers and the mildly lunatic Dr. Marten's Air Wair clunkers, a line of punked-up workboots and shoes. This means the tiny shop is mobbed.

99X is one of the most affordable of the next-wave boutiques. Gina wholesales a slew of accessories—socks, makeup, fishnet and lace panty hose, hats, black cotton gloves, sunglasses—that she sells in the shop for $2 to $5. She also manufactures a few separates featuring crazy fabrics—some original 1960s prints, others with an Americana theme—at $14 to $40. The Body Map and Guns and Butter labels round out the stock, often marked down.

Gina has a wonderful selection of shoes, mostly eccentric English imports for men and women, and an immense range of jewelry from young designers, some local and some European.

Silly stuff starts at $3, while chic Tri Axis and Pauletta Brooks jewelry is rarely over $50 and mostly well under. A box is filled with clothing marked down to $1 to $10. Mail orders available on the Dr. Marten's. — S.C.

99X, 210 East 6th Street, 460-8599. Open Wednesday to Saturday, 1 P.M. to 8 P.M.; Sunday, 2 P.M. to 6 P.M. AE.

YUZEN

W H E N the free-form futurism of the East Village has just about unraveled you, contemplate Japan and its formal tradition. A spectacular silk kimono is always hung in the window, arms spread wide on a dowel. That's Yuzen's specialty, kimonos. All in good condition, all elegantly displayed. Most are vintage, twenty to sixty years old, and carefully chosen in Japan.

In addition to the more familiar luxurious silks are the practical cottons. Full robes, jackets, and the kind of pants worn by Japanese shopkeepers and firemen—some vintage, some new—are available for adults and children. Prices begin around $30. Robes made of printed cottons are called Yukatas; robes of yarn-dyed woven ikat patterns are called kasuris. The store itself is named for a resist-dye technique used on the silks. Owner Don Walker will distinguish processes for the novice.

Incidental items include ties made from vintage kimono silk, purses, scarves, obis, and wall hangings. On their buying trips in Japan, the owners occasionally find an exceptional piece of antique furniture that winds up in the store. At one point there was a lovely tansu chest used in the tea ceremony.

Antique kimonos average $60 to $150, though outstanding items from the nineteenth century may run as much as $3,000.
— S.C.

Yuzen, 318 East 6th Street, 677-0791. Open daily, 1 P.M. to 11 P.M. AE, MC, V.

ONA

S A T U R D A Y afternoon and Paula's salon is in full swing. Lari Shox, one of the store's featured designers and a pioneer of hand-painted clothing, is sitting with a young designer from the Upper East Side who is desperate to know just what makes this neighborhood so magical. A man comes in seeking a place where he can do some silk-screening. Lari is himself trying to track down a poster of Eddie van Halen wearing one of his painted "eye" suits. Some people come in to shop.

Run by house designer Paula Chandler, Ona offers clothing and accessories from a cross section of young designers. Whimsical hats in leather, fake fur, linen, and straw are $20 to $80. A twist of straw netting is a turban by Jill van Dyke; a black jersey "rasta" hat featuring long fabric braids is by Shox. Paula is behind the counter of one-of-a-kind jewelry she has selected with her keen instinct for untried talent. Prices range from $15 to $150, but most items are under $50.

Simple, clean jersey dresses by Paula and Kathy Inukai begin around $40. Kat P. Scent is always outlandish. She revived the peace symbol motif (thanks a lot, hon) and invented real brassiere-topped sundresses. Classy spring coats from Martha McGill run up to $160 and tend toward the voluminous. David Greene paints jacket backs with such celebrated icons as Elvis and Marilyn. And, of course, more Shox. — S.C.

Ona, 64 Avenue A, 777-0570. Open Tuesday to Saturday, 1 P.M. to 8 P.M.; Sunday till 6 P.M. AE, MC, V.

LANDEAUX STUDIO X

"Y O U just can't live in Texas if you don't have a lotta soul." Well, Doug Sahm may have stretched it a bit with that line, but there do seem to be certain plots of earth where the soil is more fertile (though not necessarily arable). Landeaux Studio X is the brain bairn of Roedeanne Landeaux, a Texan whose transplant to the heart of the Lower East Side may have enhanced the urban sophistication of her designs, though not at the price of a quality one would hesitate to call *soul* in clothing but could. She puts into her fashions many of the qualities one would look for in a lover: They have style, are often breathtakingly beautiful and intelligent, can be worn unselfconsciously. They embrace the lines of a female body (women do have curves and rarely run to six feet) and lay gentle on the skin, fabrics ranging from shimmering featherweight silks to thick textured cotton jac-quard. (She calls this her all-American line since it is United States-made but conjures a rough-hewn Mexican peasant weave.) Styles range from dropped-waist dresses to harem pants to Laura-Ashley-goes-lamé shifts. Further titillation of the flesh may be achieved with her handmade silk lingerie. She also makes a few items for babies—shirts, pants, dresses—in cotton or silk.

Prices for ready-to-wear dresses begin at $50 to $250 for cottons, $90 to $400 for tailored separates. Unique charmeuse-lined, bias-cut silk eveningwear may run up to $800. Landeaux Studio X offers couturier service, too often dressing weddings, films, and entertainers. For quality, vision, and attention to detail, this place is a treasure trove.   — S.C.

Landeaux Studio X, 78 East 1st Street, 254-1700. Open Tuesday to Friday, noon to 6 P.M.; Saturday, 1 P.M. to 5 P.M. AE.

SHRIMPTON & GILLIGAN

VISION and revision. A cool room this, Shrimpton & Gilligan. "It's based on French wallpaper," Angel Zimick, one of the two house designers, explains, though she cannot recall the period, "like they used in music halls." Painted by John Fischer, the walls and multicolored fake marble floor feature crests, with the tools of a tailor's trade—scissors, needles and pins, bolts of fabric, thimbles—replacing traditional emblems. Angel is in the workshop at the rear of the store where she is creating her fall fashions, which she describes mostly with negatives: "Not uptight, not bitching, not snobby" in mood, and "not heavy or bulky" in fabric. For a neat little long-sleeved rayon blouse with a 1940s sculpt, she stresses shape, not period. When she does use unnegated adjectives they are words like "humorous" and "charming," and for fabrics, "sporty." Specifically these are naturals and rayons, cotton knits and woven jacquards, an Italian linen that blends in sheen with a little Lurex. Angel's partner Chris Isles leans more toward prints, from carrots to cartoons. Both like shifts and simple lines. Dresses average $75 to $100 for summer and $100 to $200 in winter. T-shirts begin around $25.

Recently, Angel and Chris added men's clothing, when they discovered most of their customers were male. Tony Vermillion liberates male anatomy with backless tees and drapey sweatshirt updates, while Jack Pell for Aire cuts beautifully textured cottons into pleated slacks, sport shirts, and suits.   — S.C.

Shrimpton & Gilligan, 70 East 1st Street, 254-1249. Open Monday to Saturday, noon to 8 P.M.; Sunday till 7 P.M. AE, checks.

DESIGN EAST

O N E doesn't want a kid growing up without a sense of sass. Courage, yes. Obedience, not really. Not even a dog should be too obedient. Self-reliance is important, too. One must watch those smother-mother tendencies to grow a good thinker. Even from the beginning the little bugger has to be swaddled with humor if he is to come out fighting. Design East, a little storefront run by a couple of young artists who silk-screen irreverent images on T-shirts and sweats, to the rescue. They make their mark on clothing for brats of all ages, from infant to adult.

Want an image that shows the folks back home you've been to the Apple? "New Yolk" features a skillet with two fried eggs. "Regular" (in New York coffeeshopese, that's with cream and sugar) shows a steaming cup of coffee. The martini glass and television set speak for themselves. New designs include colorful roadscapes and toasters. Beach towels, tote bags, and scarves round out the line. One of the original boutiques cum galleries, Design East also offers sculpture and rubber pins that are worth checking out. In the neighborhood where graffiti went from misdemeanor to big business, it's nice to find wearable art still at democratic prices, usually $10 to $20 for adults, $6 for kids, with pins $2 to $4.   — S.C.

Design East, 7 Second Avenue, 598-0046. Open Tuesday to Sunday, noon to 6 P.M. during the winter; till 7 or 8 P.M. during the summer.

THE BROADWAY CORRIDOR

INTRODUCTION BY
Stephanie Chernikowski

Broadway, long regarded as the Great White Way because it's the center of the theater district—oft heralded in song, on stage, and at the cinema for its bright lights and big-city sophistication—began as a wagon trail. While the midtown strip of this street that runs the length of Manhattan may be better known, the last few years have seen the lower reaches snatch a little notoriety of their own. Between the Gap clothing store at 8th Street and the huge Tower Records at 4th Street, with its adjacent street market—overflowing toward Canal Street as new stores open to the south—Broadway is jammed solid with pedestrian traffic on weekends. Some come to shop along this corridor, where it seems a new store is born every week; others come to dine in the glitzy restaurants serving international cuisines.

Shopping is youth oriented, catering to the New York University student population that lives nearby. It follows the

THE BROADWAY CORRIDOR

1 Zoot Clothiers
2 Unique Clothing Warehouse
3 Cheap Chic
4 Antique Boutique
5 Street Market
6 Maripolitan

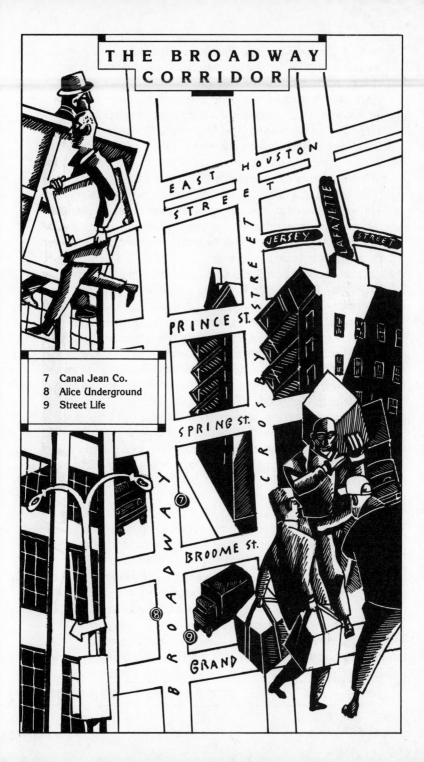

THE BROADWAY CORRIDOR

7 Canal Jean Co.
8 Alice Underground
9 Street Life

lead of Unique Clothing Warehouse, the street's first major department store for the hip, but is increasingly varied: some cheap, some retro, some Seventh Avenue. Kavala at 1 Astor Place is well stocked with moderately priced current fashions for moderate men and women. Good shoes aren't expensive. They do free alterations. The Gap at 8th Street and Wings at Bond Street have basics like jeans, sweats, and sportswear. Wings is particularly recommended for international visitors who want American standards like Levi's, Danskins, or Calvin Klein undies at a discount. Le Chateau at Houston is a popular Canadian chain that manufactures reasonably priced "fashion-forward" menswear and womenswear, including shoes. Below Houston, Mano a Mano carries better menswear at reduced prices in an upscale environment.

Conran's on Astor Place, the Pottery Barn at 4th Street, and Broadway Panhandler below Houston are good for contemporary home furnishings and tablewear and kitchenware at reasonable prices. Conran's, the largest, is the most varied and the best for furniture. Pottery Barn has biannual sales with serious markdowns. Panhandler imports a lot of kitchenware, including all-metal Mouli graters, difficult to find even in France. Those willing to pay more for the extraordinary should take a side trip to Jerrystyle (34 East 4th Street). Though it's essentially an interior designers' showcase (and it's quite a show), its "ancient modern" lamps and objects are for sale. S and S Antiques just south at 339 Lafayette specializes in vintage furniture and memorabilia, from Deco through the 1950s, with a little bit of anything else that fits. It's eccentric and often exceptional.

Back on Broadway, at 743, Star Magic, with its maps and globes (celestial and terrestrial), crystals and talismans, jewels and telescopes, brings the sky within reach. Totems of transportation to unexplored terrains are guaranteed to capture the imagination. Those who prefer reading about this world will find the Kiosk at 753 a well-stocked newsstand, a source for the imported and the arcane. Don't miss Untitled II at 3rd Street, though be warned it can be habit-forming. Carrying art and photography books, but mostly postcards, they stock the most current and the rare, the artful and the delightfully tasteless, from high art to post punk. Cinemabilia (the name tells the story) is upstairs at 611.

And, of course, there is Tower Records, "the largest record store in the known world." They don't have everything but they do have a hell of a lot, including frequent in-store appearances by rock stars signing their latest hits or running up their charge accounts. On weekends the place is so jammed you'd think they were giving it away. An annex on 4th Street at Lafayette discounts classical tapes and records.

Dining in this neighborhood is best for those who enjoy sipping blue margaritas in a glossy environment while waiting for a table. Bar Lui has nouvelle Italian food and Bayamo serves Asian-Caribe cuisine. Caramba offers Mexican fare. Betty Brown's serves retro junk food and ice cream to those who missed their chance for a sugar rush at David's Cookies up the street. Bitable has fresh salads and pitas for a healthy lunch. To the east on 4th Street, Acme specializes in regional American cooking in a rough-hewn room. If your budget is limited or you want a more relaxed atmosphere, head half a block west on Waverly to Eddie's for a burger or to the Waverly Coffee Shop, a student dive serving soups and sandwiches.

Most of the historical interest in the area—like most of the interesting theater—is off Broadway. Begin at Astor Place with Cooper Union, a tuition-free private school for art, architecture, and engineering, founded in 1859 by an idealistic industrialist named Peter Cooper. Abraham Lincoln, Susan B. Anthony, and Mark Twain spoke here. Today it continues to be a prestigious design academy. In the center of the street, the large movable cube, officially named The Alamo, is a participatory sculpture by Tony Rosenthal. Shove it.

Those intrigued by the rich and famous will want to amble a block down Lafayette to see the faded splendor of the Colonnades Row, former home of Cornelius Vanderbilt, Warren Delano (FDR's grandfather), and John Jacob Astor. At his death, Astor was the richest man in America, his wealth amassed by slaughtering beavers (see the commemorative tiles in the Astor Place subway station), then buying up most of Manhattan. It is claimed that his only deathbed regret was not having bought it all.

Across the street from the Colonnades is the Public Theater, housed in a building Astor constructed (he did leave his mark on the neighborhood) ostensibly as a library for the poor, though the hours were not to a workingman's convenience. Home of Joe Papp's New York Shakespeare Festival, the Public is one of New York's most important Off-Broadway theaters, with fare ranging from the original production of *A Chorus Line* to works by Samuel Beckett. Stop by to see what's running. A limited number of half-price tickets go on sale on the day of performance. Its Shakespeare in the Park (Central Park's Delacorte Theatre) offers annual summer productions of Shakespeare and other classics—Raul Julia and Meryl Streep's *The Taming of the Shrew* was fiery—free to anyone willing to wait on line for tickets.

At 13 Astor Place, where the District 65 Union building now stands, 30 people were killed and 150 were injured in 1849 when riots erupted between fans of rival British and American actors. This is a town that takes its arts seriously. Crowds now gathered across the street at Astor Place Hair Designers may look ominous but tend to be more docile. In business since the 1940s and capable of cutting a 1950s DA style worthy of James Dean, this real American barber shop survived the contempt of the 1960s unscathed and unchanged to become the darling of the East Village. Now hordes of retro freaks and arch punks seeking asymmetry come from hither and yon to stand on line (they don't take appointments) for hours waiting for an $8 clip job (without wash; $10 with); $10 for women or $12 with wash. They still give shaves.

For redeeming social value, stop in to the New Museum just below Houston at 583 where you may see displays by contemporary artists. Check the events scheduled. They often sponsor tours of artists' lofts.

To reach the Broadway Corridor by subway: Take the BMT R to 8th Street or the IRT 6 to Astor Place. By bus: Take the M1 up Bowery or down Park Avenue South; the M3 or M5 down Fifth Avenue; the M101 or M102 up or down Third Avenue; or the M13 crosstown to Astor Place.

■   ■   ■

ZOOT CLOTHIERS

"WE are retro, not antique," they will insist at Zoot, pointing out that most of their wares are from the 1940s, 1950s, and 1960s. They are similarly quick to note that, as the nation's largest supplier of these goods, they are often called upon to dress films, music videos, and the stars. They number among their customers Bruce Springsteen, Madonna, PeeWee Herman, and Whoopi Goldberg, who shops with her mom. Their selection is vast, with clothing well arranged and easily viewed.

About 80% of their stock is vintage. Dress up in formals: tuxes, $35 to $100, and prom dresses, $30 to $50. Dress for the street in bowling shirts, $15, madras or seersucker sports coats or letter jackets, $25 and up. Of the new stock, most is their house-manufactured separates, $20 to $30, in trendy cuts and fabrics. There are some pretty snazzy military-styled rubber raincoats imported from France selling for $35. Accessories include classic fringed rayon scarves for $12.   — S.C.

Zoot Clothiers, 734 Broadway, 505-5411. Open Monday to Saturday, 10 A.M. to 10 P.M.; Sunday, noon to 8 P.M. AE, MC, V, checks.

UNIQUE CLOTHING WAREHOUSE

EVERYONE knows that the youth of America hangs out in shopping malls. For that matter, most of America centers its social activities around these complexes. Who would have expected New York kids, with the best stores and entertainment in the world, to feel deprived? No mall to call their own. The answer to their dreams: Unique Clothing has declared itself a shopping mall.

Unique Clothing Warehouse opened in 1973 and was true to its name. Big and stuffed with inexpensive clothing and accessories, it catered to the less-than-affluent students, artists, and musicians who were starting to crowd into the neighborhood, particularly into the East Village. It specialized in vintage and military wear, as well as early punk and new wave. You could even hear local punk bands like Talking Heads and Television on the sound system.

Today, a few doors up Broadway at 726, in its splashy new glass-fronted emporium, the music has become more synthesized, the clothes more off-the-rack—major labels like UFO, Pandemonium, Reminiscence, and French Connection—but it's still hip. Unique has brought the East Village to a larger audience by opening Wonderland, a boutique featuring young area designers; and Artwave, a do-it-yourself service dedicated to keeping painted clothing a participatory democracy. Accessories range from Maripolitan jewelry to wigs and sunglasses to a new cosmetics department. There are also good sale racks.

Cheap Chic, at Unique's old location, 718 Broadway, is paradise for bargain hunters, selling many of the same brands' current closeouts at genuinely "drastic reductions."   — S.C.

Unique Clothing Warehouse, 718 and 726 Broadway, 674-1767. Open Monday to Saturday, 10 A.M. to 9 P.M.; Sunday, noon to 8 P.M. AE, MC, V, checks.

ANTIQUE BOUTIQUE

A N T I Q U E Boutique, which encourages its customers to "be a legend in any time," claims to be the largest outlet for vintage threads around. So does its competitor up the street. Truth aside—both back up their claims with impressive stock—the competition seems an asset. Antique Boutique is a sprawling space filled with nostalgiabilia: clothing, jewelry, hats, gloves, lamps, kitchenware. It features clothing for men and women who want to dress like Marilyn Monroe or James Dean—some vintage, some restyled, some reproduced new. Vintage wares are cleaned and screened to come to you in near-mint condition. Baseball and bowling shirts ($12 to $20) are in one room; sports jackets, slacks, and tuxes in another. A classic white tux runs around $45, brocades and cutaways with tails can push $120. For women, they have a good stock of dresses and reproductions of vintage accessories, particularly hats and jewelry.

Downstairs is a bargain basement where outtakes that didn't qualify upstairs are sold cheap. Women's squaw and circle skirts can be had for around $7.99, dresses for $12.99 to $19.99. Down here the white tux jackets are $19.99 and men's khaki slacks are $6.99 to $15. Kimonos are $15 to $40. The major sale here is the two-for-one offer that comes at the end of July.   — S.C.

Antique Boutique, 712-714 Broadway, 460-8830. Open Monday to Wednesday, 10:30 A.M. to 10 P.M.; Thursday to Saturday till midnight; Sunday, noon to 8:00 P.M. AE, MC, V, checks.
    Other branches: 227 East 59th Street, 752-1680. Open Sunday to Friday, noon to 8 P.M.; Saturday, 10:30 A.M. to midnight.

STREET MARKET

E V E R Y Saturday and Sunday, the parking lot next door to Tower Records is transformed into a street market where licensed vendors bring their wares. Merchandise and quality vary, but it is a good place for a keen shopper to find bargains. From bags to belts to bonsais to homemade brownies and pizzas—they're here and they're for sale. Many vendors show up weekly; with others, catch it while you can.

A few of the artisans are excellent: See if the leather luggage is still being sold. Table after table displays jewelry—most new, a little antique, some imported—from laminated map pins featuring your fave geographical region to large Indian semi-precious stone bracelets to original handcrafted wares. There is a wide selection of T-shirts, many unique: Look out for the one with the curse in Polish.

Closeouts and seconds from name-brand socks and clothing manufacturers sell for well below retail: Esprit, Street Life, Sante, Gap. Watch for defects. A young Japanese designer sells silk-screened cotton and fleece separates for under $20. Imported sweaters from Mexico are well made and relatively inexpensive.

Vendors spill over up and down Broadway: more socks and a Pandora's box of jewelry. A Granadan artist spray paints T-shirts while you watch. Just remember, Pedro & Alejandro, whose couture is internationally admired, were discovered at a street market. Trust your eye.   — S.C.

Street Market, Broadway between Great Jones and East 4th streets. Open all day Saturday and Sunday, year-round. Cash.

MARIPOLITAN

M A R I P O L, née Marie Paule, is a legit downtowner, having done time—usually it ran from about midnight till dawn—during the glory days of the new-wave club scene. Her "too much is never enough" aesthetic—she heaped the rubber bangles on one Material Girl way back before the kids caught on—is no doubt the product of those days. Mix it up with her love of Chanel and fascination with the 1950s, and you have Maripolitan, a mini-museum of modern pop that features, along with her latest gems, a bit of local art and fashion craftsmanship. Clothing by Steven Anger and hats by Sherry Vigdor are often modestly priced sample pieces.

Maripol's classy chain mail and thick crosses series alludes to the Crusades. Mesh cuffs, $50 to $70, and belts for $3 to $300 stand opposite a rack of end-of-the-season earrings—lots of fluorescent plastic and rubber hoops and geometrics, many from her Maripolitan label—marked down to $3. A pillbox on a mesh bracelet adorned with an iridescent eye is $60. An "Around the World" charm bracelet for $70 features her fave totems: French poodle, phone, key to the city, Virgin Mary. Similarly 1950s-ish magnetic bracelets, jewel-encrusted stretch bands for him or her, claim healing powers. Relieve stress and improve circulation, while still looking cool, for a mere $14 to $16. Earrings, from cowboys and Indians to luminous Italian vitriol glass depicting crosses and exploding planets, average $12 to $24. The lady whose eye styled Blondie's *Parallel Lines* and Madonna's first two album covers ain't bad. — S.C.

Maripolitan, 59-65 Bleecker Street, 475-2277. Open Monday to Saturday, noon to 7 P.M. MC, V, checks.

CANAL JEAN CO.

I T ' S big, it's bright, it's cheap, and it's all to a disco beat. One of the original downtown department stores, Canal Jeans (now located on Broadway, though originally on the street of the same name) began as a glorified Army/Navy store with basics like jeans and T-shirts, webbed belts, cheap sunglasses, and in-house dyed shirts. Located near the now defunct Mudd Club, once the new-wave Studio 54, it offered neighborhood night-crawlers threads and eccentric accessories in which to meet the dawn.

Now it has a little bit of everything, but mostly trendy new and vintage clothing and accessories for young Americans: from recycled military trenchcoats ($29.95) and gabardine shirts ($8) to new $5 sneakers and $10 "Beatle boots." At the door are large area rugs imported from Turkey for $29, cotton T-shirts for $4.99, and name-brand socks and hosiery at serious reductions. Toward the rear is a wide selection of discounted lingerie and bathing suits. Cotton jersey dresses and overalls run around $20. Vintage clothing includes kimonos (even some for children) for $20 to $40, end-of-the-season blazers reduced to $5, and antique white nightshirts imported from Europe for $8 to $15.

Accessories include: wigs; cosmetics; a large variety of bags, and jewelry—plastic fish earrings, rhinestone bracelets, 99¢ aluminum bangle bracelets. As one customer commented, "You can spend the day here,"...and not come out impoverished. Bins outside the store feature garments for $1 to $2.

— S.C.

Canal Jean Co., 504 Broadway, 226-1130. Open Sunday to Thursday, 10 A.M. to 7 P.M.; Friday and Saturday till 8 P.M. AE, DC, Discover, MC, V, checks.

ALICE UNDERGROUND

I T S original Victorian boudoir atmosphere has gone to chrome, edged out by shiny racks of more merchandise, but if anything its stock of vintage clothes has improved and the prices stay reasonable. Outside are bins of army pants for $6, men's white shirts for a buck, and cord jackets for $5. Inside, the house cat, Cleo, pines for her buddy, Max, locked in the basement till he recovers from an illness, but they sneak a game of footsies under the crack in the door. It is a comfortable shop with clothing prettily presented—an old wooden vanity still holds gloves; racks display clothing without overwhelming.

Thursday is delivery day, when the cleaners bring in all the new stock that will hit the floor by Friday. Ladies' print rayon dresses from the 1940s go for around $40; a slew of cotton frocks from the 1950s are around $12; party dresses in failles, tulles, and laces average $25. A rack holds jeans going for half price, $6. Leather and suede jackets run $30 to $35, with bomber jackets for $125. Furs and fakes are $30 to $60. End-of-the-season markdowns are 50%.

There are some wonderful chenille bedspreads for behind closed doors—the real thing—$15 to $45, with robes to match, as well as some affordable silk lingerie. Brocade smoking jackets and rayon robes for him are $20 to $25. There's a small selection of children's clothing, too.   — S.C.

Alice Underground, 481 Broadway, 431-9067. Open daily, 10 A.M. to 7 P.M. Checks.

Other branches: 380 Columbus Avenue, 724-6682. Open daily, 11 A.M. to 8 P.M.

STREET LIFE

T H E S E guys are innovative. Street Life was, for what it's worth, among the first designers to start painting clothing. They splashed and stenciled cotton camp shirts, tees, sweats, and sneakers to become the dribble that started the deluge. Now they manufacture and distribute mostly men's and women's casual wear with a flair, often in cotton, occasionally in unexpected fabrics like brocade mattress ticking and acetate coat lining. Lines are usually simple and clean but current. Men's pleated slacks and oversized jackets run about $40 per. Bermuda shorts and shirts are $34 and $24, respectively. For women there are oversized cotton and challis shifts in interesting prints for $40, baker's smocks for $32, and circle skirts for $24. The end-of-the-season markdowns are phenomenal, with a $10 rack and $5 barrels a constant. Street Life proves that clothing may be utilitarian and durable without being boring.

While it features its own line, Street Life also carries accessories from other manufacturers "if they are exceptional." Case in point is their bags, which have ranged from colorful vinyl totes in Carmen Miranda prints to classy leather carpenter grips. Shoes, when they have them, are fun and moderately priced. Shop to music by Roxy Music and Bryan Ferry. — S.C.

Street Life, 470 Broadway, 219-3764. Open Monday to Saturday, 11 A.M. to 7 P.M.; Sunday, noon to 6 P.M. AE, MC, V, checks.

S O H O

INTRODUCTION BY
Lynn Yaeger

I f a compulsive shopper fell asleep twenty years ago and just now woke up, she would find that a whole new shopping neighborhood, more varied and interesting than she could ever have imagined, had sprung up in an area where formerly only factories and warehouses stood.

Soho today, with its teeming weekend crowds of tourists, artists, shoppers, and ordinary residents; its cast-iron buildings and art galleries; its cobblestone streets sporting new high-tech glass restaurants, is a shopper's dream come true. For seekers of the chic and unusual, this eclectic neighborhood has stores with a wide range of stylish merchandise, from neo-street punk to near-couture. There are clothes available that are identical to the ones on Madison Avenue—only here they are next to English chain mail shirts for men. And here you can see au

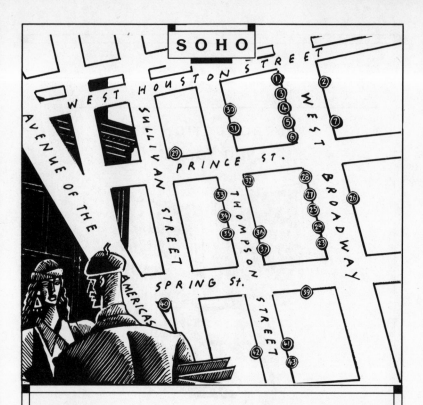

1 IF	23 Harriet Love
2 Le Grand Hotel	24 Paracelso
3 Henry Lehr	25 Miso
4 EX Jun	26 Beau Brummel
5 Susanne Bartsch	27 Dianne B.
6 Xavier Danaud	28 Joovay
7 Victoria Falls	29 Mood Indigo
8 Tootsi Plohound	30 Liza's Place
9 Back in Black	31 Betsey Johnson
10 Agnès B.	32 Paris/New York, Rita Kim
11 Tootsi Jr.	33 Ecco
12 Wendy's Store	34 FDR Drive
13 Parachute	35 Peter Fox
14 Comme des Garçons	36 Bomba De Clerq
15 Dianne Benson Men & Women	37 Bébé Thompson
16 Steve's Soho	38 Putumayo
17 La Rue des Rêves	39 Hollywood Legend
18 Charles Chevignon	40 Detail
19 Norma Kamali	41 Tous les Caleçons
20 The Second Coming, Ltd.	42 Tous les Caleçons
21 Le Boudoir Giambrone	43 Victoria DiNardo
22 Lilit Eclectiques	

courant designer clothes in the shops, then look down the street and see them being worn by some bright young thing lunching in the window of a former paint factory.

Soho was originally discovered and settled by artists, and a casual lower Manhattan mood still pervades the area, despite the presence of high-priced stores and restaurants. It's a stimulating, exciting place to visit art galleries, eat in restaurants, and spend your money—and whether you have $50 or $500 to blow, you're sure to find something wonderful here that will worm the cash right out of your pocket.

This guide seeks to describe the clothing and accessories stores that are especially distinguished for their merchandise and ambience—those that prove most seductive to the hearts and minds of the peripatetic shopper. But don't overlook the other shops along the way—for instance, Ad Hoc Softwares at 410 West Broadway for unusual linens, spectacular lace curtains, and special bed and bath accessories, and Dean and Deluca at 121 Prince for gourmet food. Think Big at 390 West Broadway, with its giant pencils and gargantuan paper clips, is especially worth noting if there are children in your party. Strictly for adults are the huge furniture emporiums, spanning styles from French country to Art Deco, that also dot the landscape. Look for them on Wooster and Greene streets.

It's hard to believe that only twenty years ago Soho was a quiet New York neighborhood, industrial east of West Broadway and residential Italian to the west. You can get a glimpse of the old neighborhood by taking a walk on Sullivan Street. Here, candy stores and butcher shops are still open for business, and people live in tenement apartments instead of high-tech lofts. Stop for a cappuccino at Cafe Borgia II at 161 Prince Street, then go directly across the street and look into the Vesuvio Bakery at 160—an Italian bread bakery that has stood unchanged, inside and out, for the last fifty years.

On the streets east of West Broadway, check out the fabulous cast-iron facades of the nineteenth-century factory buildings that became the first lofts and art galleries when Soho was young. These cast-iron buildings are rapidly being turned into condominium lofts, to accommodate the large number of people who want to live in Soho for the style and space that drew artists to this area in the first place.

Don't attempt to cover all of Soho in one day. This is a neighborhood where so many galleries, shops, and restaurants have opened in the last few years that you can spend weeks exploring the visual and gustatory delights. If you have only one day to spare, make sure you take enough breaks to keep up your sagging shopping spirits. When your eyes start to glaze over at the endless array of price tags, refocus them on a canvas or sculpture, or close them entirely behind a brimming espresso. Soho shops keep late hours—usually 11 A.M. to 7 P.M.—and some shops close on Mondays, like the art galleries. Most are open on Sunday, however.

If we consider Soho to be bordered by Houston Street on the north, Canal to the south, Sixth Avenue to the west, and Broadway to the east, you could cover the shops beginning from the top of West Broadway, then circling from east to west as you work your way down. Start the morning off with coffee and a bite at the Cupping Room Café, 359 West Broadway. Or if you're a different sort of shopper, start off with a shot and an omelette at Fanelli's, one of the oldest bars in the city, on the corner of Prince and Mercer. Stop at the Wine Bar at 422 West Broadway for much-needed midafternoon refreshment, or if you're saving all your money for clothes, keep in mind the Canal Street Coffee Shop (at West Broadway and Canal), where delicious French toast and coffee will set you back less than $3.

If you can spring for an expensive dinner, try the unpretentious Raoul's, at 180 Prince Street, for excellent hearty French food. There are lots of glamorous, pricey restaurants in Soho—just be on the lookout for peach-colored walls and a $200 flower arrangement in the window.

After a long hard day of shopping (and maybe even checking out a gallery or two), there's nothing nicer than collapsing under a heap of packages, with just your little face peeking out at the top, and sipping a gin rickey or munching on genuine French fries with sublime abandon.

To reach Soho by subway: Take the IND A, C, E, or K to Spring Street; the IND B or D to Broadway-Lafayette; the IRT 1 to Houston Street; the BMT R to Prince Street; or the IRT 6 to the eastern edge of Spring Street. By bus: Take the M1 up Centre Street or down Park Avenue South; the M5 down Fifth Avenue; the M6 down Broadway or up Church Street; the M10 down Seventh Avenue to Houston Street; or the M21 crosstown to West Broadway.

■   ■   ■

IF

A L T H O U G H it's not readily apparent if you're just drifting past, IF, on West Broadway a few doors down from Houston, contains the very best of the best—French and Japanese designers of the absolute first rank, hanging unpretentiously within reach of your grubby little hands. This is the dream store for the starving fashion-conscious population of Toledo or Kansas City—all the clothes you see in *Vogue,* waiting for you to try on, and without the overbearing Madison Avenue atmosphere or the chained-to-the-rack tactics of a department store.

Designers on parade include Anne Marie Beretta, Thierry Mugler, and Yohji Yamamoto. IF was one of the first stores to feature the complete works of Azzedine Alaïa, the designer of moment on both sides of the Atlantic. Wonderful Robert Clergerie shoes ($120 to $200) and also the new line of Alaïa shoes are another feature at IF.

There's a big men's department in the back room, with clothes from a variety of designers but specializing in the hard-to-find Gaultier for men. Actually, there are men's clothes here you won't see anywhere else—like a one-piece man's gladiator bathing suit with shoulder straps. (There are no mirrors in the try-on rooms, which is how you get to see a man in a gladiator suit with shoulder straps.)

As you would expect, prices here are high—the same amount you'd pay for these clothes on the Rue Montaigne or on East 60th Street. However, there are remarkable end-of-season sales, when lots of clothes are slashed to below-wholesale prices, often around $100. There's even a $50 rack.

The fitting room is a cunningly disguised confessional lifted from a defunct church somewhere—check under the lace panel and see the giant cross. Here you can silently ask forgiveness for your vanity, gluttony, and venality before emerging and trudging shamefacedly up to the cashier.

— L.Y.

IF, 474 West Broadway, 533-8660. Open Monday to Saturday, noon to 7:30 P.M.; Sunday till 7 P.M. AE, DC, MC, V, checks.

LE GRAND HOTEL

THIS large, long, brick-walled store is located right at the gates of the city of Soho—on West Broadway just off Houston Street. Le Grand Hotel was one of the first stores in Soho, and the (relatively) old girl has seen a lot of shops come and go, up and down the avenue. But Le Grand Hotel continues to flourish, thanks to the classic quality of its stock—special-occasion dresses and shoes for actress and model types.

The beautiful evening clothes here run to brightly colored satin taffeta and hand-beaded pastel silk ($250 and up). A portrait of a black ballerina (the owner's mother), circa 1920, stares serenely down from its perch high above the frenzied shoppers, who bite their lips and view themselves dubiously in turquoise chiffon and stocking feet.

Satin and rhinestone slippers ($120 to $180), as well as more conservative shoes in plain pink or apple-green leather ($100 and up), are available to go with the dresses. Modernist oversized costume jewelry and finer jewelry are here as well.

The salespeople are certainly eager to assist you. In fact, personal service at Le Grand Hotel is so personal it verges on the overbearing.

— L.Y.

Le Grand Hotel, 471 West Broadway, 475-7625. Open Tuesday to Friday, noon to 7 P.M.; Saturday till 6:30 P.M.; Sunday, 1 P.M. to 6 P.M. AE, MC, V, checks.

HENRY LEHR

464 West Broadway, 460-5500. See index for main listing.

EX JUN

E X Jun has beautiful Japanese clothes for the man who has everything—assuming he doesn't have a heliotrope rayon suit.

This minimalist steel and granite store carries the design staples of the Japanese new wave—trenchcoats in changeable taffeta with enormous shoulders; small-collared, small-patterned shirts ($120 to $180); sweaters that are hip takeoffs on 1950s high school cardigans—everything an homme de world can't live without and things a woman would die for too.

Philip Glass-type music plays in the background, and a video screen above shows pictures of an endless, rolling surf. Life is timeless—we are mere pebbles on the ocean beach of time—why not spend all our money on clothes?

There are some things expressly for women here, but many will buy the men's zoot suits and T-shirts and never make it to the back of the store where luscious Japanese women's clothes with the "George Sand" label are displayed.   — L.Y.

EX Jun, 458 West Broadway, 475-9312. Open Monday to Saturday, noon to 7 P.M; Sunday till 6 P.M. AE, MC, V, checks.

SUSANNE BARTSCH

I F Prince Ludwig of Bavaria and Boy George fell in love and got married, their issue would shop at Susanne Bartsch.

This cracked-tile emporium, with its stage set arches and Disneyland architectural detail, is a must-see for any shopper in Soho. You enter through a long hallway, paved floor to ceiling with smashed bathroom tile. There aren't many clothes in evidence, and it's unclear at first just what this madhouse is. Upstairs, though, suitably avant-garde clothes complement the extreme setting.

The emphasis here is on English fashion, especially the neo-punk clothes of Vivienne Westwood. Here is one of the most complete selections of Westwood clothes in town. An interestingly cut Westwood jacket (around $250) or shirt would complement any wardrobe and, removed from its setting and its brother and sister clothes, look almost normal in your closet.

Also at S. Bartsch are funny French and Italian designs, and a wonderful selection of fantasy hats shaped like giant envelopes or felt bird cages to stick on your head ($75 to $150).

Before descending the staircase and departing through the funhouse corridor, look out the second-floor window for a bird's-eye view of Soho below.

Sales are held in January and July.   — L.Y.

Susanne Bartsch, 456a West Broadway, 674-3370. Open daily, noon to 7 P.M. AE, MC, V, checks.

XAVIER DANAUD

XAVIER Danaud is a store with superb French style to make you look like Catherine Deneuve or Anouk Aimée and feel like a million francs. This is the grown-up style of France— droopy, layered knits, clothes to make you seem like a chic adult and not the oldest Madonna/Cyndi Lauper look-alike on the block.

There's a large collection of Charles Jourdan sportswear here—wool knit oversized tops and skinny bottoms, or speckled-print silk dresses with padded shoulders ($150 to $300).

The shoes are au courant frenchies by Xavier Danaud and Charles Jourdan—unusually sleek and flattering, never clunky and teenaged or marginally grotesque ($90 to $140). The less-expensive ($60 to $90) Seducta shoe line is available also, styles like plain kid shoes with clear heels shaped like little crystal tops of Chrysler buildings and Cap d'Antibes wedgies with Carmen Miranda trim for scarlet toenails to peek from seductively.

Sales are held in June and at the end of December.   — L.Y.

Xavier Danaud, 454 West Broadway, 254-8080. Open daily, 11 A.M. to 7 P.M. Closed Mondays during August. AE, DC, MC, V, checks.

VICTORIA FALLS

E V E R Y T H I N G in this big, white, bleached-brick emporium is pale-colored and romantic. These are giant baby clothes for great big toddlers who work, eat in restaurants, and live in their very own apartments.

For winter, Victoria Falls has full, silk broadcloth blouses ($160 to $180) and wool skirts ($160 to $180) and jackets ($220 to $280), as well as delectable stiff linen blouses ($145 to $160), all made for the store in the updated pseudovintage style that is its specialty. In warmer weather, Victoria Falls really lets loose with linen and lace fantasies, along with vaguely 1920s drop-waisted silk crepe dresses the store calls "South of France" dresses ($260). Featured here, too, is the singular jewelry of Wendy Gell—like cupid brooches studded with dime-store gems set in gold spray-painted splendor. One season recently offered teeny hand-knit sweaters with puffy sleeves and glass buttons, many imported from England, where teeny hand-knit sweaters are a way of life ($130 and up).

Hanging high up near the ceiling in the back of the store are authentic dresses from the turn of the century through the Roaring Twenties—exquisite for a wedding party, or maybe even the office Christmas party.

A white cockatoo snoozing in a giant cage under the antique dresses serves to remind you of the timeless beauty of God's creatures (and also of how good you would look in a feathery white dress). — L.Y.

Victoria Falls, 451 West Broadway, 254-2433. Open Monday to Saturday, 11 A.M. to 7 P.M.; Sunday, 12:30 P.M. to 6 P.M. AE, MC, V, checks.

TOOTSI PLOHOUND

T O O T S I Plohound on Prince Street is the place to rush to when you have a last-minute date and need a pair of inexpensive, fabulous shoes to set off your outfit.

Tootsi has a large selection of women's and men's shoes in unusual materials like metallic florals and orange suede. Satin tuxedo pumps (about $70) would improve even the dreariest outfit. Glitter flats ($38) could lead a double life—at the prom and at the beach at 5 A.M. once you've changed into your after-prom satin blue jeans outfit.

There are lots of shoes here (by Freelance and other trendy, young companies) that are usually light and comfortable, as well as ultrafashionable, with a sense of humor. For once you can afford to be up-to-the-minute because these shoes are extremely cheap compared with their shoe stepsisters from the likes of Maud Frizon and Manolo Blahnik.

In summer, Ms. Plohound shows espadrilles in riotous variety ($35 to $38). In winter, ridiculous boots make you laugh at the weather (and at your own two feet).

The store itself is small and friendly, with loud rock music, a youthful sales staff, and equally youthful customers. A vast collection of socks lines the walls. This is the spot for those pink ankle socks with yellow palm trees you've been looking for.
— L.Y.

Tootsi Plohound, 124 Prince Street, 925-6641. Open Monday to Friday, noon to 8 P.M.; Saturday, 11 A.M. to 8 P.M.; Sunday, noon to 7 P.M. AE, MC, V.

BACK IN BLACK

B A C K in Black on Prince Street sells the popular jewelry of the last hundred years. Here you'll find some of the real treasures of the new middle-classes of the nineteenth century— memorial jewelry made with the hair of the deceased in a precious brooch or locket; or the touching, small 9K gold ring ($100 to $200) that was the heart's delight of an English girl 100 years ago.

Back in Black also has the English girl's daughter's Edwardian cameo and her husband's pocket watch, as well as the next generation's flapper "festoon" necklaces and new-fangled wristwatches ($150 to $350).

Also available in this small store is a profusion of Bakelite and plastic jewelry from the 1930s and 1940s ($25 and up)—very fashionable today, and just as affordable as it was fifty years ago, to the joy of our own grandmothers.

If your mother refuses to give them to you, her 1950s crystal earrings and fake pearl necklaces are sold here also.

Sales are held in January and after Labor Day, with 20% to 30% markdowns. · — L.Y.

Back in Black, 123 Prince Street, 473-3010. Open Tuesday to Sunday, noon to 6 P.M.; Saturday till 7 P.M. AE, MC, V, checks.

Other branches: 928 Madison Avenue, 737-4896. Open Monday to Saturday, 11 A.M. to 6 P.M.

AGNÈS B.

THE white-tiled emporium of Agnès B. on Prince Street is the place to go first when the airline loses your luggage and you don't have a thing to wear. Here are hip, French working girl fashions—a pleasure to wear, and never dowdy or boring.

Agnès, the designer, specializes in reinterpretations of Gallic classics—long pleated skirts in natural fibers (around $100), big trenches, and striped polos ($54). She often keeps designs active for ten years or more, showing the identical items in Lurex or leather or pink gabardine as the seasons go by. It's always possible to pick up a short or long pretty skirt and a well-cut oversized tee or blouse here.

The atmosphere is calm and friendly. A large communal fitting room for women allows you to see yourself as a Parisienne and submit to the critical and/or admiring glances of your fellow shoppers.

Right next door, in the newly expanded menswear department, you'll find bright paisley shirts, big cotton boatneck pullovers ($120) with matching cardigans, and terrific pleated pants. Mini polos and pleats are available for babies and children also, so you can dress your little Pierre or Nicole appropriately for their first day of school at the Lycée Française.

Sales are held in January/February and July/August.   —L.Y.

Agnès B., 116 Prince Street, 925-4649. Open Monday to Saturday, 11 A.M. to 7 P.M.; Sunday, noon to 6 P.M. AE, MC, V, checks.

Other branches: 1063 Madison Avenue, 570-9333. Open Monday to Saturday, 10 A.M. to 6 P.M.; Sunday, noon to 6 P.M.

TOOTSI JR.

THIS spacious, sunny Prince Street store has high-fashion clothes for baby, including au courant Japanese designer fashions in case your baby is sick of Paris and bored with Milan.

The real specialty at Tootsi Jr., though, is the expansive kiddie shoe selection—all the shoes your baby needs to go with its wardrobe, but was having such terrible trouble finding. Here at last are baby tuxedo pumps ($48), baby floral party pumps, baby metallics ($34)—in many cases, exact replicas of the shoes worn by mommy (and daddy), only these are just 6 inches long. The three of you can have matching footwear, and baby no longer has to toddle along behind you, ashamed of itself in those insipid pink and blue booties.

If your baby is a rare, iconoclastic, Jack Kerouac type who prefers to go barefoot and shrieks its head off at shoe try-on time, there are toys here you can buy in a hurry to distract him or her while you cram recalcitrant little feet into ruby-red tap shoes ($34). — L.Y.

Tootsi Jr., 110 Prince Street, 925-8931. Open Monday to Friday, 11 A.M. to 7 P.M.; Saturday till 8 P.M.; Sunday, noon to 7 P.M. AE, MC, V, checks.

WENDY'S STORE

T H E big, heavy bunny rabbit on the sidewalk outside Wendy's Store will have the little ones shrieking with anticipation before you even get inside. This is a veritable department store for the well-dressed toddler. Basic outfits like T-shirts and baby jeans ($14 and up) are available, as are the ubiquitous, exquisite French smocks and hand-knit sweaters ($75) that are the dernier cri in babydom. Lots of little incidentals are for sale, too—little girls' jewelry, baby dishes, funny socks, toys, books.

Plastic raincoats and matching umbrellas with duckie handles ($8) will have your three-year-old praying for rain (and may have you wondering if a twenty-eight-year-old woman can carry off a minuscule duckie umbrella).

This is the place to go if you need a gift for a little kid. Wendy's Store is large, friendly, and eclectic, so you're sure to find something suited to your taste and price range. The staff is friendly and knowledgeable and will patiently explain to you for the fiftieth time why a newborn baby needs a twelve-months size. They love screaming babies here, so you needn't leave yours outside, tied up next to the rabbit. — L.Y.

Wendy's Store, 131 Wooster Street, 533-2305. Open Tuesday to Saturday, 11 A.M. to 7 P.M.; Sunday till 6 P.M. AE, MC, V.

PARACHUTE

T H I S absolutely huge Wooster Street store, sort of a giant duplex Soho loft, is filled with the merchandise teenagers dream of—hip clothes that have a foreign air and would not be out of place at Area or Palladium. There are racks upon racks upon racks of merchandise for men, women, and children.

The clothes themselves run to large padded shoulders, sharp leather jackets, well-cut pleated pants ($80 to $150), shirts with stand-up collars and snaps down the front—generally a space-man effect—slightly derivative of Claude Montana and employing a palette of rich jewel tones like amber and turquoise. The fabrics are often shiny and silky.

This store is so big that it usually has clothes in a wide variety of shapes—long and short dresses ($100 to $200), endless padded-shoulder jackets, skin-tight skirts, and always coats. A specialty here is oversized, seasonless trenchcoats with huge shoulders and lots of buttons and buckles ($200 to $600). These are the ideal coats for the unisex layered look.

Although not cheap, these clothes are by no means as expensive as the haute Soho houses like Comme des Garçons or Dianne Benson. A teenager, or you, could probably save up for and afford practically anything in the store.   — L.Y.

Parachute, 121 Wooster Street, 925-8630. Open Monday to Friday, noon to 8 P.M.; Saturday till 7 P.M.; Sunday, 1 P.M. to 7 P.M. AE, MC, V, checks.
   Other branches: 309 Columbus Avenue, 799-1444. Open Monday to Friday, noon to 9 P.M.; Saturday till 8 P.M.; Sunday, 1 P.M. to 8 P.M.

COMME DES GARÇONS

N O shopping trip to Soho should be undertaken without a stop at Comme des Garçons. Despite its French name, this is the showcase store of Japanese designer Rei Kawakubo.

This is a cavernous place with a resolutely minimalist decor—gray stone floor and walls, clothes displayed starkly on wooden dowels. Infuriatingly diminutive saleswomen, deadly chic in their Japanese frocks, are generally friendly and help offset the severity of the atmosphere.

The clothes themselves are the very best of the Japanese *nouvelle vague* that hit these shores with such a vengeance a few years ago. Styles change, of course, from year to year, but basically these clothes are oversized and loosely constructed, employing a somber palette (although occasional warm-weather collections have sported startling pastels). Asymmetrical pleats and unusually placed slits (even holes) have been known to characterize the women's clothes ($200 to $500). They may look a bit odd on the hanger, but once on the human body, the beautiful cut and graceful drape of these garments become apparent.

The men's clothes run to oversized trenchcoats (around $635), sweaters, and zoot suits, and magnificent, huge shirts. Somber ties ($55 to $65) are available for the faint of heart.

In its early years, Comme des Garçons used a lot of natural, hand-dyed fabrics, but of late it has been pioneering with synthetics—an aberration to the fashionable, upper-class American consumer, but oddly free-thinking in the eyes of the younger, more liberated shopper.   — L.Y.

Comme des Garçons, 116 Wooster Street, 219-0660. Open Monday to Saturday, 11 A.M. to 7 P.M.; Sunday, noon to 6:30 P.M. AE, MC, V.

DIANNE BENSON MEN & WOMEN

THE long, dark, cavernous interior of this store on Wooster Street has been described as "urban primitive" (or maybe it was "primitive urban"?). Anyway, this is one of those places where everything for sale looks hipper and more avant-garde than anything you've ever owned. And no wonder—here find racks of Alaïa, shelves of Crolla's nouveau dandy clothes from London, the toasts of Paris like Jean Charles Castelbajac, and the new line of Miss Maud shoes by Miss Maud Frizon herself (about $185).

Additionally, one-third of the store's not inconsiderable 3,600 square feet is given over to the collected works of Issey Miyake, including his never-before-seen-in-this-country Asha line of clothing and linens. And for fans of the voluminous smocks and abbreviated knits of Dorothée Bis, Dianne Benson offers one of the most complete collections outside France.

This isn't one of those high-fashion stores where practically everything available is for women and there are a few woe-begone racks of men's stuff off in a corner. There's lots for men here, and some of it is quite extraordinary, like the silk pajamas and walking sticks of Saville Row tailors Gieves & Hawkes—just the thing for the elegant sleepwalker.

Dianne Benson also features fabrics by the yard by Tokyo designer Juniichi Arai. These tucked and pleated, naturally dyed wools, linens, and cottons are beloved by haute Japanese designers. But a caveat for home sewers—at $65 to $100 a yard, let's not have any slips of the scissors.   —L.Y.

Dianne Benson Men & Women, 102 Wooster Street, 219-9760. Open daily, 11 A.M. to 7 P.M. AE, D, MC, V.

Other branches: See index for Dianne B. stores, each of which features different merchandise.

STEVE'S SOHO

I F you've been fishing all summer for that invitation to Fire Island, and he's finally asked you, but you haven't a thing to wear, and you have to catch the 5:07 out of Penn Station, and it's now 2 P.M., rush to Steve's men's store on Wooster Street.

Here is everything you need—espadrilles, cotton drawstring pants ($32), purple cotton socks, nice T-shirts—and don't forget a cute little bathing suit. If it's breezy drinking those margaritas on the wraparound deck, pick up an oversized, Shaker-knit cotton pullover in perky pink or sunny yellow ($44). And buy a big canvas carryall to pack it all up in.

Steve's is good for a ski house share, too, with reasonably priced pleated pants, nice wool sweaters, and good warm stylish jackets. The salespeople are nice, and there's just enough imported and highly styled merchandise to keep things interesting.   — L.Y.

Steve's Soho, 97 Wooster Street, 925-0585. Open Monday to Wednesday, 11 A.M. to 7 P.M.; Thursday to Saturday, noon to 8 P.M.; Sunday till 5:30 P.M. AE, MC, V, checks.

LA RUE DES RÊVES

"T H I S is our new line from Istanbul and Paris," the salesman says to you as you enter this densely populated, tropical jungle habitat store. You were not aware that collections were being presented in Istanbul, but then, you would be hard put to guess where some of the items here originated—the purple suede minidresses with 12-inch fringe, the "tropical leathers" in yellows and lime greens ($170 to $450), or the "wig hats" in Tina Turner styles and colors for $35.

This is a crowded, noisy place at all times. It's crammed with merchandise, lots of cats at your feet, and, you will swear, shrieking parrots flying above your head—everything but the bloodhounds snapping at your rear end. Most of the fashions are bright, hot American night-out taste, sort of Charlie's Angels go to Area. But if you force yourself to search carefully and try to ignore the hysterical atmosphere, it is actually possible to find some less obtrusive items, like a beige linen dress with padded shoulders ($275) or a nice blue panne velvet suit with a tunic and a straight skirt.

This place is not cheap, but somebody's got to pay for all that cat food and birdseed. Cruise by the windows before going in. A recent display showed a pair of what was described as "orange dropped-crotch pants," to give you an idea of the delicate sensibility at work here. — L.Y.

La Rue des Rêves, 139 Spring Street, 226-6736. Open Monday to Saturday, noon to 6:45 P.M.; Thursday and Friday till 8:45 P.M.; Sunday, 1 P.M. to 5:45 P.M. AE, MC, V, checks.

CHARLES CHEVIGNON

CHARLES Chevignon is the store for the hip, young, French sister of the woman who shops at Agnès B.—the place to achieve the Princess Stephanie, as opposed to Princess Caroline, look. Here is where you'll spot the leather jacket you've been saving up for over the last fifteen years. These jackets, worn equally well by men and women, are French versions of motorcycle and air force leathers, priced at $500 to $600. To pair with the jackets, Chevignon has straight skirts for women and tweedy trousers for men.

Also available are humorous printed pants and highly styled sweaters. In addition, Chevignon carries a house line called "Un apres-midi de chien" with jeune-fille style, round-collared blouses; smock dresses ($120); and school blazers in yellow and hot pink ($195). Beautiful leather shoulder bags, also good for men or women, are in stock here also.

Charles Chevignon has another store in Paris, but if you can't make it to that one soon, stop by on Spring Street.

Sales are held in late July, with markdowns to 70%—L.Y.

Charles Chevignon, 146 Spring Street, 334-8010. Open daily, 1 P.M. to 7:30 P.M. AE, MC, V.

NORMA KAMALI

113 Spring Street, 334-9696. See index for main listing.

THE SECOND COMING LTD.

T H E Second Coming bills itself as a vintage department store. Curvaceous, overstuffed Art Deco furniture, left over from a Fred Astaire movie, greets you when you walk through the door. These glamorous living room and parlor sets (all for sale) put you in the right mood to foxtrot over to the good selection of vintage clothes available.

The Second Coming specializes in day clothes for women. There are lots of 1940s and 1950s dresses in black rayon velvet or, especially, in brightly printed fabrics with the unconventional designs of the Truman and Eisenhower eras—pink elephants on brown rayon, ballerinas, carousels, or nutty indescribables like pink and purple abstracts on chartreuse ($75 to $125). There are enough dresses here for you to find one that fits you. There's also a good collection of beaded sweaters, as well as men's baggy white shirts, sport coats, and suit jackets ($50 to $150).

In the back of the store are racks of antique shoes to accompany the clothes in the front. There are classic 1950s flats in patent leather with little bows (pre Rainier-Kelly) and thick-heeled, heavy, lace-up saucy walker grandma shoes for heavenly orthopedic comfort (about $30).

This is a big store, so after you dress up in a vintage outfit and shoes, you can stroll up the staircase, gaze longingly at the Deco furniture on the mezzanine, and check yourself in the various dressing table and armoire mirrors before making your final selections. — L.Y.

The Second Coming, Ltd., 72 Greene Street, 431-4424. Open Monday to Saturday, noon to 7 P.M.; Sunday, 1 P.M. to 6 P.M. Closed Sunday during July and August, AE, MC, V, checks.

LE BOUDOIR GIAMBRONE

I N a small New Hampshire town in the 1950s, a certain country doctor was known to walk to town each week to get his Sunday paper—dressed for the occasion in pajamas, robe, and bedroom slippers. Thirty years later in New York City, you might find it just as difficult to remain indoors if you owned a pair of striped silk satin green-and-pink pajamas from Le Boudoir Giambrone ($112). These pjs simply shriek to be let out into the light.

Le Boudoir Giambrone is a jewel-box store featuring women's lingerie designed by Donna Giambrone. The usual house line consists of coordinated silk tap pants, slips, camisoles and teddies ($50 to $60), all of exquisite quality in the best lingerie colors—peaches and cream, or black. It is impossible not to like these things.

Striped silk or satin and lace robes ($150 to $300) are so beautiful that you don't want to drip coffee or smudge *The New York Times'* newsprint on them. Just put them on to answer the door, get the big bag of croissants you just had delivered, and wink at yourself in the mirror. Other things for sale here include white summer nightgowns that just might get to go outside to see the Fourth of July fireworks.

Le Boudoir Giambrone has lingerie parties for Christmas and Valentine's Day, when men only are invited to watch models parade around in underwear. This spectacle is supposed to help men buy a present for you. If you think this sounds like a good idea, tell your favorite man about it. Just make sure he comes home with a camisole, not a fishy expression and a model's phone number in his back pocket.

Sales are held in January and July. — L.Y.

Le Boudoir Giambrone, 60 Wooster Street, 418-9693. Open Tuesday to Saturday, noon to 7 P.M.; Sunday till 6 P.M. AE, MC, V, checks.

LILIT ECLECTIQUES

LILIT Eclectiques is the type of shop found only in New York, or possibly Paris. On Wooster, one of the few cobblestone streets left in the city, and up a flight of stairs, this store is crammed to the gills with necessities of an earlier age. Here is the definitive collection in New York (maybe anywhere) of antique Louis Vuitton trunks (from $600). Once, ladies and their maids traveled the oceans with these fabulous, fitted suitcases. You could stuff ninety pairs of shoes, or a dead body, in one of these and nonchalantly have the porter haul the thing into your cabin.

Now you travel on People Express with two pairs of jeans and a leather skirt in a duffel bag, ready for six months in Europe. Still, your heart skips a beat when confronted with these trunks. What to do? Buy one. They are perhaps the ultimate fashion accessory. Keep one in your apartment instead of the Conran's armoire you thought you would have to buy. If you ever leave your husband, you can throw everything in your antique Louis Vuitton trunk and have it shipped to California, where you are going to start a new life. Just keeping things in your trunk at home will impart to them a glow of fashion superiority, a *je ne sais quoi* sure to be noticed with envy by the other clothes in your house.

Lilit Eclectiques also has a collection of silver cigarette cases, vintage toilet cases, and dressing table accessories with ivory handles. Evening purses with marcasite clasps ($100 to

$150) are heartbreakingly beautiful and a lot cheaper than the Judith Leiber copies sold at Saks Fifth Avenue.

A large number of authentic paisley shawls and heavily embroidered silk piano shawls are also available here. These can be draped over you on a chilly shipboard evening, or perhaps during a drafty People Express flight. Some people like to use them as home-decorating accessories, folded elegantly on an old divan. They would also look nice draped over an antique Louis Vuitton trunk. — L.Y.

Lilit Eclectiques, 55 Wooster Street, 966-0650. Open daily, 1 P.M. to 6 P.M. AE, V, checks.

HARRIET LOVE

H A R R I E T Love is the grand doyenne of the antique clothes business in New York, and possibly the world. While you were saving up for white Courrêges boots, Harriet was scouring Europe for convent-made white nighties and convincing society ladies that they were just the thing for summer Southampton supper parties.

Before Harriet, old clothes were the ratty velvets hippy mamas wore. A generation of us trudging around Lower Manhattan at this very moment in 1940s coats and 1950s dresses owe our closet to Ms. Love.

Her shop on West Broadway is disarmingly small, given her reputation. Here you will find a judiciously edited collection of vintage clothes, everything in very good condition. There are men's clothes available, mostly from the 1940s and 1950s. The women's day clothes (from $90) date from about the same era, but the evening things can stretch as far back as the early years of the century—you might luck into a spectacular beaded 1920s dress, in case you are up for an Academy Award ($250 and up). The emphasis, though, is on cocktail hour classics from the 1940s and 1950s.

This is definitely the place to go if you are new to vintage clothes and just developing an eye. It's not the cheapest place to shop for these clothes, but better to get your feet wet here than make a tragic flea market mistake. The very knowledgeable salespeople will tell you how to care for vintage treasures, steer you toward things that may actually fit you, not laugh when you come out of the (tiny) fitting rooms, and tell you how the thing you have on is supposed to look.

There is also a fine selection of jewelry, with an emphasis on early twentieth-century pewter and sterling silver, and 1930s, 1940s, and 1950s costume pieces. Vintage lizard, alligator, and crocodile handbags are also available. The stock changes often, so stop by frequently.   — L.Y.

Harriet Love, 412 West Broadway, 966-2280. Open Tuesday to Saturday, noon to 7 P.M.; Sunday till 6 P.M. AE, MC, V, checks.

PARACELSO

T H E clothes at Paracelso are for the woman who still has her SDS button pinned inside her knapsack—the one who stays up late at night listening to her Phil Ochs records and reminiscing. These are natural-fiber, full-cut clothes, many of them made in what used to be known as the Third World. The fabrics have a hand-woven, hand-dyed look, and there are plenty of scarves and shawls ($39 to $120) to go with the long dresses ($39 to $120), full skirts, and pretty, detailed blouses ($45 and up). They are distant cousins of the made-in-India ethnic clothes of the 1960s. If you hate everything in style now, and you long for a raw silk, long pleated smock, you can probably find it at Paracelso.

This is also a good spot for you if you promised God at birth that you would never do aerobic exercises. These loosely cut clothes actually look better on the slightly Rubenesque figure.

An outfit from Paracelso is, on its own terms, just as classic as a pleated skirt and cashmere sweater. The calf-length, natural-fiber smock dress, with black tights and flat shoes, has been a standard American look for the past twenty years. Paracelso is an excellent source of slightly exotic, any-season clothes. Prices are moderate, so if you need that special graduation outfit for commencement from the Naropa Institute, you have found your store.   — L.Y.

Paracelso, 414 West Broadway, 966-4232. Open Tuesday to Saturday, 12:30 P.M. to 6:30 P.M.; Sunday, 2 P.M. to 6 P.M. AE, MC, V, checks.

MISO

T H I S pleasant, spacious store specializes in the new American work clothes—not smarmy little suits and bow ties, but clothes a woman can actually wear to work and not hate herself in the morning.

Miso has things like long pleated rayon skirts in lavender with a discreet print ($72), and plain, generously cut silk blouses ($60 to $120). Now that the dress-for-success 1970s are over, it's okay to wear these things on the job. Even if you're a doctor or a lawyer (or an Indian chief) you could probably get away with one of Miso's calf-length, padded-shoulder dresses ($120 to $170), and you might like it enough to wear it on weekends.

This place does a land office business twelve months a year. It could be that after spending a few hours trying on the Japanese and English clothes along West Broadway, women grab a cup of coffee and then head down to Miso to actually buy something. When it comes to parting with their money, lots of people seem to prefer going home with a nice cotton or wool sweater or well-cut gabardine trousers, rather than risking a fortune and potential ridicule on a hopsacking dress with a Lurex collar.

It's almost impossible to get out of Miso without swooning

over the toy counters. Lots of old-fashioned wooden and mechanical toys are here at very reasonable prices. There's also a small selection of clothing for children—unfortunately, the little hand-knitted sweater with Humpty Dumpty on the front ($75) will not fit you, even though it's your favorite thing in the whole store.

Sales are held at the end of the summer and winter seasons, with markdowns from 30% to 50%.   — L.Y.

Miso, 416 West Broadway, 226-4955. Open Monday to Saturday, 11:30 A.M. to 6:45 P.M.; Sunday, 1 P.M. to 5:45 P.M. Closed Sunday and Monday during July and August. AE, MC, V, checks.

BEAU BRUMMEL
421 West Broadway, 219-2666. See index for main listing.

DIANNE B.

T H E delightful Dianne B. shop on West Broadway is the flagship store for women's fashions designed by Dianne Benson herself. Although Dianne has done a small collection for several years, she has recently greatly expanded her repertoire, and her entire line (plus some experiments) is for sale here.

These clothes are usually hip, comfortable designs in natural fabrics—suitable for casual office and definite weekends. Dianne staples include generously cut jumpsuits and beautiful, oversized, artist smock-type shirts with little collars and big sleeves.

The store has a few non-Dianne items as well, like Italian

sweaters. This is an excellent source for clothes you'll probably wear a million times, and the prices are reasonable—traveling from $75 for tailored slacks up to $300 for a coat.   — L.Y.

Dianne B., 426 West Broadway, 226-6400. Open Monday to Saturday, 11 A.M. to 7 P.M.; Sunday, noon to 6:30 P.M. AE, D, MC, V.
   Other branches: See index for other Dianne B. stores, each of which carries different merchandise.

JOOVAY

J O O V A Y, perhaps the tiniest store on West Broadway, has the prettiest, most resolutely feminine lingerie and sleepwear in Soho. This is not one of those new-wave underwear stores with black lace G-strings and bikini panties advertising illegal sexual practices in the window. There's a demure sensibility at work here—more Plaza than Chelsea Hotel, if you purchase your lingerie to correspond with imagined trysting sites.
   The emphasis is on bias-cut silk satin, frothy teddies ($85), and confectionary cottons with hand-embroidered detail ($30 to $80). A quiet, happy dignity pervades these teddies and tap pants—this is real Laurie Colwin lingerie. Look up—lots of finery is hanging on racks high above your head.
   Sales are held in January and July/August.   — L.Y.

Joovay, 436 West Broadway, 431-6386. Open daily, noon to 7 P.M. AE, MC, V, checks.

MOOD INDIGO

P A S T the huge variety of Fiestaware dishes and the silver cocktail shakers shaped like the Hindenberg, Mood Indigo has a groaning counter of Bakelite and other jewelry from the middle years of the twentieth century. The hilarious Bakelite baubles run to 4-inch red fox terrier brooches with rhinestone collars, or plastic green and orange palm trees to decorate the front of your T-shirt. There are also lots of wide Bakelite bracelets carved to look like ivory, except that they're hot pink and canary ($25 to $125).

Mood Indigo also sells men's enamel cuff links, especially nice in lavender, that would add a touch of archaic splendor to the most prosaic shirts. There is also a good selection of chrome jewelry with the Mexican-Deco Frida Kahlo look of the Depression years.

Metal-and-enamel powder compacts sporting the Trylon and Perisphere on their covers ($45 to $65) look as if they've lain unused for decades waiting for you to buy them and present them to some breathless young thing who can't remember the 1964 World's Fair, let alone 1939.

The prices here are reasonable—always less than $100 and sometimes much less—making this jewelry cheaper than inferior reproductions of the self-same styles.   — L.Y.

Mood Indigo, 181 Prince Street, 254-1176. Open Tuesday to Sunday, noon to 7 P.M. AE, MC, V, checks.

LIZA'S PLACE

L I Z A sold clothes on the second floor of the now-defunct Soho antique market for years. Her gorgeous hand-beaded 1920s dresses ($250 and up) hung incongruously from the disintegrating walls. Now she is happily ensconced in more suitable digs on Thompson Street. Her shop specializes in vintage evening and wedding wear—flapper dresses, velvets, gossamer whites. The prices are not low, but this is the place to shop when you want a very special dress for a once-in-a-lifetime occasion.

Liza also has accessories such as beaded bags and antique shoes. Recently, couture 1930s Paris silk dresses with matching silk jackets were on sale for $500. I suppose there are other places to see such clothes, but Diana Vreeland won't let you try things on.

— L.Y.

Liza's Place, 132 Thompson Street, 477-6027. Open daily, noon to 8 P.M. Checks.

BETSEY JOHNSON
130 Thompson Street, 420-0169. See index for main listing.

PARIS / NEW YORK, RITA KIM

THIS tiny pink store on the best block of Thompson Street has French dimestore accessories you can't find anywhere outside of France. If you've always regretted not buying more Gitane cigarette lighters and Eiffel Tower earrings ($14 to $16) on your last trip, quit bawling and stock up at Paris/New York.

Here at last is the Tintin line of dishes you'd almost stopped looking for—little cups and bowls featuring Tintin and his doggie riding in a sidecar, plus drinking glasses for that first diablo menthe in the morning.

As for clothes, Paris/New York has classic La Samaritaine-type work smocks ($45) for artists and artist look-alikes both male and female. Also, at one point, an absolutely ducky leopardskin plastic rain poncho ($25) that you might even wear in the sunshine, and—to top it off—a plastic shopping bag carryall shaped like a TV with a screen in front. Lots of other amusing carryall bags are for sale here also, as well as Gallic junque jewelry. — L.Y.

Paris/New York, Rita Kim, 120 Thompson Street, 925-0073. Open Saturday and Sunday only, noon to 6 P.M. MC, V.

ECCO

111 Thompson Street, 925-8010. See index for main listing.

FDR DRIVE

T H I S small, unprepossessing shop is the quintessential Soho boutique—a former Chinese laundry, it now holds a variety of witty and unconventional antique and modern clothes that will thrill and delight the classically chic man or woman shopper.

FDR Drive used to sell mainly antique clothes. This could be the spot to find a 1910 workdress, and if you've never even seen one, you don't know how perfect they are for beach and summer parties. Luscious white organdy armistice blouses ($100 to $200) and petticoats are always on hand, as well as spectacular white embroidered-on-lace flapper wedding dresses.

More recently, FDR has been introducing a modern line designed by and for the store. There are Claudine à l'Ecole smocks with sailor collars ($300), Chanel-type silk satin sleeveless halter blouses with plenty of brass buttons, silk black-on-black printed bathrobe dresses ($365), and violet linen oversized shirts at $160 for men (but craved by women).

There's also a large showcase of antique jewelry, as well as lots of eccentric vintage hats from the turn of the century through the 1940s.

As if the stock wasn't ingenious enough, the people who own and run this store are incredibly knowledgeable about clothes. They have a quirky, original style and will gladly swap clothing stories and trade hints with you by the hour. You can while away the afternoon here, trying on beautiful old and new things and gabbing with the owners on such subjects as tea-dyeing and where to find cut-rate Chanel makeup. — L.Y.

FDR Drive, 109 Thompson Street, 966-4827. Open Tuesday to Sunday, 1 P.M. to 7 P.M. AE, MC, V, checks.

PETER FOX

I F you are summoned to an audience with the queen or with the pope, and you need a pair of court shoes, go to Peter Fox. They have black and white satin court shoes with silver buckles and fashionable eighteenth-century Louis heels ($150).

If you are dashing from lunch at Gandalfo to supper at Woods with Sean Penn and Madonna, change on the plane from your court shoes into lace-up white mesh boots with black suede spots, also from Peter Fox.

The shoes here, with their adorably pointed toes, cunning little laces, and twisted little heels, made of the very finest kidskins and fabrics, have an almost couture, custom-made look. Often models include elements of shoe styles of the past, like buttoned straps or high laced shanks.

Thus, these shoes look good with lots of different things you own—your favorite antique dresses as well as ultramodern space-cadet day and evening clothes. If you crave a pair of pixie pink lace-up boots with triangular toes, splurge at Peter Fox ($190). (After all, you can keep them for years. They're not exactly going to go out of style.)

The men's division, reached by a separate entrance but right next door to the women's shop, has beautifully cut shoes for men—white bucks, graceful shoes for day with minimally extended soles, and for les pieds de résistance, side-laced Fred Astaire dancing pumps in devastatingly soft kid ($115).

These are small stores—really storefronts—and they tend to get pretty crowded with more than three or four shoppers inside. Try to visit on a weekday if possible, to avoid the Saturday throngs.

These shoes are not cheap, but neither are you when you see something you want. — L.Y.

Peter Fox, 105 Thompson Street, 431-6359. Open Monday to Saturday, noon to 8 P.M.; Sunday, 1 P.M. to 8 P.M. AE, MC, V, checks.

BOMBA DE CLERQ

UPON entering this little sweater store on Thompson Street you will suddenly remember why you never wanted 50,000 things in your closet. Why all the endless shoes and hats and bargain clothes you own only serve to depress. Why what you really always wanted was a tiny, timeless, very expensive wardrobe expressing the timeless, classic style that you alone (well, maybe a few others) possess.

Bomba De Clerq carries an exclusive line of expensive sweaters in beautiful natural fabrics and colors ($150 and up). These are elegant down to such details as two tiny pearl buttons closing their square necks. The cut is sometimes elongated, sometimes short and boxy.

Bomba De Clerq has one other store—on Via Dell'Oca in Rome—but the charm of these sweaters is that you really can't tell where they come from. They look like the beautiful, faded, time-worn favorites that come out of your best friend's closet year after year and make you sick with envy.

A plain cashmere from Bomba De Clerq, in a lovely soft color, may set you back a pretty penny—but you could give all your other sweaters to the Salvation Army and take them as a tax deduction.

The long ribbed cashmere cardigan with pearl buttons down the front is the most beautiful sweater in the world ($440). You could give up smoking for a year and, with the money you save, buy this sweater. Hang on to your last pack of Gauloise and let them peek out of the front pocket.

These sweaters fit men as well as women, and most styles are gender neutral.　　　　　　　　　　　　　　　　　　— L.Y.

Bomba De Clerq, 100 Thompson Street, 226-2484. Open Tuesday to Sunday, noon to 6 P.M.; till 7 P.M. during the summer; and by appointment. AE, MC, V, checks.

BÉBÉ THOMPSON

Y O U R closet is probably full of mismatched pants and tops, ill-fitting skirts and dresses that don't quite make it. Your baby has noticed this, remarked disdainfully to itself about the state of your affairs, and does not wish to find itself in a similar predicament. If your *bébé* is a chic, soigné type, who would rather have a few expensive, well-loved items than a hodge-podge of desperate attempts like *pauvre* mama, take him or her shopping at Bébé Thompson.

For your littlest Francophile, Bébé Thompson has smock dresses ($68) and Pierrot suits from the popular Petit Faune line, made up in Liberty cottons with Liberty baby espadrilles to match—perfect if your baby is spending the summer on the French Riviera with Brigitte Bardot.

If your child only wears natural fibers and turns up its adorable little nose at machine-made sweaters, you can get it handmade cotton or wool outfits ($52) at Bébé Thompson. If baby is going to Palladium, there are leopard-print suede booties here. Your baby doesn't want to be the only one at the sandbox without a genuine reproduction rayon Hawaiian baby shirt ($22). You may be a stupid American, but your baby is a citizen of the world and wants an elegant, seasonless wardrobe to match. Next year, your baby's classic clothes will still be in style—and won't that be lucky for little Pierre and Nicole down the block, since by next year your little baby, nobody's fool, will be a big strapping tyke who needs a whole new Soho wardrobe.   — L.Y.

Bébé Thompson, 98 Thompson Street, 925-1122. Open daily, noon to 7 P.M. AE, MC, V, checks.

PUTUMAYO
147 Spring Street, 966-4458. See index for main listing.

HOLLYWOOD LEGEND

H E R E is the store for the man who believed his mother when she told him antique clothes have cooties. Everything in this store is from the 1930s to the 1960s, and none of it has *ever* been worn. It's all factory fresh, even though the factory may have gone out of business fifty years ago.

Here are men's suits ($150 to $400) in absolutely perfect condition—and these are the exact same models worn by the likes of Al Capone and Jean Paul Belmondo. Along with the suits, there are pleated tweed pants and Little Richard sport coats, nifty 1950s shirts and sweaters, and wonderful leather-trimmed football jackets ($130) that would delight men and women alike.

The pristine condition of this stuff is really something to see, especially if your former experience with antique clothes runs to the moth-eaten, mysterious-smelling variety. And the selection is vast—the place is jammed to the rafters with merchandise.

The wildly overenthusiastic salespeople here may make you feel as if you're dodging a hail of bullets just to be able to try on a few items in relative peace. But it's worth weathering the storm to take a crack at these treasures.   — L.Y.

Hollywood Legend, 178 Spring Street, 925-5799. Open Monday to Sunday, noon to 7 P.M. AE, MC, V.

DETAIL

O N Spring Street near Sixth Avenue, at the far western end of Soho, is Detail, the best place in New York City for outré costume jewelry. This English store is headquarters for the accessories of the New British Empire—that wild island where school-leavers stand in the dole line with pink plastic pigs dangling from the three holes in their bisexual ears. If your idea of fashion heaven is Annabella and Bow Wow Wow, then Detail is your kind of store.

The stock is ever-changing, but a casual visit might yield multicolored metal neck chains that would set Coco Chanel spinning in Pere Lachaise (for the marginally more mature shopper, modernist metal jewelry is also on display). Papier-mâché is the material of choice for lots of big, flat, bright earrings in funny shapes like flattened bubbles or paramecia. And you're sure to find something special for that certain someone—like fried egg earrings.

Most everything is under $100, and a lot is less than $50.
          — L.Y.

Detail, 204 Spring Street, 925-8982. Open Monday to Saturday, noon to 7 P.M.; Sunday till 6 P.M. AE, MC, V.

TOUS LES CALEÇONS

I F you are possessed of a lithe and youthful figure, stop in at Tous les Caleçons for casual clothes for men and women with Gallic flair in French navy blue, black, and white. There are two basic design themes—men's underwear and Marseille sailor.

The underwear influence was extremely prevalent when the store first opened—the big items were gaily printed Gallic boxer shorts snatched up by girls to wear at the beach and (horrors) in town as well. Recently this theme has been expressed in ribbed cotton knits (men's underwear material), done up in unisex tank tops, toreador pants ($44), and tight dresses with deep holes in the sides—the *ne plus ultra* of Côte d'Azur charm.

If you are hell bent on a life before the mast, striped mariner boatneck T-shirts, a boheme staple for the last hundred years, are available in classic blue and white combinations ($48).

For town, short, Chanel-type jackets and skirts with lots of brass buttons were recently at very cheap prices—about $120 for the whole suit—which, with $1 pearls from 14th Street, could give Karl Lagerfeld a heart attack and save you $700.

Tous les Caleçons is at two locations. At 59 Thompson find men's clothing with an emphasis on sous-vetements. At 72, the collection is largely women's casual wear. — L.Y.

Tous les Caleçons, 72 Thompson Street, 219-3465. Open Monday to Friday, 1 P.M. to 7 P.M.; weekends, noon to 7 P.M. AE, MC, V, checks.
Other branches: 59 Thompson Street, 226-7512. Open the same hours.

VICTORIA DINARDO

O N C E, millinery stores dotted the avenues. Those were the days when no woman set foot outside her door without an appropriate hat, when a new spring or autumn outfit was always accompanied by suitable headwear, when the status of a woman could be ascertained by the plumage on her head.

Those days are gone forever. Now, hat lovers are usually reduced to haunting department store counters, and you can walk around as bareheaded as a boy, even on Easter Sunday, and no one will blink an eye.

The custom-made hat store of Victoria DiNardo, on Thompson Street, is among the last of a dying breed. Here you will find a wonderful collection of hats in various felts and straws (from $45), sold over the counter or made up to suit your individual needs. Victoria will reproduce the designs you see in the store, or she will work with you on your own bizarre ideas. She can supply the fabrics or use yours.

Victoria says she has had an avalanche of orders from brides recently, so if your concession to these reactionary times includes wedlock but you draw the line at orange blossoms, Victoria can design a bridal headpiece for you with silver antenna.

Prices at Victoria DiNardo are fairly reasonable, with straw boaters in the $80-to-$90 range. If this sounds like a lot, remember that this made-to-measure hat was created for you alone, and, not unlike the bespoke riding jacket or English leather boots, is an item that has nothing to do with fashion and everything to do with style.   — L.Y.

Victoria DiNardo, 68 Thompson Street, 334-9615. Open Tuesday to Sunday, noon to 7 P.M.; daily during the summer. AE, checks.

ORCHARD
STREET

INTRODUCTION BY
Linda Dyett

There are many New Yorkers who are functionally incapable of buying at retail prices. For them, the only place to shop is Orchard Street—the tumultuous cut-rate clothing bazaar that stretches for two-thirds of a mile at the heart of the old, moldering Lower East Side. On Sunday, when it's closed to auto traffic, the street becomes America's original shopping mall, dazzling in its multitudinous variety of goods, the hustling savvy of its shopkeepers, and the pluck of its clientele. Here it is possible to buy anything wearable—from tube socks and house dresses to Gaultiers and storefront couturier frocks.

Some of the shops have been smartened up, given high-glitz or high-tech decor, but a lot of the smaller ones—the marts for underwear and hosiery, especially—are still equipped with their original creaking wooden floors, toppling piles of cardboard boxes, and ornate, old-fashioned cash registers. They're shabby but totally authentic. Browsing in these ancient places berthed into tenement storefronts, you'll feel both isolated in a time warp and exposed to the shopping transaction at its most primitive: The storekeeper makes his bid, you acquiesce or evade. There are no feigned friendships down here, no pleasantries exchanged. It's strictly business. No place in the world is like Orchard Street, except maybe marketplaces in Africa and the Middle East, and London's Petticoat Lane.

Although the open-market tradition of *hondling*, or bargaining, is no longer widely prevalent on Orchard Street, it still persists, to some extent, and is worth trying. If you find something you like that looks expensive, don't express ecstatic joy over it, but tell the shopkeeper you might be interested if the price were low. If he says absolutely no, forget it. If he starts to negotiate, you're on. It's always helpful to mention that you'll pay with cash rather than credit cards or checks. The store can use cash immediately, so it's a bargaining point for you.

Orchard Street, nearby Essex and Allen streets, and the narrower streets that cross them, specialize in odd lots and manufacturers' overstocks. Prices are usually 20% to 60% less than you'd pay uptown (though a lot of the merchandise down here doesn't even get sold uptown). You can find plenty of shops spewing out low- and moderate-priced American brands of men's sportswear—jogging suits, *Miami Vice* and other leisure looks that've become mainstream. The majority of women's stores cater to career types and sell upmarket standard brands such as Tahari, Evan Picone, Harvé Benard, Spitalnik, Nicole Miller, and Albert Nipon, which are unloaded mostly from local wholesalers and jobbers.

But there's also a new breed of Orchard Street storekeepers—recent émigrés from Russia, South America, and North Africa who arrived with fashion flair and mysterious wholesale connections in Paris and Florence. It's at their stores that you can encounter fabulous imports. Several men's shops have steady supplies of leftover suits, jackets, shirts, sweaters, and shoes from Italian designers and better manufacturers—names like Ferré and Versace, even—and from the factories that produce their clothes.

A couple of women's and children's stores offer classic

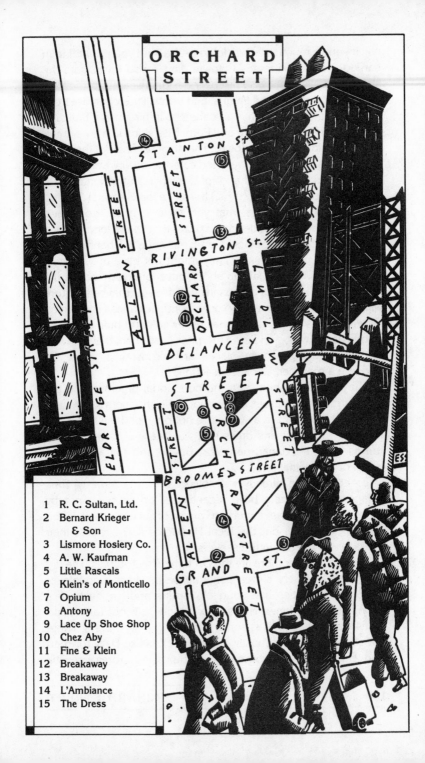

ORCHARD STREET

1 R. C. Sultan, Ltd.
2 Bernard Krieger
 & Son
3 Lismore Hosiery Co.
4 A. W. Kaufman
5 Little Rascals
6 Klein's of Monticello
7 Opium
8 Antony
9 Lace Up Shoe Shop
10 Chez Aby
11 Fine & Klein
12 Breakaway
13 Breakaway
14 L'Ambiance
15 The Dress

Italian- and French-tailored clothes—the kind you might find in carriage-trade businesses uptown. And if you investigate the street carefully, you'll also discover designerwear from the likes of Gaultier, Armani, and Mugler, and oddball merchandise from the high-ticket Americans—silk sheaths in bizarre but beautiful prints from Pauline Trigère and Perry Ellis shirts in a lime green that just didn't work uptown. The trick is finding the stuff. Window displays don't always indicate the quality and breadth of the wares inside. (And a lot of the labels in the window are coyly covered with white cards.) If a place looks semipromising but you don't see quite what you have in mind, go in and announce your wildest desires. Explain that you're looking for a bargain-priced Versace jacket, an Emmanuelle Khanh blouse, or an Italian plaid kilt skirt. They might not have the slightest inkling of what you're talking about, but more often than you'd imagine you'll be in for a pleasant surprise—or maybe the store will have something made by your favorite designer's contractor. Several shops (such as the ones reviewed here) hide their best goods under wraps and save them for customers they know to be connoisseurs. These places are almost like clubs. To become a member, just keep asking.

The lure of the hunt and the occasional precious find are what attract adventurous and iconoclastic shoppers to Orchard Street. It helps to have a subtle eye not only for the avant-garde but also for last year's dress that was really a gem but went unnoticed by the department store buyers and now is selling at a fifth of its original price.

To add to this already well-spiced stew, a couple of East Village-type designers have recently set up shop on nearby Stanton Street. The suburban dress-for-success ladies find them bewildering, but the local Hispanics seem to like their styles, as do the adventure seekers.

Then, of course, there are the Orchard Street staples. The dry goods and hosiery stores continue selling vast amounts of undershirts, panties, bras, long johns, slips, and "model coats." Brands include Hanes, Health Tex for kids, Lily of France, and Christian Dior, as well as some interesting new imports. There are shoe shops, too, mostly offering brands like Bally for men and Bandolino for women. And the fabric stores are still around, the biggest and best of them probably being S. Beckenstein (118, 125, and 130 Orchard Street).

Walk east to Essex Street and you'll discover rows and rows of narrow shops selling electronics, sports equipment, china, and Jewish ecclesiastical goods—including yarmulkes in a staggering array of colors. Walk west along Grand Street and you'll find a number of bed and kitchen linen shops, offering not only shams and ruffles but the latest chic designers' sheets, toilet seats, dish towels, and eiderdowns. Probably the best-stocked of these marts is Harris Levy at 278 Grand.

Grand Street is actually where it all began. In the mid-nineteenth century, the Lower East Side was New York's major shopping turf, and the finest department stores—including Lord & Taylor—were located on Grand. The wholesalers, textile companies, and needle trades thrived just to the south on Canal. These businesses were run by Western European Jewish immigrants who'd been specialists in the garment business before they arrived in America. When Eastern European Jews started appearing in vast numbers during the 1880s, they too settled here. But they weren't skilled. Many could survive only by operating pushcarts, where they sold the odds and ends they salvaged from the wholesalers. When they got enough capital, they invested in their own pocket-size shops, which began appearing on Hester Street and later spread to Orchard. This is the origin of America's garment trade.

Even today, the retailers remain Jewish, most of them, though the majority of residents are now Hispanic, joined by a gathering wave of artists and designers spilling south from the East Village.

This section of the Lower East Side headed into decline around the turn of the century, when the fancy department stores moved uptown. And though it remains in disarray, it's slowly being spruced up by a new generation of tenement dwellers who are high on energy if low on cash. Fortunately, some of the historically important and architecturally magnificent old structures remain. The original *Jewish Daily Forward* building is at 175 East Broadway. Congregation Anshe Slonim, still standing at 172-176 Norfolk Street just south of Houston, is the oldest synagogue in New York, built in 1849. Its now crumbling Gothic Revival structure is said to have been modeled on the Cathedral of Cologne. Further south, the large Eldridge Street Synagogue, with a cathedrallike rose window and a facade that combines Romanesque, Gothic, and Moorish styles, is in the process of being refurbished. These edifices remind you of the New World hopes and desires brought by a mass influx of immigrants. Architectural remnants of the past abound, especially east and south of Orchard Street. This neighborhood, just teetering on renovation, deserves a long tour before it changes.

The old Jewish eateries are part of the charm and make perfect stops for a snack or lunch. For midmorning babka and coffee, try Gertel's Bake Shop at 53 Hester Street. It's got table service and a disheveled tea-room environment. For lunch, there are several Jewish delicatessens. Katz's, 205 East Houston, at the corner of Ludlow, is a vast L-shaped place with self-service as well as waitered tables. Don't get them confused or the waiters will bark. Schmulke Bernstein's at 135 Essex dispenses similar fare but is smaller. The neighborhood used to have many dairy restaurants serving perfect gefilte fish, scrambled eggs, glasses of cream, and fruit desserts. Now only a few remain. Fortunately, their waiters are still surly, in the great tradition of Jewish father-figure waiters. The large and famous Ratner's, at 138 Delancey Street, not far from the Williamsburg Bridge, is frequented by tourist busloads. You might prefer the smaller Grand Dairy Restaurant, 341 Grand, where the apple blintzes are superb and the seltzer supply endless. By midafternoon you'll want tea and a fresh knish, which you can get at Yonah Schimmel's, 137 East Houston at Forsyth.

If you like Rumanian food with *schmaltz* (that's fat), try Sammy's, 137 Chrystie Street, for dinner. Or you could go to one of the newer establishments. The Hat, 108 Stanton at the corner of Ludlow, serves good Mexican food and margaritas; and La Luncheonette, 131 Essex, has nouvelle French.

To reach Orchard Street by subway: Take the IND B or D to Grand Street and walk east; or (the best route) take the IND F train to Delancey. That way, before you commence clothes shopping, you can take a detour to buy a sour pickle from one of the barrels at Guss Pickles, 35 Essex Street, then head a bit further south until you hit Canal. Turn right, and you'll soon be at the very start of Orchard Street. By bus: Take the M101 or M102 up or down Third Avenue/Bowery; the M15 up or down First Avenue/Allen Street; or the M14 across 14th Street and down Avenue A/Essex Street to Delancey Street; or the M21 across Houston to Essex Street.

If you like jostling crowds, by all means go on a Sunday, though you may have to wait in line outside the more popular shops. If you seriously want to explore the interstices of the stores and ferret out the unique wares, try a weekday instead. But don't choose Friday afternoons. A lot of these shops close early for sabbath. Nearly all are closed Saturday.

■ ■ ■

R. C. SULTAN LTD.

THIS is a long, narrow shop with an old-fashioned, wood-paneled office cubby up front and metal shelves that line every conceivable inch of wall space. They're crammed with thin, fragile cardboard boxes and bigger plastic ones—more practical but less romantic—containing all manner of business and play socks, stockings, panty hose, tights, and anything else the foot would wear.

Hanes panty hose are the house specialties for women. Virtually the full line is here—in ultra, everyday, and stretch sheer to fit all sizes. Prices average about $2.25 per pair. The exotica includes Le Bourget textured panty hose, about $5 per pair; and Perry Ellis anklets and knee socks, going for 20% to 30% less than uptown prices.

The men's department is stocked with the entire line of Christian Dior socks, plus lots from Burlington, Pierre Cardin, Yves Saint Laurent, and Henry Grethel. The underwear labels read Hanes, Jordache, Playboy, and BVD. Here, too, everything is discounted by 20% to 30%.

Sultan's has frequent closeouts that lower the prices even more. That's when cashmere-blend and pure cotton argyle socks go for $2.50 or so. But this stuff won't leap out at you. You have to ask for the specials and the luxury goods. They're hidden away. But the staff respond instantly and know exactly which box to reach for.   — L.D.

R.C. Sultan Ltd., 55 Orchard Street, WA5-9650 and WA5-9651. Open Sunday, 8 A.M. to 5:30 P.M.; Monday to Friday, 9 A.M. to 5 P.M.; Friday till 3 P.M. during the winter. AE, MC, checks.

BERNARD KRIEGER & SON

"I'M one of the few handkerchief authorities left in New York," boasts Joe Krieger. His store, Bernard Krieger & Son, has been in business since 1936 and is possibly the last of the old-time accessories dealers. It's not fashion city, but it's a good source for certain staples at rock-bottom prices.

Men's and women's cotton and linen handkerchiefs come plain and fancy—some with elaborate Chinese openwork, others with floral prints. Personal favorites are the men's colored slips, as they're known in the trade, with little border patterns like Roman keys. Prices start at $4.50 per dozen, which is the only way they're sold, and go up to $60 for men's large Swiss voile handkerchiefs that would cost over $10 apiece if you could find them uptown.

Krieger's also carries felt, straw, and cloth hats and visors for women. The best of them are the basic wool felt, angora, and crocheted cotton berets, $4 to $10.

In the scarf showcases are silk prints by major American designers, $15 to $20; elegant paisley silk mufflers that reverse to wool, about $20; and Russian-style wool challis squares with colorful florals, $4 to $6.

Glove selections are pretty basic. Cashmere-lined leathers go for $30 or so, and cotton lace styles are about $5.   — L.D.

Bernard Krieger & Son, Inc., 316 Grand Street, CA6-1929 and CA6-4927. Open Sunday to Thursday, 9 A.M. to 4:30 P.M.; Friday till 4 P.M. Checks.

LISMORE HOSIERY CO.

NOTHING'S been changed at Lismore Hosiery Co. in the fifty-odd years it's stood on the corner of Grand and Ludlow streets. The black and white tile floor and the dark woodwork are still intact. The cardboard boxes piled everywhere look like they've been at a dangerous tilt for decades. There's an old-timer who comes in to savor the atmosphere. To please him, the owners go through a pretend- *hondle* routine, though they don't really bargain these days. But at Lismore's prices, no one's complaining.

A lot of the merchandise is Lismore's house brand, much of it difficult to find elsewhere downtown. Men's cotton lisle ankle socks, in up to eight colors, go for $20 or so per dozen, or you can buy them by the pair. Pima cotton ankle and over-the-calf styles are about $4 and $4.25. Ladies' pure cotton anklets are under $2.

There's a full line of nylon stockings—mesh; 70-denier service weight; ultra, dress, and business sheer; and some with dark seams. These are $12 per dozen, and they come in boxes of threes. You'll want the orange boxes, with Lismore's own logo.

Samples of the fancier goods—colorful, patterned panty hose and leg warmers, heavy cotton anklets to go over panty hose, and San e Origin Japanese socks—hang from clotheslines. The "foxes" are attracted by this merchandise, explains the owner. — L.D.

Lismore Hosiery Co., 334 Grand Street, OR4-3440. Open Sunday to Thursday, 9 A.M. to 5 P.M.; Friday till 2 P.M. Cash only.

A. W. KAUFMAN

Y O U enter A. W. Kaufman, currently in its third generation as the world's narrowest and most cluttered lingerie outlet, and instantly you're overwhelmed by plastic-scented claustrophobia. Polyurethane bags, all tied at the bottom to protect the night-gowns and peignoirs, are squashed together on the floor and ceiling racks. Every inch of shelf space is crammed with cardboard boxes filled with small unmentionables. Slips, knickers, and wickedly cut silk panties seem flung with abandon all over the counters. Ben and Burt Kohn, the father and son who run the business, are men of the world who don't flinch when you ask for the risqué styles.

The specialties are Hanro's Swiss-made cotton, silk, and wool jersey teddies, bikinis, briefs, and camisole sets, bargains at $5.50 to $60; and cotton and cotton-flannel nightgowns, priced from $28.75 up to $60 or so. Many of them bear the label Eileen West for Queen Anne's Lace.

It's a perilous struggle through the bags and the other customers to get to the nightgowns and trousseau sets in the back and upstairs. Varied brands are carried, the most prominent being Christian Dior. At the department stores, his lingerie prices start around $100. Here they're as low as $60.

Some of the best buys are the classic all-cotton-terry wrap robes, $36 and up; and the tailored silk pajamas, $100 and up.

— L.D.

A. W. Kaufman, 73 Orchard Street, 226-1629. Open Sunday to Thursday, 10 A.M. to 5 P.M.; Friday, 10:30 A.M. to 3 P.M. AE, MC, V.

LITTLE RASCALS

T H E two most sophisticated childrenswear shops on Orchard Street are uneasily situated next door to each other. Both specialize in European imports, but their aesthetics are totally different.

Little Rascals deals in odd lots and closeouts from Italy and France. Its look is tailored and traditional, for kids sized from six months to fourteen years.

Summer dresses and playsuits have gentle stripes and small floral prints, while the winter goods are black and brown velvet smocks, panel-pleated navy skirts, braid-trimmed loden coats with red heart buttons, and gorgeous wool check dresses and suits with Peter Pan collars. Inferior versions of these classics go for at least $75 when you can find them in department stores. Here the prices are $20 to $50. Also tough to locate elsewhere are cotton lace knee socks (about $5), the kind European children wear with strappy brown sandals.

Speaking of which, there's an excellent all-Italian shoe department with basics like black ankle boots and perfect Mary Janes. Prices range from $45 to $60.

Out-of-season clothes are often on half-price sale. So in the summer you can buy an elegant wool tweed Italian coat or a rabbit fur coat for $100 to $150. These are definitely bargains.

The owners and staff are Russian émigrés who like to treat long-standing and big-spending customers kindly. Don't expect to bargain with them unless you fit into one of these categories.

Sales are held in January and July, with markdowns of 20% to 50%. — L.D.

Little Rascals, 101 Orchard Street, 226-1680. Open Sunday to Friday, 10 A.M. to 6 P.M. AE, MC, V.

KLEIN'S OF MONTICELLO

THIS is a store for spunky, sassy, natural-fiber Club Med kids—or for parents who wish their progeny would behave that way. The ambience is workshop modern, with metal industrial shelving, Swedish hanging lamps, and long wooden tables, on which to perch the smaller tots while they're being wardrobed.

The main manufacturers imported here are New Man, Naf Naf, Bourget, Chipie, and Trotinette from France; Landman from West Germany; and the sort of Japanese goods you can buy in Fusen Usagi way up on Madison Avenue. Klein's is possibly New York's best source for primitive-print rompers or East Village graffiti-print coveralls for the under-twelve crowd.

The only American goods to pass the shop's stringent fast-forward test are brightly colored appliqué jogging suits by Marsha and Christine Foley's beautiful handmade sweaters.

Prices are discounted but high anyway. Most substantial outfits are at least $50 and can go up to $200.

A junior department for anyone over five feet tall and past the age of eleven has the goods for a West Coast shopping-mall look—oversized jersey message shirts, print coordinated tops and shorts, and stone-washed jackets. Their prices are comparatively reasonable, at $25 to $75.   — L.D.

Klein's of Monticello, 105 Orchard Street, 966-1453. Open Sunday to Friday, 10 A.M. to 5:30 P.M. MC, V, checks.

OPIUM

C A L L I N G the shop Opium was a trifle heavy-handed, but you'll forgive the Russian émigré owner, Ada Todd. This is one of those enchanted Orchard Street sources of elegant Italian classics and some heavy-duty designer wares. They're definitely special. You won't find them elsewhere on the street.

To name names that sell here for half their uptown prices: items from Gaultier's summer collection are about $120 to $450. (Opium evidently couldn't swing a deal for the winter stuff.) And Luciano Soprani's silky rayon knits—oversized cardigans and novelty pullovers with fabulous cuts and cunning necklines—may cause insanity if you can't afford them at about $200 apiece.

Also frequently in stock are elegant retro-style dresses and skirts from Compagnie n.g., and saucy little French and Italian afternoooon dresses and silk blouses, all priced from $100 to $200.

Then there's a slew of classic Italian suits, jackets, and separates in good fabrics with menswear tailoring. Particularly wonderful are the wool-blend blouses, tartan trousers, and straight linen skirts. Prices range from $75 for the pants to $150 through $300 for the suits.

If you're due for a winter coat, don't fail to come here first.

They've got reefer and shawl-collar styles, sometimes in cashmere blends, from Armani's contractors. These go for about $200. Even more interesting is the occasional stunning greatcoat with proper military collar and swirling skirt from Gianmarco Venturi that sells for about $350.

You have to call in regularly and be the pursuer in your relationship with Opium. The best stuff can get snapped up hours—maybe minutes—after it goes on the racks.

Sales are held in January and July, with some markdowns below cost. — L.D.

Opium, 104 Orchard Street, 533-8394. Open Sunday to Friday, 10 A.M. to 6 P.M. AE, CB, DC, Discover, MC, V, checks.

ANTONY

O R C H A R D Street has a number of men's stores selling Italian designerwear—maybe not the best Armanis and Versaces, maybe not the very newest cuts. But they do carry high-quality goods at reasonable prices.

Antony, a little shop with silver-toned dressing cubicles, was one of the first of these Italian import businesses. It sells a wide and changing range of Italian designer discounts. The sports shirts from Ferré and his ilk, pricemarked at over $100, are randomly put on sale. So are all the other goods. Lusciously soft sweaters (some reversing to jackets), made in those peculiar wool-linen-cotton-silk-synthetic blends only the Italians can concoct, officially start at $75. There are cashmere coats (marked at $300 to $350), jackets with leather treatments (around $100), and wizard suits priced at $275 to $400 but occasionally sold two-for-the-price-of-one. They come single- and double-breasted, in linens, gabardines, flannels, tweeds, and sensational plaids with vivid color arrays. Tailoring is traditional, with handsewn lapels and other fine details. The labels read Mino, Lombardi, Hilton, and sometimes Giorgio Armani.

Also on hand are Van Laack dress and sports shirts in gorgeous cottons and blends, marked at $50 to $75, considerably less than they cost on Madison Avenue.

Emporio, located at 88 Orchard Street, one block south, is actually Antony's shoe and leisure wear department. The footwear styles are avant-garde and/or raffish, in softest leathers and canvas, priced at $50 to $120. Absolute bargains.

Uomo, a brother shop at 52 Orchard Street, 226-3666, sells merchandise similar to Antony's.   — L.D.

Antony, 106 Orchard Street, 477-0592. Open Sunday to Friday, 10 A.M. to 6 P.M.; and by appointment. AE, Discover, MC, V.

LACE UP SHOE SHOP

T H E Orchard Street women's footwear marts are massive disappointments on the whole. But one store is worth frequent visits. It doesn't carry the upper empyrion of European shoe designers, but Lace Up Shoe Shop, on the corner of Delancey, sells the very next level down—killer chic shoes and boots bearing labels you'd never fantasized would wend their way to the Lower East Side.

"Don't mention brand names," urges Larry Hecht, the owner of this high-tech, glass-tiled, red and gray discount store. (Its wares sell for 20% to 30% less than they do uptown.) Okay, but here's a hint. There's a full line from a Frenchman, known as the king of pumps, who's also famous for his tarty-looking, high-heeled mules. His sexy spikes are the highest around, though they're actually comfortable and come in a wide range of colors. Here, his prices are $60 to $250. A subdivision of his company, named for a fellow Frenchman, does a more informal line with lot of fabric coverings, platform soles, open toes, and unusual color combinations. These shoes sell here for $60 to $140. Or you can buy them for full retail prices at their own Soho boutique.

Also on hand are selections from an Italian famed for his classic, expensive shoes; from several American designers; and from a less-touted but worthy line by the company that manufactures Saks's Fenton Last and Bergdorf's Delman footwear.

Very fetching handbags from the Frenchmen sell for $140 to $250.

Don't even dream of coming on Sunday, or you'll find yourself standing outside in a queue.

Sales are held in January, February, and around the Fourth of July, with markdowns of 50% to 80% and two-for-the-price-of-one specials. Cash only on sale merchandise.   — L.D.

Lace Up Shoe Shop, 110 Orchard Street, 475-8040. Open Sunday to Friday, 9 A.M. to 5:30 P.M. MC, V, checks.

CHEZ ABY

A B Y Cohen and his family, multilingual natives of Morocco (they speak up to six languages), run one of the best-stocked women's shops on the Lower East Side. It's two connected stores, really, since Chez Aby has done so well that it's expanded. The space is strictly workaday—tightly packed racks of French and Italian imports, mostly classics. But a lot of it is manufactured by suit contractors to some of Italy's top designers.

The suits, dresses, separates, sweaters, and coats are sold at low markups—sometimes at half the price you'd pay in Soho or on Madison Avenue. For under $50, you can find a wool flannel or gabardine skirt with triple kick pleats or kilt details. Suits, sometimes with ornate frog closures on the jackets, start at under $100. They can go up to $1,000 when they're by designers whose names must remain shrouded in mystery.

The cute French dresses by Hug An'Co and Henry Leparque

(who used to be Anne Marie Beretta's designer) recall the little bourgeois frocks worn in Eric Rohmer movies. The more sedate Italian dresses—wool plaids with Peter Pan collars and swirly skirts, and summer linen coatdresses with shawl collars—are the sort Anouk Aimée has worn in most of her films. Dresses are priced from under $100 to about $300.

The best items are the sumptuous silk suit blouses with complicated necklines and odd colors, like chartreuse. They cost $50 to $200.

If you don't see what you want, ask. They've got plenty more in the basement.

Officially the hours are by appointment. You can drop in, but you'll very likely get better service if you call in advance. — L.D.

Chez Aby, 77-79 Delancey Street, 431-6135. Open Monday to Saturday, 10 A.M. to 6 P.M.; Thursday till 8 P.M.; Sunday, noon to 6 P.M. AE, DC, Eurocard, JCB, MC, V, checks.

FINE & KLEIN

FINE & Klein, Orchard Street's premier handbag retailer since the mid-1940s, has acquired mythic status. Every guidebook heaps on superlatives. It's always besieged. Yet several recent visits to this large, cluttered store were unimpressive. Frumpery reigned everywhere. Most of the goods came via major distributors, with the labels reading Koret, Meyers, Dooney & Burke, Bagheera, and Carlos Falchi—middling or overrated department store fare. But a plea to have them open the cardboard boxes did yield the occasional beauty—enough to put Fine & Klein conditionally on the A-list. Besides which, they'll special-order most major manufacturers' bags—the kind you see in department stores—and discount them by a third or more.

For about $50, you can get a very large—but not huge—buttery soft kidskin shoulder bag in envelope or satchel style.

Mr. Klein says these are made locally by a Russian émigré. Evening styles include Whiting & Davis's impeccable metal mesh bags for $20 to $100, and many, many minaudières—gold and silver boxes in all sorts of shapes, from seashells to eggs and animals, starting under $50 and ranging up to $1,200.

The most perfect bag in the store is an Italian lizard envelope with an adjustable shoulder strap, its only embellishment a gold Deco clasp. It's about $400, which sounds outrageously expensive, but uptown you probably couldn't get it for $600.

Upstairs are attachés, men's bags, belts, and a jewelry concession with designer and antique baubles.   — L.D.

Fine & Klein, 119 Orchard Street, OR4-6720. Open Sunday to Friday, 8:45 A.M. to 5:30 P.M. Checks, money orders.

BREAKAWAY

A lot of the Orchard Street women's shops cater to budget-minded careerists who swoop down on the Ellen Tracys and the Harvé Benards. Breakaway, a large two-branch store, sells plenty of these goods. It also stocks some interesting, higher-priced, nonbusinessy items that are avoided by the regular clientele. After they've sat on the racks for around three weeks, they pass into Breakaway's automatic markdown system and spiral downward until they reach $25 or $35.

These immovable bargains, along with leftovers shunted in ignominy from a more prestigious uptown sister store, reach their final resting place on the third-floor mezzanine. There, among genuine detritus no one would want, you may find pay dirt—like Lolita Lempicka wool sweaters for $25.

Other scorned merchandise includes Jacques Gevertz's wonderful French blazers and skirts, at the presale price range of $100 to $250; classic Italian and German sportwear that initially sold for $25 to $300; Anne Marie Beretta's great-looking winter coats, originally $250 and up; and pretty print dresses by Nicole Miller and Sara McNamara, priced about $58 and up.

The basement fur department offers private-label ranch mink coats for as little as $1,750. An on-premises fitter will repair, too.

Sales are held at the end of each season, and there are special holiday promotions on furs. — L.D.

Breakaway, 88 Rivington Street, 598-4455. Open daily, 9 A.M. to 6 P.M. AE, CB, DC, Discover, MC, V, checks.
Other branches: 125 Orchard Street, 475-6660. Open the same hours.

L'AMBIANCE

L ' A M B I A N C E is a pioneer—the first brave storefront couture boutique to descend on the Orchard Street area. Its owners, Luis Reyna and Michael Martin, are neophyte designers who also do all the sewing. Their wares—utterly basic, unadorned dresses and separates—seem intended for the bargain-hunting businessladies who regularly haunt the street. None of the clothes are particularly avant-garde, but all of them have such simplicity that they bcome appealing.

Typical fare is round-neck and deep U-back tops and shifts with drop shoulders and elbow-length roll-up sleeves. These can be office wear or dressy, depending on the fabric. In calf-length black jersey, the shift is excellent after-hours club material. Skirts come in slim elastic-waist and trumpet styles. Everything's done in cotton, silk, rayon, and wool, and prices range between $20 and $70. They've got accessories, too—leather berets and bellboy hats, $5 to $25.

Like dozens of Lower East Side shops, L'Ambiance is small. But here everything is organized, with a dressing room carved out at the back and a jewelry case at the cash register. — L.D.

L'Ambiance, 86-88 Stanton Street, 533-4820. Open daily, 11:30 A.M. to 6 P.M. MC, V, checks.

THE DRESS

T H E minimalist post-Memphis decor should be a dead give-away. The Dress is no ordinary Lower East Side apparel mart. It's a designer atelier with a limited selection of extremely avant-garde clothes. Unsuspecting seekers of cut-rate Harvé Benards stumble in and inquire "Is this all you have?"

It's fitting that The Dress should have set up shop in the shadow of Orchard Street. Amy Downs and Mary Adams, its designer-owners, are exploring the limits of fashion and the essence of dresshood; and where better to accomplish these noble tasks than in the very heart of the shmatte trade, home of the housedress? They're also looking for an eclectic clientele, which they certainly can attract on the Lower East Side. Their customers range from teens buying prom dresses to fashion intellectuals in feverish pursuit of the leading edge.

Adams creates the tamer, ladylike stuff—organdy and velvet frocks, blouses, and skirts with big collars and fitted bodices— they evoke the late 1950s. Her peplum numbers look like pretty Albert Nipons as reinterpreted by Issey Miyake. She also designs wedge- and beachball-shaped handbags in canvas and naugahyde.

Downs started out as a fiber artist with a specialty in pieced fabrics. You can still buy her long patchwork kimono coats with abstract hieroglyphics. But lately she's been playing with trends. Her fitted patchwork plastic and vinyl cowpunk outfits are her comment on Tough Chic, and her bolero suits with full, short skirts suggest cartoon images of good girls. Downs's belts, trimmed in fake fur and decorated with cat collars, look like fetish pieces. She also designs oversized stovepipe and wide-crowned Emma Goldman driving hats.

Adams's prices go from $55 to $300; Downs's from $50 to $600 (for the kimono). Hats and bags are $10 to $75. All styles can be sewn to order in the workroom at the back.   — L.D.

The Dress, 103 Stanton Street, 473-0237. Open Wednesday to Sunday, 1 P.M. to 6 P.M. Cash only.

CHINATOWN

INTRODUCTION BY
Elaine Louie

There are two worlds in Chinatown, one visible, the other hidden behind the nondescript, often shabby buildings that make up this area bounded by Canal Street, East Broadway, and Worth and Bayard streets. To most people, Chinatown means exotic curio shops filled with fans made of paper, finger puzzles of straw, and vials of queen bee essence—and restaurants. But the strength of Chinatown lies in the fact that it is a living community, made up of Chinese doctors, lawyers, herbalists, acupuncturists, launderers, clerks, and, obviously, restaurateurs, cooks, and waiters. What Chinatown is *not* is just a tourist place, even though its phone booths are shaped like pagodas. To plunge into the area's shops and restaurants is to explore a vital culture.

Chinatown begins its day at 7:30 A.M. when the streets are seemingly deserted and unusually clean. But at Hee Seung

Fung, the best teahouse in Chinatown (46 Bowery), the Chinese are having their breakfast, which may consist of fresh, wide slippery noodles wrapped around beef or shrimp, or congee, the rice gruel, accompanied by twists of fried bread. The food is bland early in the day and increases in both spiciness and variety as the day goes on. Most of the other shops and restaurants open between 9 and 10, and slowly the streets begin to fill, usually first with Chinese residents and later in the day with others.

There are three kinds of places to lure anyone to Chinatown. The first are the emporiums that sell clothing, dried foodstuffs, and home accessories. What's fascinating about these stores is not the quality, which is inconsistent and ranges from mediocre to excellent, but the variety and the fact that they reflect a great deal of what mainland China, in particular, sees fit to export to the United States. In these emporiums you don't look for high fashion, but perhaps basics like superbly silky cotton T-shirts or padded silk comforters. They usually carry extremely well-priced, sometimes absolutely cheap, kitchen items like bamboo chopsticks, clay pots, and porcelain teapots. Toys include tiny straw figures suitable for hanging on Christmas trees, and seashells filled with paper flowers. Drop the shell into a glass of water, and the flowers emerge and expand. These shells are toys that Chinese mothers have given their children for generations past. The best emporium of all is Pearl River Products Emporium, at 277 Canal Street; the best source for Chinese food specialties is Kam Man, down the street at 200 Canal.

Some people come to Chinatown for pure 24K gold jewelry. Here you will find the delicately worked ornaments and charms that Chinese give each other for birthdays, weddings, and anniversaries.

What's most seductive in Chinatown are the food suppliers, the vendors as well as the restaurants. Not only does the area have the greatest variety of Chinese regional cuisines, including Hakka, Cantonese, Szechwan, and Mandarin, it also has the raw or cooked specialties to be taken home. Only in Chinatown can you find hairy melon, baby spring ginger, and salted fish. On the streets, fish vendors sell shrimp that cost half the price but taste twice as sweet as those sold uptown. In the windows of food

stores hang racks of barbecued ribs and entire roasted pigs, their skins golden and crackling. It's around these food places that you will find the largest concentration of people, shopping for their food daily. They are not looking just for bargains but for quality—the glossiest eggplants, the liveliest crabs. They jostle and push to reach the most perfect vegetable.

Still, they will stand in line fairly patiently waiting for a table in the restaurants, which play an important role in the community. The poorest Chinese man may be seen eating a pork bun and a cup of tea at 10 in the morning, savoring each bite. At night, there will be extravagant banquets featuring an array of ten to fourteen courses, proceeding from cold appetizers to Peking duck to noodles that symbolize long life. Except for those who are so wealthy as to have their own chefs at home, most Chinese prefer to do their lavish entertaining at restaurants because there they can eat complicated dishes—like Peking duck and winter melon soup served in a sculpted melon shell— that are too time-consuming to make at home.

Even ceremonial occasions are celebrated in restaurants. For example, when a baby is one month old, the family will hold a party at a restaurant. Guests will bring *lai see*, a few dollars tucked into red (for good luck) envelopes, and the baby will be taken from table to table by the mother. For a wedding banquet, the bride, who may have been married in a Western dress, will arrive at the restaurant in a Chinese *kwah*, a long heavy silk jacket embroidered with birds, chrysanthemums, and peonies, worn over a *cheong sam*, the Chinese dress slit up the thigh.

Much less public is gambling. At home or in gambling houses, the Chinese play mah-jongg, poker, or pai gow. In gambling houses, which are plain basement rooms with linoleum floors, 99% of the gamblers are men. Women tend to play cards at home or in the casinos of Atlantic City.

Among the better restaurants are Hee Seung Fung Teahouse at 46 Bowery, Siu Lam Kung at 18 Elizabeth Street, and Tai Hong Lau at 72 Mott Street. But the way to judge an unfamiliar restaurant is to peer in the windows and see how many Chinese people are actually eating there. The Chinese have a word-of-mouth grapevine and follow the chefs as they roam from one place to another. If there are a lot of Chinese diners in one restaurant, assume that the food is quite good. If there are not, don't go in.

While English is spoken in most of the restaurants, many other shops in the area have shopkeepers who speak only Chinese. These include the apothecary shops, which makes shopping for dried sea horses a risky business. Still, many items can be bought on impulse, without the benefit of the Chinese language. At stationery shops, there are pretty bright pink gold-embossed envelopes decorated with Chinese cherubs and lanterns with golden tassels. Since Chinatown is small and congested, it's fun to comparison shop. You may find Chinese pajamas for toddlers for $9 at one store and $7 at another. So prowl. And when you're tired of walking, stop and have a roast pork bun with a cup of tea, or a Chinese egg custard, called *don tot*, with a cup of coffee. One of the great surprises of Chinatown is that, at many of the coffee shops, the restaurateurs brew some of the best coffee in town.

The main arteries of Chinatown are Canal and Mott streets and the Bowery. Start at the corner of Canal and Mott and walk south, marching west to Mulberry and east to Bowery and beyond.

To reach Chinatown by subway: Take the BMT N or R; or the IRT 6 to Canal Street. By bus: Take the M6 down Broadway or the M1 up Church and Centre Street to Canal and head east; or the M101 or M102 up or down Third Avenue/Bowery to Canal and head west.

■   ■   ■

PEARL RIVER
CHINESE PRODUCTS
EMPORIUM, INC.

T H I S is one of those all-encompassing and amazing China-town emporiums that offers soup to nuts, along with cotton T-shirts, silk comforters, embroidered cotton sheets, backpacks, preserved olives and fruits, woks, chopsticks, steamers, and Christmas tree ornaments. Prices are not only cheap, sometimes they are downright ridiculous. Suffice it to say that it is a perfect store for impulse shopping, even if you're broke and don't think you need a thing.

Start with socks for kids. Uptown, a pair of plain white all-cotton socks can run you $1.25 to $4. Here, there are packets of three pairs—one pink, one blue, and one white—for $2.25. Sleeveless T-shirts for men and women are in fine, silky cotton and cost a mere $4.50 each. At that price, you can afford to dye the shirts yourself in every color of the spectrum. Or do what some Los Angeles people did: As they faced a hot summer, they ordered twelve white T-shirts for each member of the family, and on every miserable doggy day, they put on a fresh, spanking-clean white shirt as often as needed to feel pristine and immaculate. Come winter, there are pure wool V-neck long-sleeved pullovers for men in rust or brown for $18.50, and brocade padded jackets for children and adults, $25 to $70.

There are adorable children's pajamas here, with the top fastened by frogs and decorated with an embroidered bear, duck, or Chinese tot, pigtails blowing in the wind. They come in blue, pink, yellow, or celadon green ($7 to $8 a set). There are also pure cotton underpants for men or women, and silk shirts. In slippers, there are the well-known black canvas Mary Janes or velvet slip-ons, often adorned with a beaded rose.

If the fashion fails to excite you (high style is not the big draw), there are good accessories for the home, such as shocking pink silk comforters with lavish red and gold embroidery for over $100 (price varies according to elaborateness). There are also pure cotton sheets embroidered with dragons and phoenixes, as well as tablecloths, napkins, and towels.

The housewares and food section features clay pots, woks, teapots, enameled tin dishes and thermoses, porcelain, preserved olives and plums, canned baby corn, and bags of cellophane noodles. If shopping makes you hungry, you can buy a bag of preserved plums or lemon peel, which the Chinese eat as snacks throughout the day.

At the checkout counter, there are lots of inexpensive impulse items that children love, such as tiny straw men and women in theatrical poses that can be hung as Christmas tree ornaments and small wooden pencil sharpeners in the guise of brightly painted little girls, panda bears, or ducks. — E.L.

Pearl River Chinese Products Emporium, Inc., 277 Canal Street, 431-4770. Open daily, 10 A.M. to 7 P.M. AE, MC, V.
  Other branches: 13 Elizabeth Street, 966-1010. Open the same hours.

LEE CHEONG
CORPORATION

CHINATOWN is the place to buy pure 24K gold jewelry that is so soft as to be utterly malleable, but so brilliantly colored that it makes the more practical 14K and 18K gold look almost pedestrian. The Chinese love the 24K gold precisely for its purity, and they make ample use of its malleability.

Because the gold is soft, extremely delicate patterns and designs can be beaten into the metal to make ornate bracelets, rings, pendants, and charms. For little children, there are tiny goldfish charms with movable, highly detailed scales. There are bracelets on which are stamped or hammered intricate floral designs. The Chinese give these pieces of gold on special occasions. When a child is born, he or she may receive a gold bracelet. A bride traditionally receives a dowry of gold jewelry from her future mother-in-law.

This shop is representative of the Chinese jewelry shops lining Canal Street, with a large, varied, and typical array of charms, pendants, rings, earrings, and chains. The proprietors speak English and will tell you that a child's bracelet is around $50 and a wedding ring is priced anywhere from $60 to $80.

— E.L.

Lee Cheong Corporation, 217 Canal Street, 966-4870. Open daily, 11 A.M. to 6 P.M. AE, MC, V.

BOK LEI TAT TRADING CO., INC.

F O R anyone who is interested in the Oriental martial arts, this is one of the major places to go. There are kung fu outfits in black or white, with tops and pants priced at $19.99. These can be used for actual kung fu practice or for lolling around the house on a hot summer day. For a little four-year-old boy who wishes to probe the martial arts or simply to scare the wits out of his parents, there is a small Ninja outfit, complete with a black mask that covers most of the face ($29.99). A handsome item is a black satin club jacket with a dragon embroidered on the back ($50).

— E.L.

Bok Lei Tat Trading Co. Inc., 213 Canal Street, 226-1703. Open daily, 9:30 A.M. to 7:30 P.M. AE, MC, V, checks.

Other branches: 27-33 West 23rd Street, 741-8833. Open Tuesday to Sunday, 9:30 A.M. to 6:30 P.M.; Monday, 11 A.M. to 6 P.M.

THE FINANCIAL DISTRICT

INTRODUCTION BY
Susan Flinker

The hub of international finance and home to the country's stock and bond markets, these streets are electric. You can almost *feel* the wheeling and dealing. And you never know if the person who just whizzed past you just closed a $50 million oil futures deal.

The financial district isn't known as a big shopping area, but those in the know make it their business to get down here—frequently, if possible. That's because some of the best discounts in the city for fashions and accessories await. Maybe the discounters settled here because the financial district is the wheeler-dealer capital of Manhattan, and it's deals aplenty you'll find at these outlets. Probably the other (read "real") reason that huge discount stores thrive here is because of relatively inexpensive rents in comparison with other neighborhoods on the island. They pass the savings on to us.

THE FINANCIAL DISTRICT

1 Job Lot Trading Corp./Pushcart
   Stores
2 Gorsart
3 Syms
4 Mernsmart
5 Century 21 Department Store
6 Brooks Brothers

THE FINANCIAL DISTRICT

7   Laura Ashley
8   Ann Taylor
9   Fine Design
10 Banana Republic
11 Aca Joe

Five stores in particular are musts if you come to the Wall Street area. Each was selected because it provides excellent values on all manner of clothing and accessories. Three are on Church Street, the main shopping drag; the others are directly off it, or close by. At Syms, one of the most famous off-price operations in the country, crowds flock to pick up imported Italian designer sundresses at a fraction of their regular retail price, or, for men, an extensive collection of name-brand suits.

The faithful of Century 21 Department Stores come for the constantly shifting array of merchandise, including up-to-the-minute footwear from the likes of Norma Kamali, Perry Ellis, and Vittorio Ricci—all of it at fabulous prices.

Upscale professional men make their way to Gorsart for excellent quality, traditionally styled business and weekend wear, made by top manufacturers for the store's own label at prices far below Paul Stuart's or Brooks Brothers's. Others who like their look a bit more updated make Mernsmart a source for a wide selection of men's name-brand clothing, from Daniel Hechter to Calvin Klein, also at discount prices.

And Job Lot Trading Corp./Pushcart Stores is in a class by itself, an impulse buyer's dream that carries everything from schlocky home fashions to fragrances to designer socks.

The lure of bargains is a great leveler, so you find all types of shoppers passing through the financial district—from area workers to those who make a special trip downtown, from corporate vice presidents to the guys who work in the mail room, to artists who live in nearby Tribeca.

And if you come down here, you may want to combine sight-seeing and shopping, even if you live in New York. There are many tourist attractions and historical stopoffs that can make your day especially memorable. The financial district played a vital role in the history of not only the city, but the nation as well. From Church Street, walk south along Broadway to the head of Wall Street. There you'll find Trinity Church, chartered in 1697, where such famous figures as Alexander Hamilton and Robert Fulton are buried. Also on Wall Street is The New York Stock Exchange. Inside is a two-tiered visitor's gallery where you can sit and watch the action on the trading floor.

There are also some interesting places to eat down here, with their own impressive histories. Fraunces Tavern, at the corner of Broad and Pearl streets, dates back to 1719. It serves up classic American cuisine for breakfast, lunch, and dinner. Legend has it that George Washington toasted his officers farewell here in 1783.

Upscale Oscar Delmonico's, at 56 Beaver Street, opened in 1836. The menu is Northern Italian fare. Or you can skip the history and go for some good, cheap eats. Hamburger Harry's at 157 Chambers Street (near Church) does great burgers, and it's a fun spot just to hang out and have a cool drink or two. Ye Ye at 127 Chambers does the near-impossible: serves a great Chinese meal for around $6.

While you're in the neighborhood, you can eat and at the same time see spectacular views at the World Trade Center's Windows on the World restaurant complex. And at the extreme east side of Fulton street (which intersects with Church), walk over to the South Street Seaport. You can shop or sample foods of the world from scores of concessions (the food is better than the shopping).

If you want, you can easily walk a couple of blocks north from the financial district to artist and lofts land—Tribeca. A popular spot there for lunch and dinner is Exterminator Chili, at 305 Church Street, which serves four kinds of chili, from "residential" (mild) to "industrial strength" (hot). Or try Cafe Americano, 105 Hudson Street, an art gallery/dance club kind of restaurant, where you can lunch for about twelve bucks. They also do fun fashion presentations, featuring the work of local talent, to inspire your shopping. For a more elegant lunch or dinner, hip downtowners favor The Odeon, 145 West Broadway, for French food in a refurbished deco cafeteria.

Since the financial district is at the skinniest tip of the island, many subways go right through it. Take the IND A, C, E, or K to the World Trade Center; the BMT N or R to Cortlandt Street; the IRT 1 to Chambers Street, 2 or 3 to Park Place, or 4 or 5 to Fulton Street. By bus: Take the M1 or M6 down Broadway or the M6 up Church to Warren Street; or the M22 across Chambers to Church.

You can start your shopping expedition here at the corner of Church and Warren streets, the site of Job Lot Trading Corp./Pushcart Stores. Continue south on Church to Murray Street, where Gorsart is, one more block to Park Place for Syms, then two blocks to Mernsmart, at Vesey and Church streets. Three more blocks down Church to Cortlandt and you're at Century 21 Department Store.

■   ■   ■

JOB LOT TRADING CORP./ PUSHCART STORES

CHECK your dignity at the door. You'll definitely find this store a guilty pleasure. The ambience is more than no-frills—with its grimy walls and wooden pushcarts filled with everything from potato peelers to jockey shorts, Pushcart is downright grungy. But it is still a fun place to shop because of the possibility of finding surprises like a long-sleeved Danskin leotard for only $2.99.

Pushcart handles every imaginable kind of close-out and business liquidation. Things move in and out with incredible speed, and you *can't* go in to look for a specific item. But this place is great for hunting up an unexpected fashion basic. For example, on one day you can walk in and find men's Jordache denim blouson jackets for $19.99, suggested retail $48; or Bonjour men's briefs made to sell for $5, $1.99 here; or crocheted anklets in fashion colors for 79¢ instead of their $2.25 preticketed price. Ramie and cotton short-sleeved sweaters for women might show up here at $6.99, regular prices $24 to $32. Yet the next day you'll be lucky to find Burlington Leg Looks panty hose at a third of their retail price, some boxed hankies for $1.50, and an Izod polo shirt for $5.99. Or for women, weekend wear like Gabrielle's oversized orange and white color-block tees for $5.99, elsewhere $20.

A word of advice—examine everything very carefully before

you ring up your purchases. Damaged goods are not un-
common. There is a refund policy, though, in case something
gets by.   — S.F.

**Job Lot Trading Corp./Pushcart Stores, 140 Church Street, 962-4142.
Open Monday to Saturday, 8 A.M. to 6 P.M. MC, V, checks.**
   **Other branches: 412 Fifth Avenue, 398-9210. Open Monday to Friday, 8
A.M. to 6:30 P.M.; Saturday, 9 A.M. to 6:30 P.M.**

GORSART

I F your style is Brooks Brothers or Paul Stuart, check out
Gorsart. It's a shop with a lot to offer the man who has to dress
the part of the high-powered executive during the week, and has
to maintain the image on the weekends.

Gorsart has been a well-kept secret in retailing for sixty-five
years, operating strictly by word of mouth. It's where lots of
judges, bankers, brokers, and lawyers go to get outfitted. The
emphasis here is on private-label garments with excellent
construction and sumptuous fabrics. The goods are made by
top manfacturers of tailored clothing (suits) like Hertling, Hickey
Freeman, and Arthur Freedberg. Dress shirts come from Eagle,
Sero, Kenneth Gordon, and others. You'll also find selections
that you'd see up on Madison Avenue, but discounted by about
20% or better. They can do that at Gorsart because of all that
money they save on advertising and lower rents than uptown.

The overall fashion statement here is traditionally conservative
clothing, but with a *slight* updating. For example they'll sell
pleated trousers, which is considered contemporary by traditional standards of business dressing. Everything from socks to
formalwear and outerwear to prep extraordinaire golfing pants
awaits. And if you're not quite sure what you need, you can trust
the sales help. They're very knowledgeable about proper business attire and what will fit your physique. If you're in a
profession like banking, finance, the law, or in any other

---

corporate environment where very traditional dress rules are observed, Gorsart is a great find.

Prices for summer suits in light worsted wools and cotton/wool blends are $200 to $390, with a cotton seersucker suit going for about $170. Blazers (which are a strong point—most are of beautiful imported Scottish fabric) are $150 to $240. A button-down shirt of Sea Island cotton that sells for $80 uptown is $60 here. The same kind of savings can be had for well-known shoe brands. A pair of classic preppy Alden tassel loafers that is $150 uptown sells for $110 here. Outerwear, like a double-breasted London Fog raincoat, $175 elsewhere, is $130 at Gorsart.

There's no charge for alterations (in fact, Gorsart has over thirty in-house tailors on call). To avoid crowds, avoid weekday lunch hours.

Storewide sales are held in January and July.   — S.F.

Gorsart, 9 Murray Street, second floor, entrance next door to 9 Murray Street, 962-0024. Open Monday to Friday, 9 A.M. to 6 P.M.; Saturday till 5:30 P.M. Closed Saturday during July and August. MC, V, checks.

SYMS

BLUE·COLLAR workers vie with the pinstripe crew for the fashion finds at Syms. One of New York's most famous off-price operations, Syms is five floors of black walls and an almost overwhelming number of pipe racks and bins. It is absolutely no-frills shopping—even a little bleak—and really trend-conscious shoppers will do better elsewhere. But where Syms's strength lies is in presenting a huge assortment of solid, mainstream clothing and accessories—fashion staples for men, women, and children—all discounted.

On the women's floors you'll find sportswear, dresses, and suits from Calvin Klein, Nicole Miller, Ellen Tracy, Ralph Lauren, and other major names; as well as shoes with labels such as 9 West, Maud Frizon and Hippopotamus. An idea of the values: A

Regina Kravitz rayon jumpsuit that retails for $140 elsewhere is $79 here. A Perry Ellis Portfolio short-sleeved cotton knit sweater goes for $35 here, suggested retail $65.

Handbags and lingerie are some of the best deals you'll find. Multicolor Liz Claiborne clutch bags are $13 here, $24 elsewhere. A white leather satchel with gold accents from Meyers is $99 here, $180 at department stores. And lingerie is about 50% suggested retail, too, from names like Lily of France, and bras from Warners and Bali. Some discounts can be even steeper in lingerie.

There's basically the same grab bag of major brand and designer names for men. Styles for both sportwear and suits range from the conservative to more contemporary. Daniel Hechter, Pierre Cardin, Nino Cerruti, Bill Blass, and After Six are well represented. For example, a Pierre Cardin wool suit that sells for $240 in most men's stores is $139 here. A Henry Grethel silk tie is about half price at $7.

Try-ons are permitted in fashion departments. Avoid shopping at Syms during weekday lunch hours, when it can be really crazy. If you come on Sundays, you can even find parking on the street. — S.F.

Syms, 45 Park Place, 791-1199. Open Tuesday and Wednesday, 8 A.M. to 6:30 P.M.; Thursday and Friday till 7:30 P.M.; Saturday, 10 A.M. to 6:30 P.M.; Sunday, 11:30 A.M. to 5:30 P.M. Checks.

MERNSMART

F O R men who are dressing for success, Mernsmart is a great place to shop. And while you won't be able to put together an extremely directional fashion statement, you'll find plenty of mainstream to "contemporary-plus" top designer and brand names here at discounts ranging from 20% to 60% off regular retail.

Basically, all areas of menswear are represented, from office looks to sporty weekend wear, to what you have to wear underneath it all. They feature a large selection of suits in the $120 to $270 range. A Calvin Klein 100% wool suit in gray and white stripes with European-cut boxy non-vent jacket sells for $250. Regular retail is $320. A wool European-cut double-breasted suit from Daniel Hechter can go up to $240. Here, it's $180. A sophisticated silk mustard-and-blue striped tie from Geoffrey Beene sells for $18.50 elsewhere, $8 here. There are similar savings on silk ties from Cacharel and Paco Rabanne.

If you want to go more "cas," as in *casual*, Mernsmart's got the goods. Pleated linen trousers from Calvin Klein, $110 elsewhere, are $50 here. WilliWear cotton tunic tops, $60 elsewhere, go for $35. Pastel striped long-sleeved cotton-knit crew- and V-neck pullover sweaters from Ron Chereskin are $40 here, $55 elsewhere.

Unlike most off-price or discount stores, Mernsmart does have major sales on key holidays, so you'll save even more. Yes, lunchtimes are the busiest here during the week.   — S.F.

Mernsmart, 75 Church Street, 227-5471. Open Monday to Friday, 9:30 A.M. to 6:30 P.M.; Saturday till 6 P.M. AE, MC, V, checks.

CENTURY 21
DEPARTMENT STORE

I F paradise were a store, it would be called Century 21. This place is a shopper's fantasy come true. Not only is it an off-price operation featuring a fabulous selection of designer and name-brand fashions, but its atmosphere is just as pleasant. The store was renovated a few years back, so don't be shocked if you see marble flooring almost everywhere you look.

As if that weren't enough, Century employs tons of easy-to-spot blue-smocked salespersons. And as soon as you can say "Excuse me, but . . ." you'll have two or three people eager to check stock for you. Since in most discount—and department—stores salespeople are scarce, this is a big plus.

They don't call this store Century 21 *Department* Store for nothing. Everything your little heart desires is here from undies to accessories, shoes, cosmetics and fragrances, beauty supplies, housewares, and, of course, the latest in updated, contemporary sportswear. And the savings are impressive. They carry better sportswear names, junior manufacturers, and designer labels than found in most major department and specialty stores. For example, a Rebecca Moses slinky knee-length cotton and rayon dress that's regularly $220 goes for $129 at Century 21. Or kicky Betsey Johnson cotton leggings and body-hugging long-sleeved top separates: $30 here; $45 elsewhere.

Women's shoes are exceptional from a value and fashion standpoint. From positively avant-garde to basic work and glitzy dress styles, it's all here. You'll find everything from Vittorio Ricci $200 high-fashion pink pumps for $97, to $90 Joan and David leather flats for $50. There's always great footwear from Perry Ellis, Norma Kamali, Freelance, Sasha of London, Ralph Lauren, and so on, all at equally good prices.

The men's area isn't as extensive in terms of selection, but what they do carry is great for both conservative and very contemporary dressers. The discounts here can go up to the 50%-off mark. You'll find suits like unconstructed, padded-shoulder linens by Verri Uomo. Dress shirts for work are plentiful, including those by Jeffrey Banks, Nino Cerruti, Perry Ellis, Henry Grethel, and more—in other words, what you'll find in the men's department of Saks or Bloomingdale's, for a lot less. There's activewear and furnishings, in addition to other fashion categories.

The kids' department is not to be missed, either. There are top names at great prices. Gianfranco Ruffini shorts for boys usually sell for $24.99. At Century 21, they're $5.97. And the savings go on and on.

As with most other shops in the neighborhood, lunchtime is packed to the rafters with shoppers. No fitting rooms on the premises, so there are no try-ons. But there is a cash-refund policy. Don't miss out on the home fashion areas, as well. They're just as impressive—name brands from Lenox China at 20% off to Ralph Lauren towels at 30% off suggested retail prices. New stock arrives daily. — S.F.

Century 21 Department Stores, 12 Cortlandt Street, 227-9092. Open Monday to Friday, 7:45 A.M. to 6:10 P.M.; Saturday, 10 A.M. to 4:30 P.M. Closed Saturday during July and August. AE, MC, V, checks.

BROOKS BROTHERS
1 Liberty Plaza, 267-2400. See index for main listing.

LAURA ASHLEY
4 Fulton Street, South Street Seaport, 809-3555. See index for main listing.

ANN TAYLOR
25 Fulton Street, South Street Seaport, 608-5612. See index for main listing.

FINE DESIGN
89 Fulton Street, South Street Seaport. 406-3661. See index for main listing.

BANANA REPUBLIC

Pier 17 Pavilion, South Street Seaport, 732-3090. See index for main listing.

ACA JOE

Pier 17 Pavilion, South Street Seaport, 406-0770. See index for main listing.

CHELSEA

INTRODUCTION BY
Susan Flinker

Chelsea is a neighborhood of contrasts. It's a little funky. It's a little chic. It's a little industrial. It's very residential. At one end, you'll find stretch limos parked in a conga line outside the trendy bistros that have lately come to this neighborhoods' previously industrial blocks off Fifth Avenue. At the other end are prostitutes working the West Side Highway. And sandwiched in between are neat, six-story middle-class apartment buildings, interspersed with a few low-income housing projects.

Chelsea is in the middle of a major image overhaul. Up until three or four years ago, it was considered the kind of neighborhood where it wasn't safe to walk at night. Then came the influx of upscale renovators and mass condo converters, bringing with them the specialized gourmet takeout shops, little boutiques, and trendy eateries. But even with what people are calling the revitalization of Chelsea, the area hasn't lost its quiet residential

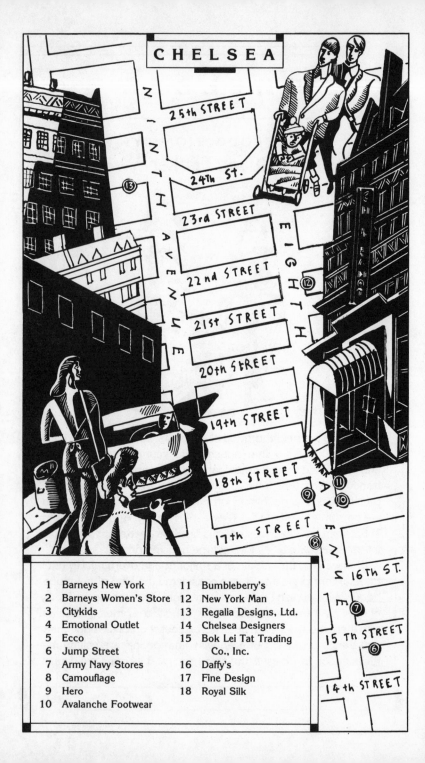

CHELSEA

25th STREET

24TH ST.

23rd STREET

22nd STREET

21st STREET

20th STREET

19th STREET

18th STREET

17th STREET

16TH ST.

15Th STREET

14th STREET

NINTH AVENUE

EIGHTH

quality, especially on the side sreets. Many young families have gravitated here because of affordable condo prices, so little kids riding tricycles, grandparents proudly pushing baby strollers, and business-suited daddies with toddlers in hand are common sights on these tree-lined streets. Yet it's not unusual to see a Chanel-suited woman sauntering down Seventh Avenue into Barneys New York (one of the most seductive temples of consumerism in the city) and right behind her a postpunk space cadet in black leather.

The older population remains a strong presence here, too, expecially fourth-generation Irish residents, amid more recent Latin immigrants, predominantly Puerto Ricans and Cubans. Throughout the neighborhood, twenty-four hour banking machines will ask you if you want to conduct your transaction in English or in Spanish.

Chelsea's not teeming with fashion stores of the kind you'd see in the East Village or Soho. But its growing reputation as a shopping center is attracting a wide spectrum of female pilgrims, in search of everything from a good deal on a pair of shoes to contemporary officewear from the Emotional Outlet; from the artsy-craftsy womenswear at Bumbleberry's to sensibly priced middle-of-the-road looks at Royal Silk. Modern beaux brummels scout out the perfect silk tie at Camouflage. Jeans and T-shirted yuppie parents in their thirties clutch their little ones en route to Citykids, with its selection of cuddly terry cloth bathrobes and sharp little jogging suits. Of course, Barneys on Seventh Avenue is the anchor, summoning ultrapreppies in chinos and Weejuns, as well as avant-garde Eurochics who dress in exotics from Gaultier or Comme des Garçons—plus every other fashion preference in between. It has its own special mystique.

Besides fashion stores, there are some other terrific shops here that shouldn't be missed. Gear, the first retail space of this nationally known home fashion resource, at Seventh Avenue and 17th Street, is great for country-inspired home textiles, ceramics, or just browsing. Nearby is Jensen Lewis, at Seventh Avenue and 15th Street, specializing in trendy Eurostyle furniture and living accessories. Farther west and uptown is the Pottery Barn on Tenth Avenue and 26th Street, a good source for things you can't find around town—like discontinued pieces—as well as current stock.

For books, the Barnes & Noble Sale Annex at 18th Street and Fifth Avenue is legendary for its astounding bargains on remaindered books on every imaginable subject, and is also known as a singles' scene.

But for all these outposts of contemporary life, Chelsea's past is visible everywhere. The area was named by a captain, Thomas Clarke, after a soldiers' hospital near London. In 1750, he established Chelsea, his farming homestead, here on what today is 22nd and 23rd streets, around Ninth and Tenth avenues. The neighborhood retained an English village atmosphere until the 1840s, when the Hudson River Railroad tracks were constructed along Tenth and Eleventh Avenues, and when Clarke's grandson, Clement Moore, decided to break up his patrimony, selling off the property in building lots. The railroad brought an industrial flavor to the neighborhood that still remains—auto parts, plumbing supplies, electronics, printing and graphics, and a slew of huge storage warehouses operate from 17th Street up through the Chelsea border at 26th Street.

Yet there are still some streets in Chelsea that invoke a gracious era, lined with two- and three-story, nineteenth-century brick townhouses, trimmed with charming black wrought-iron balconies and window guards. Most of these are found in the low 20s from Ninth to Tenth avenues, where you can also see elegant, well-manicured four-story brownstones with their original arched facades intact. They're worth looking over after a shopping expedition here.

By the 1880s, 23rd Street had become Manhattan's entertainment center, with lots of theaters, restaurants, and cafés in the immediate vicinity. Author O'Henry lived here. So did the legendary Lily Langtry, in the original London Terrace townhouses that in the 1920s became the mammoth London Terrace apartments, spanning 23rd Street between Ninth and Tenth avenues.

But Chelsea's most famous landmark is the Chelsea Hotel at 222 West 23rd Street. It has been home to such diverse personalities as couturier Charles James and Nancy Spungen, murdered there by her boyfriend, the Sex Pistols' late bass player, Sid Vicious. In front are plaques commemorating residents Brendan Behan and Thomas Wolfe.

In the 1960s, mega-scenemaker Andy Warhol filmed part of his epic, *Chelsea Girls*, in this part of town. Not that his was the first movie to be produced here. In fact, Chelsea was a center of the fledgling cinema industry. Mary Pickford shot some of her earliest movies here, including *Tess of the Storm Country*.

In a way, the entertainment-center 1880s Chelsea is being reborn today. Locals, downtowners, uptowners, and out-of-towners flock to its lively nightspots such as Limelight, housed in the little brownstone Church of the Holy Communion at Sixth Avenue and 20th Street. Private Eyes, the video dance club, is on the same block. The renowned performance-arts space The Kitchen has settled here, on 19th Street between Tenth and Eleventh avenues. On Eighth Avenue at 19th Street, the Joyce Theater plays host to some of America's most important medium-size and avant-garde dance troupes.

There are many interesting restaurants in the area as well, in case you want to plan a post-shopping evening around dinner and clubhopping. For a really nice supper in a nonstuffy setting, try L'Acajou, 53 West 19th Street, for classy French bistro fare, a good wine list, and a fun bar scene. Roxanne's, 158 Eighth Avenue, serves good French food in a charming room. Claire, 156 Seventh Avenue (there's also a branch in Key West), offers seafood with style. Miss Ruby's Café, 135 Eighth Avenue, features a completely new American regional menu every few weeks.

An old neighborhood favorite is Café Andalucia at 160 Seventh Avenue, where classic Spanish chicken and rice runs only about $8. If you're looking for a sushi outlet, head over to Meriken, at the corner of Seventh Avenue and 21st Street. Decorated in mint-green pastels and neon à la *Miami Vice* years before Crockett and Tubbs ever existed, this restaurant offers a nice Japanese lunch for around $12. If it's tall, exotic drinks you're after, check out the stylish Rick's Lounge on Eighth Avenue near 17th Street, or the bar at Rogers and Barbero, a block south. Or for a good old American steak, there's Harvey's Chelsea Restaurant, 108 West 18th Street. Its quaint 1880s ambience typifies the best of what Chelsea was and what it is today.

You could start your tour at Barneys, on the corner of 17th Street and Seventh Avenue. From there you might circle down Seventh Avenue, go west on 15th Street and up Eighth Avenue for more adventurous fare. Then head east to Fifth Avenue for Royal Silk and Fine Design for more traditional clothing and Daffy's for fabulous fashion discounts.

To reach Chelsea by subway: Take the IND A, B, C, E, F, K to 14th Street; or the IRT 1 to 18th Street or the 2 or 3 to 14th Street. By bus: Take the M10 up Eighth or down Seventh Avenue to 17th Street or the M14 across 14th Street to Seventh Avenue.

■　■　■

BARNEYS NEW YORK

O N E hundred twenty-five in-house tailors and fitters stand waiting to alter over 30,000 suits ranging from the stalwartly conservative to the monumentally trendy. Where else, but at Barneys New York? The largest men's specialty store in the country, this Chelsea institution (for some sixty-five years) has reached legendary status.

If you can zip it up, splash it on, or toss it nonchalantly over your shoulder, you'll find it at Barneys. In a sense, the store is a testament to the modern man's God-given right to care as much about his appearance as women always have.

Basically, *any* man can find something to suit his taste here. The merchandise assortment is mind-boggling. Every current direction in men's, boys', and young men's fashion is represented in depth—from the avant-garde's own Jean-Paul Gaultier to the preppy romanticism of Ralph Lauren to the office polish of Hickey Freeman. And Barneys buyers look for the unusual. It was one of the first stores in the country to carry Milan designer Giorgio Armani in 1976.

Want to drop mega-hundreds on an imported silk paisley smoking jacket, or over $200 for a pair of Yojhi Yamamoto rubber-soled work shoes? No problem. If in the back of your mind you remember something about Barneys New York being a discount operation, forget it. Those days ended when Fred Pressman (son of Barney) took over nearly twenty years ago. Now you pay top dollar for everything. But the service and the ambience are impeccable. Salespersons are there to assist but aren't pushy, and the interior of the store is immaculately maintained—you won't see smudgy glass cases here—and lavishly appointed (for example, with wooden throne chairs) to make shopping a very civilized experience.

Barneys also has one of the most famous after-season clearance sales in retailing. Every January most of the top designer collections go for 50% off original prices.

Even though Saturdays and evenings are crowded, you can still shop without much annoyance. If you'd like it a little quieter, weekday afternoons from 3 to 5 P.M. are choice hours.   — S.F.

Barneys New York, 106 Seventh Avenue, 929-9000. Open Monday to Friday, 10 A.M. to 9 P.M.; Saturday till 8 P.M.; Sunday, noon to 5 P.M. AE, Barney's, MC, V, checks.

BARNEYS WOMEN'S STORE

W H E N the women's division of Barneys New York was housed on the penthouse floor of its men's store, it concentrated on the *top* international and American talent working in fashion. But in 1986, when womenswear moved around the corner to its own store, housed in six turn-of-the-century brownstones whose facades were maintained to preserve the character of the neighborhood, Barneys aggressively began cornering the market in all areas. Sure, you'll still be knocked out by the high-end pieces (and prices) from Chanel, Yves Saint Laurent, Azzedine Alaïa, Gianfranco Ferré, Jean-Paul Gaultier, and company on the fourth, fifth, and sixth floors. In fact, after noting a couple of $1,100 and $1,300 price tags on silk nightgowns, you may go into shock. But Barneys has greatly expanded its moderate-priced collections as well. About half the merchandise is private label, which is generally less expensive, and you won't see yourself coming and going in it. English type tailoring is featured on the second floor, with the Barneys New York label next to Patricia Clyne and Ralph Lauren. On the third floor, where the clothes have a more Italian feel, a private label suit could be $400, gabardine skirts and pants $130 to $175, and silk blouses $110 to $150. On these floors professional women can find tailored clothing that's designed specifically for them, rather than picked up from men's apparel. And standard alterations are complimentary.

The main floor has a good shoe department with such desirable labels as Manolo Blahnik, Maud Frizon, Stephane Kélian, Robert Clergerie, and Roger Vivier. There are other sorts of accessories, of course, plus a well-edited cosmetics department. The Chelsea Passage department from the original Barneys (carrying fine linens, china, silver, stationery, gifts for the home, antique quilts, etc.) now occupies about half the main floor.

If your budget makes all this elegance for window-shopping-only, head to the adjacent CO/OP department, two floors of less expensive, more junior merchandise, featuring labels like Kenzo, Basco, WilliWear, Yohji Yamamoto, Matsuda, and Norma Kamali, plus the CO/OP private label. Prices range from around $500 for outfits from Katherine Hamnet and Workers for Freedom, to the under-$75 sweaters in the Top Shop, and under-$100 shoes.

While the CO/OP is modern in design, the main part of the women's store is soothing and elegant, with Art Deco and Weiner Werkstaette pieces and a central skylit atrium that illuminates all the floors, as in a French department store. The lower level has a café serving breakfast, lunch, tea, and dinner (the store is open till 9 P.M.). Also there—and also open till 9 P.M.—is the Roger Thompson beauty salon, where you can get a manicure or a facial as well as a great haircut at prices ranging from $35 for no-appointment service to $60 for the top cutters to $85 for Mr. Thompson himself. And the people are unusually nice for a fashionable New York salon.   — S.F.

Barneys women's store, 17th Street east of Seventh Avenue, 929-9000. Open Monday to Friday, 10 A.M. to 9 P.M.; Saturday till 8 P.M.; Sunday, noon to 5 P.M. AE, Barney's, MC, V, checks.

CITYKIDS

O K A Y , you don't want to dress your *enfant terrible* in the same old department-store fare. But considering how fast children grow, you don't want to invest your life savings in an ensemble from a tony Madison Avenue boutique.

Citykids might be the solution, offering fun, upbeat, and unpretentious selections. Here you'll find everything from vintage brocade tuxedo jackets ($50) for post-toddlers to plush, velvety terry cloth robes in charcoal gray ($40).

Owner Ken Goldstein says half the fashions (for sizes newborn to 10—the latter will fit a seven-year-old, give or take a bit) are imported. You'll find pieces like a cotton batik paisley print overall for little girls' sizes (ages four to seven) from Austria's Creation Stummer ($44). Much of the stock comes from small children's clothing manufacturers that you won't find in department stores—like a toddler's three-piece white cotton fleece outfit, the jacket pink ribbon and eyelet trimmed with pink hearts and rhinestones at the shoulder; and underneath shorts and a sleeveless T-shirt with pink ribboning around the straps ($45), from a company named Janet.

About a quarter of the fashions here are from their own Citykids line. Goldstein has an in-house artist who hand paints basic sweats, T-shirts, rompers, and sleeveless tank tops with urban scenes, like a skyscraper or a bright yellow cab riding down the street. Prices for hand-painted items range from $12 for an infant size T-shirt to $28 for an older child's sweatshirt. Another in-house designer creates contemporary clothing— less hip, say, than the mass-market house Esprit, but more "tiny adult" looking than Garanamals. An example of a Citykids creation: elasticized, high-waisted cotton cropped pants, in a pink-and-blue floral print reminiscent of English country upholstery fabric ($28).

There is a good collection of children's shoes here as well, featuring imported leather and kicky sneaker styles.

Citykids also carries an extensive toy collection, ranging in price from 25¢ for a tiny plastic car to $150 for a 4-foot-high plush teddybear with movable, jointed arms. Citykids is also the exclusive source for La Peluche, a French line of whimsical small plush toys (anywhere from about 6 to 11 inches high), including penguins, ducks, and rabbits, in the $25 range. There is also a nice selection of children's books.   — S.F.

Citykids, 130 Seventh Avenue, 620-0906. Open Monday to Friday, 11 A.M. to 7 P.M.; Saturday till 6 P.M. AE, MC, V, checks.

EMOTIONAL OUTLET

A shopping institution in Chelsea for just about twenty years, this flagship branch of the Emotional Outlet is aptly named. The psychic release starts as soon as you walk in, when the staff will greet you with special sales of the day and an offer of wine or coffee. There's even a Sunday brunch of bread and cream cheese at the store. Such amenities make this a particularly good place to which to drag your male companion. He can sit and watch TV, read *Esquire*, or sip a little vino while you shop.

The fashion here ranges from adventurous career clothes to weekend wear that's a bit more fun and spunky. You'll recognize the designers they sell—Cathy Hardwick, Liz Claiborne, Carole Little for St. Tropez West, and other "better contemporary" department store lines.

Downstairs, there's a terrific shoe and handbag department, featuring styles ranging from unadorned flat-heel pumps to very fashionable midcalf leather lace-up "granny" boots from well-known names.

Virtually all the stock is discounted, minimally around 10% off department and specialty store prices, although some items sell at retail price or even a bit higher. Every tag is marked accordingly, so you can figure it out for yourself. There are two major *preseason* sales of note: in March for the upcoming spring/summer season, and in September for the onset of fall/winter. Each runs for two weeks.

Seasoned Emotional Outlet shoppers know that stock blows out of the store so quickly that it pays to come in every few days to see what's new.

The store is basically a madhouse on the weekends and after 5 P.M. during the week. To avoid the crowds, aim for weekday mornings and afternoons.   — S.F.

Emotional Outlet, 91 Seventh Avenue, 206-7750. Open Monday to Friday, 11 A.M. to 8 P.M.; Saturday till 7 P.M.; Sunday, noon to 6 P.M. AE, CB, DC, MC, V, checks.

Other branches: 135 West 50th Street, 957-9340. Open Monday to Friday, 10 A.M. to 7 P.M.; Saturday, 11 A.M. to 7 P.M. 242 East 51st Street, 838-0707. 435 East 86th Street, 534-4825. Open the same hours.

ECCO
94 Seventh Avenue, 675-5180. See index for main listing.

JUMP STREET

W H E N you hear the name Jump Street, you might conjure up the image of a manic, make-your-adrenaline-rise junior sportswear stomping ground. Get that picture out of your mind. This shop is one of the more mellow women's fashion establishments you'll encounter in the city. If you like the spunky career and weekend looks that huge companies like Esprit churn out, but want a more individual look, Jump Street is for you. Key pieces are displayed on exposed brick walls, so you can get a feel for the simple, architectural shapes that owner Saundra Johnson designs.

Her fashion concept is built around two-piece dressing—for example, cotton jersey leggings with dolman-sleeved tops or pull-on skirts all in the same fabrics. It's a very easy, fashionable look that doesn't try too hard and works well for the office or hanging out on weekends. Johnson picks groups of colors that harmonize with each other, so that a pink cotton tube shirt paired with a turquoise cotton turtleneck slim tunic looks like "an outfit." Expect to pay anywhere from $70 to $90 for a two-piece combination, although you can buy tops and bottoms separately.

Johnson also carries a consistently nice group of limited-edition artwear-type appliqué tops and sleeveless jackets, designed by local craftspeople, in the $130 range. Her nephew, Rodney Epperson, does some of the dressier pieces you'll find here, like slim, body-conscious U-backed dresses in jewel-tone ribbed rayon, in a variety of lengths from minis to ankle-length for $60 to $80.

Epperson, whose clothes have sold in trendy Columbus Avenue boutiques like Charivari and Acrobat, believes that dresses shouldn't feel confining even though they are slim. So he uses fluid fabrics like jersey and rayon that show off the body yet are comfortably unrestricting. His dresses are perfect for a sunset stroll in the park when worn with a pair of sandals, and just as appropriate for a night out accessorized with high heels and bright, bold jewelry. He takes the same versatile approach to separates, creating architectural, cleancut tops ($45) that can be worn out with a belt, tunic style, or tucked in for a pared-down look with his three-panel, fit-at-the-waist, flared-at-the-calf jersey skirt ($55). — S.F.

Jump Street, 258 West 15th Street, 807-6254. Open Tuesday to Saturday, 11 A.M. to 7 P.M. AE, MC, V.

ARMY NAVY STORES

110 Eighth Avenue, 645-7420. See index for main listing.

CAMOUFLAGE

I F the behemoth Barneys or the men's areas of other major department stores are just too much for you to handle, Camouflage is a store you might want to investigate seriously.

The main strength here is that the owners offer a very well edited, very controlled statement about fashion. They offer the best pieces from American and European designers they believe are taking the right direction (an updated classic look, suave yet conservative), from Ronaldus Shamask's cashmere and wool blazers to Paul Smith's long-sleeved, modern printed shirts.

It's all for the man who wants to look fashionable, but never like a fashion victim. You'll find everything from updated chinos and football jerseys in the $45 range on up; it is possible to spend thousands on a complete ensemble—turtleneck sweater, pleated pants, blazer, and topcoat in cashmere—from Shamask. Camouflage also always carries a wide range of Perry Ellis menswear.

If beautiful silks in lovely patterned ties are your passion, you should check out the store's large collection of silks, made exclusively for Camouflage by a variety of top design houses, about $40.

Major sales are held after New Year's Day and the Fourth of July, with 50% markdowns. — S.F.

Camouflage, 141 Eighth Avenue, 741-9118. Open Monday to Friday, noon to 7 P.M.; Saturday, 11 A.M. to 6 P.M. AE, MC, V.

HERO

H E R O is a spartan, tiny little shop that concentrates on basic modern sportswear from owner/designer Henry Auvil and others.

Auvil likes funny, au courant prints—such as post-new wave and 1950s postnuclear-inspired—and that's just what he designs. You'll find graphic, hot-colored prints to pastel-toned 1950s muted patterns on T-shirts, sweats, shorts, pants, and more, for men and women.

"If you can buy it in a department store, you won't find it here," says Auvil. Catering to the young, trendy, rock-videoized customer, Hero's prices are moderate, the merchandise assortment small and precise. Bold colors in every shade and wild graphics make the real statement here, not the shape of those casual basic sweats and tees.

Prices go up to about $30 for a silk-screened printed T-shirt; pants aren't more than $50. There is a group of Auvil's limited-edition and one-of-a-kind pieces (like cotton flannel shirts imprinted with the likeness of a very famous, very dead rock star whose estate once threatened to sue Auvil for infringement!) that are slightly higher, in the $85 range.   — S.F.

Hero, 143 Eighth Avenue, 620-4084. Open Monday to Saturday, noon to 8 P.M.; Sunday till 5 P.M. AE, Discover, MC, V.

AVALANCHE FOOTWEAR

M O S T of the styles here are quietly sophisticated—for example, classic white bucks with a slightly more modern shape. One pair of bucks gets a 1960s Beatles-boot treatment, as slip-ons with elastic sides, rather than laces. There's a wide variety of traditional oxfords for the young professionals. But that's not to say that there's no fun footwear. On the contrary, Avalanche has taken classic weekend shapes and updated them. For example, preppy leather topsiders here can be bright yellow with subtle pink splatters. Or white leather basic moccasins get transformed into absolute standouts with the addition of gold-and-blue leather braiding through the sides. Canvas deck sneakers come in pastel colors as well as white. The quality of all these shoes is as fine as the quality of the well-known name brands Avalanche carries, including young, up-and-coming talent from the United States and Europe—for example, Image, a company that does styles like fun leather high-top sneakers with terra-cotta trim around the lacing and a rubber sole of pale pink, terra-cotta, and white. You'll also find the imported-from-Britain John Moore label, for Pink Flamingo leather lace-up granny boots in the $125 price range.

Prices range from $69 to $99 for casual leathers with rubber soles, to about $150 for dressier oxfords and loafers.

Avalanche has two major clearance sales, in August and January, when many styles sell for below cost. Saturdays and evenings from 5 P.M. to 8 P.M. are the busiest times here. — S.F.

Avalanche Footwear, 152 Eighth Avenue, 741-0668. Open Monday to Friday, noon to 8 P.M.; till 10 P.M. during the summer; Saturday till 7 P.M.; Sunday, 2 P.M. to 6 P.M. Closed Sunday during the summer. AE, MC, V.

BUMBLEBERRY'S

BUMBLEBERRY'S is an open, airy boutique run by Nicki Young Hoyt, who designs 90% of what's sold here. Among their specialties are whimsical artwear pieces that are craftsy but never corny. These are leisure clothes, funky and fun, Hoyt says, not high-fashion designs. They include items like boat sneakers hand painted with fruit motifs, with sweatshirts, T-shirts, and camisoles to match.

Hoyt's basic customer is the woman who likes to wear fun, not-grown-up clothes after work and on weekends, though teens might like some of her designs. This is the place to find the perfect frock to wear on a picnic in the country—her cotton scoopneck and capped-sleeve flouncy dress with a hand-painted design ($38).

Hoyt also customizes T-shirts ($50), denim jackets ($140), and sweatshirts ($50) with tapestry and lace insets or ribbed minidresses with hand-painted skirts ($36). She is known for her papier-mâché bracelets. Some have a marbleized effect, others are cuffs with "theme" collages on theater, animals, or New York City, made from cut-out pieces of newspaper and magazine articles ($20). She also takes 1-inch-round plain button earrings and dresses them up in antique lace and fabric ($6 to $8).

Prices here range from $4 for a pair of cotton socks to about $300 for an extravagant neo-Western appliquéd jacket. Hand-painted Converse sneakers run $35 ($50 for hightops), and lace-stenciled and painted evening pumps are $50 to $75. There is also a children's line, ranging from $5 for a pair of hand-painted socks to $100 for a decorated denim jacket. Most things here are one-of-a-kinds or small editions, so stock and sizes will be limited. But new things come in just about every day, depending on how creative Nicki Hoyt feels that morning.

The store's displays have the same piquant charm as its merchandise: The owners might showcase a series of bird-shaped earrings in a wooden aviary or fish shapes in a crystal bowl. Or they might take old cinema house row seats and recover them in the same fabrics that Hoyt uses for her oversized satchels or as appliqués on her intricate, one-of-a-kind patchwork quilt cowgirl skirts.

Storewide sales are held in March and August.   — S.F.

Bumbleberry's, 154 Eighth Avenue, 675-3732. Open Monday to Saturday, noon to 7 P.M.; till 8 P.M. during the summer. AE, MC, V, checks.

REGALIA DESIGNS, LTD.

R E G A L I A Designs, Ltd. caters to the career woman who's a young sophisticate, whether she's twenty-five or forty-five. Owner Donna Barba stocks this boutique with better names from the mid-priced contemporary market, from Leon Max to Gene Ewing/Bis, to more moderately priced casual weekend separates from Malavé. And while you may recognize the names of some of these designers, chances are you *won't* recognize the individual items from their collections. That's because Barba buys the pieces department stores think a little too sophisticated or trendy for career women's dressing.

Barba also carries more expensive, but lesser known European names more in the investment-dressing category, for the career woman who wants interpretations of the classics but with lots of dash. So from the French house Biscote you'll find fine wool gabardine suits made modern by strong shoulder pads, wide peaked lapels, and tailoring that emphasizes feminine curves. Details like a silk jacquard lining, rolled lapel edges, and beautiful buttons make the $350 price tag understandable.

Regalia can outfit a young sophisticate from head to toe, an astonishing feat considering the fact that the store's not much bigger than a walk-in closet. You'll find everything from campy 1940s-style swimwear by Norma Kamali to lacy lingerie from Eileen West.

And there is a real harmony among the pieces Barba collects here. You could match the colors and textures of a honey-colored rayon glen plaid Leon Max jacket with a Gene Ewing cream-colored pencil-slim linen skirt to assemble a distinctive look without looking like a walking advertisement for any one designer. Barba and her staff are helpful, without being pushy, assisting in the coordination process.

Prices for major designer names like Leon Max, for instance, are a bit cheaper than department stores'. One of his patterned knit lean sweaters would sell for $68, here it's $60. That's if you could find the exact style! Remember, the more unusual pieces get play at Regalia, and Barba brings in new goods every week. — S.F.

Regalia Designs, Ltd., 410 West 24th Street, 929-0165. Open Monday to Friday, noon to 7 P.M.; Saturday till 6 P.M.; Sunday till 6 P.M. during the summer. AE, MC, V, checks.

CHELSEA DESIGNERS

C H E L S E A Designers has been around for over ten years, and in that time it's built up a loyal following among women whose style is feminine but comfortable—and who appreciate reasonable prices.

The shop carries the exclusive designs of Peter Kent and Cathy Cunningham. Both believe in the bias-cut, no-button approach to fashion. Their pieces either slide across the body or can be wrapped for a tighter look. It's a very Japanese idea— like Commes des Garçons, but not as wild-looking. Sizing is on a one-size-fits-all basis. Most everything comes in solid neutral or go-together colors.

Kent and Cunningham love 100% silks and cottons, and use natural rayon, a fiber made from wood pulp, rather than synthetics. A tunic top with a cowl neck or a slim pull-on calf-length skirt in their rayon is in the $40 range. Silks go for $70. Customers learn of special sales through mailings.

The staff members are very helpful, to the point that if things get a bit crowded in the store, they'll break open a bottle of champagne and serve everyone in the place.   — S.F.

Chelsea Designers, 128 West 23rd Street, 255-8803. Open Monday to Saturday, 9 A.M. to 8 P.M.; Sunday, 11 A.M. to 6 P.M. AE, MC, V, checks.

BOK LEI TAT TRADING CO., INC.

27-33 West 23rd Street, 741-8833. See index for main listing.

DAFFY'S

E V E R Y day, stockroom attendants—trying to look solemn but bursting into grins of pride—wheel out racks of new clothes from vast behind-the-scenes storage areas. Could be a slew of buttery soft, cunningly retro-styled wool winter coats and jackets (none above $170) from a little Parisian manufacturer, or killer sequined vamp dresses (under $100), or gorgeously tailored men's suits from Italy (under $200). Even before the goods have reached their final destination on the selling floor, they've attracted a procession of watchful customers. Within minutes, half the items are snapped up, whisked into the communal dressing rooms (where the advice is frank and easy to come by), and very likely bought.

Daffy's (formerly Daffy Dan's) is the latest major off-price retailer to hit Manhattan. (Most of its stores are in New Jersey.) *Off-price* means that the store buys its goods at far lower than wholesale cost (often clearing out a season's worth of wares from a designer who overfabricated) and passes its enormous savings on to the retail customer. Dresses that retail in the department stores for several hundred dollars can be as low as $35 or $50 here. With 35,000 square feet on three selling levels, Daffy's features toys and clothes for children as well as men's and women's gear. The savings are 40% to 80% off regular retail prices.

There are, of course, a lot of discount houses all over the country. What distinguishes Daffy's is not only its lower-than-discount prices but also its fashion image. Some of the stuff here can be boring, but often you find racks and racks of luscious European sweaters, truly elegant mainstream evening clothes, and some interesting leathers. Most stylish of all are the clothes from forward New York designers. Daffy's also has an aggressive markdown policy for goods that don't sell right away. A cache of last season's plaid rayon smock dresses from France—nicely styled, well made—were reduced from $80 to $20.

If you love to hunt for clothes and have an eye for chic bargains, you can practically move in here.   — L.D.

Daffy's, 111 Fifth Avenue, 529-4477. Open Monday to Saturday, 10 A.M. to 10 P.M.; Sunday, 11 A.M. to 6 P.M.. MC, V, checks.

FINE DESIGN

F I N E Design offers a breath of fresh air on a typically grimy New York street. Decorated with antique pine French country furnishings, it evokes the easy, relaxed mood of the Hamptons, although it's one of a small, nationwide chain of specialty stores. The fashion emphasis here is on traditional non-flamboyant sweaters. The fibers are all natural (wool, cotton or cotton/silk blends). The shapes are all basic, from simple long-sleeved V-necks to short-sleeved crewnecks to pullovers. But best of all, the prices are very fair: An all-wool shetland shell sweater for women can run about $15. Men's pastel-hued cotton knits aren't more than $40. A limited selection of seasonal shorts, skirts, and slacks is also available, priced from $20 to $50.

Besides its own fashion group, which includes oversized cotton bigshirts for $30 and good quality cotton polo shirts in the $20 range, Fine Design's other emphasis is on home fashions. From French country floral-print cotton fabric frames to plush towels, it's a good store to shop for homey hostess and house gifts.

Storewide sales are held in January and August, with 25% to 65% markdowns.   — S.F.

Fine Design, 11 West 18th Street, 741-7498. Open Monday to Saturday, 10 A.M. to 7 P.M.; Friday till 8 P.M.; Sunday, noon to 6 P.M. AE, MC, V, travelers checks.

Other branches: 89 Fulton Street, South Street Seaport, 406-3661. Open Monday to Saturday, 10 A.M. to 10 P.M.; Sunday till 8 P.M.

ROYAL SILK

I F you've blown your whole budget on the perfect ensemble but don't have a blouse to go with it, Royal Silk can rescue you. One of the country's most visible mail-order concerns, it has a large three-floor retail outlet just at the edge of Chelsea.

Royal Silk carries an extensive collection of silks and silk blends of their own manufacture, at consistently very affordable prices.

The basic fashion statement here is classic career and weekend looks, but in the new colors of each season. Handsome pencil-slim skirts and "shorts suits" are the most fashionable pickings of the bunch. If you're the type who doesn't want to take fashion risks, Royal Silk's predominately traditional styling is for you. But that's not to say that the looks are dull. You can very easily put together a smart striped tailored shirt and a pastel-toned skirt for an under-$75 outfit that works for the office, and then goes out to dinner.

You'll find all varieties of silks here, from tweedy "matka silk" to shiny silk knits. Prices range from $6 for pure silk bow ties to around $35 for romantic ankle-grazing skirts of crushed silk, to $140 for a full-length lined duster coat with deep patch pockets. Most of their pieces can be hand washed or dry-cleaned.

Men can expect to find a nice selection of button-down silk shirts with epaulettes on the shoulder for $35, and crewneck ribbed sweaters in colors ranging from cool ice-cream pastels to safari neutrals. They're timeless fashions that never go out of—or into—style.   — S.F.

Royal Silk, 79 Fifth Avenue, 243-5507. Open Monday to Saturday, 10 A.M. to 6 P.M.; Thursday and Friday till 8 P.M.; Sunday, noon to 5 P.M. AE, CB, DC, MC, V, checks.

THE GARMENT DISTRICT

INTRODUCTION BY
David Keeps

Watchabak, watchabak, Yo, WATCH YER BACK! Turn around quickly, dart in the appropriate direction, and watch a pushcart fly by you with bolts of fabric or samples of next year's Calvin Kleins. Cross the street and you might pass a rack of polyester shmattes heading off to K-Mart. You're in the center of the garment district, a sprawling complex of sweatshops and showrooms that dominates the west side of Manhattan's midtown area and houses New York City's largest industry.

Stretching from the hallowed halls of the Fashion Institute of Technology on West 27th Street and Seventh Avenue (which in this neighborhood is named Fashion Avenue), northward through the fur district and eastward through the wholesale florists and Korean accessories importers, the

THE GARMENT DISTRICT

1 S & W Ladies Wear	11 Coco
2 S & W Lingerie	12 Martin Freedman
3 S & W Bags, Accessories,	13 Martin Freedman II
and After 5 Boutique	14 Hyman Hendler & Sons
4 S & W Coats	15 Cinderella Bridal and
5 Style Workshop	Trimmings
6 Yesterday's Yearnings	16 Sheru
7 Modiste Fur Chapeau	17 Tinsel Trading
8 Ann Taylor	18 Jay Lord Hatters
9 Macy's Herald Square	19 Job Lot Trading Corp./
10 Herald Square Bootery	Pushcart Stores

apparel district has its geographical center on the retail stretch of 34th Street, where Macy's, the largest and most adventurous retailer in the city, sits adjacent to Herald Square at the intersection of Broadway and Avenue of the Americas. The trimming, notions, bridal, and hat district lies due east off Avenue of the Americas in the upper 30s; to the west are the major designer showrooms on Broadway and the sweatshops and fabric merchants that stretch to Eighth Avenue and beyond.

This is where a hefty chunk of what America wears is conceived, created, and marketed, a business grid with an unexpected funkiness and a dress code all its own. At any street corner you may stand next to dressed-to-thrill buyers from the Midwest in paisley and pearls, leafleteers advertising cut-price Armanis, black-coated orthodox Jews, or pushcart handlers with bicycle caps and Nike gym shorts over their sweatpants.

Eating is an obsession second only to work, it would seem; delivery boys lug coffee all morning and a host of restaurants, from fancy-schmancy to dusk-to-dawn sushi bars, cater to the huge daily influx of let's-have-lunchers. Greasy coffee shops sit between kosher delicatessens and nouvelle carry-out joints on streets lined with Deco skyscrapers and modern glass-and-steel monoliths. It's an expanse that's dedicated to commerce, with more parking lots than apartments, bustling from nine to six and ghostlike at night and on the weekends.

The garment center is and isn't a shopper's paradise. Junky shoe stores and sequin-and-silk discounters abound, and the storefronts with the most mouth-watering windows display heartbreaking signs that read "Wholesale Only." There are specialty stores with custom services and hard-to-find sizes, along with discounters (including Sherwood International at 53 West 36th Street for off-price Armani and other Italiana and Good Shot at 530 Seventh Avenue for corporate suits and mainstream designer sportswear), but the retail neighborhood is not especially fashionable. Some street-level wholesalers are open to the public, the best being Alaz Sportswear (retail on Saturdays only), which stocks trendy English lines at

15 West 36th Street; and especially savvy shoppers can employ a garmento moxie—along with a good story and cold, hard cash—to snag sample and wholesale-only merchandise with a little bit of effort. But even amateur big-name hunters can easily discover which famous designers are holding open-to-the-public showroom sales, like the famous Perry Ellis seasonal blowouts (usually in April and early December) by checking for flyers in the lobbies of buildings in the 1400 block of Broadway.

The stretch of 34th Street between Fifth Avenue and Herald Square, where Macy's occupies an entire square block, is packed with street vendors hustling everything from gold chains to hot dogs and lined with budget fashion shops, a couple of which are worth a visit.

Do-it-yourselfers will thrill to the variety of yard goods stores lining the upper 30s between Broadway and Eighth Avenue, where simple cottons and crepes sit next to metallic brocaded velvets and where job-lotters (like J&A Stelzer, 239 West 39th Street) have consistently novel fabrics at remarkable prices. The button, ribbon, lace, and bead stores surrounding Avenue of the Americas offer extra embellishment at reasonable-to-ridiculously cheap prices, and a trip into the fur strip (28th to 31st streets, pushing west to Eighth Avenue) could collar you incredible savings on mink and other exotic pelts.

The garment center was formerly New York's Tenderloin district, home of organized vice during the heyday of Boss Tweed. By World War I, the skin trade migrated north toward Times Square as the well-to-do began to inhabit the Madison Square area (Broadway and 23rd Street) and department stores sprang up around the rapid transit systems that converged at Pennsylvania Station. As the mass production and marketing of clothing grew, garment manufacturers moved from the cramped quarters of the Lower East Side to huge showroom-workshop spaces in the Garment Center Capitol, a series of buildings constructed by leading wholesalers on Seventh Avenue. They not only gained space but also cut down on transport costs: Woolens and imported fancy fabrics from Europe and cotton from southern mills arrived on the East River docks to be carted crosstown to workrooms, and the finished items traveled a few blocks to the Hudson River docks to be shipped out across America. The work force was comprised of immigrant and women laborers, with a large percentage of the business dominated by Jewish entrepreneurs.

Today the industry is every bit as volatile as it was then, with businesses collapsing to be quickly replaced by new designers filling offices and warehouses that were once sewing factories, now rendered unnecessary by overseas production of goods. And yet the character of the area and its extraordinary ethnic mix maintains the same hustling vitality of days gone by.

These days, the best stores are clumped around miniature districts, to be tackled as time, interest, and foot fatigue dictate. Shopping is best attempted during nonlunch hours of the week; some stores are open on Saturday, even fewer on Sunday, and late shopping is virtually nonexistent. Begin with coffee and croissants at Eddington & Worth (333 Seventh Avenue) or a bigger breakfast among the expertly styled students at one of the several glatt kosher delis (Gefens, Deli-Art) near the Fashion Institute of Technology, where you might discover next year's big thing by investigating the student designs for sale at Kloz, located in the student union. Art Deco furniture enthusiasts will want to make a quick detour to see the incredible and cheap bureaus and cocktail cabinets at Fleur de Lis (147 West 25th Street, just east of Seventh Avenue). Then get lost for an hour or more in the row of designer discounters (largely women's clothes) on Seventh Avenue. Cross the fur district if you dare (well, maybe just $30 for some mink ear muffs, available year-round?) and head on through Macy's to your choice of the trimming district, with its panorama of doodads and men's discounters, or off Broadway to hunt for some special fabrics, shoes, and once-in-a-lifetime savings on showroom samples.

Either way, you'll want lunch at Veronica Ristorante, a bit off the beaten track at 240 West 38th Street, but well worth it for exquisite southern Italian food served cafeteria-style to an eye-catching mix of young, hip salesmen and stylists and seasoned what-makes-Sammy-runs.

To reach the Garment Center by subway: Take the IND A, C, E, or K to 34th Street; the IRT 1 to 28th Street or the 2 or 3 to 34th Street; or the IND B, D, or F or the BMT N or R to Herald Square. By bus: Take the M10 up Eighth or down Seventh Avenue or the M6 or M7 down Broadway or up Sixth Avenue to 34th Street; or the M16 across 34th Street to Seventh Avenue.

■   ■   ■

S & W STORES

"O H, my Gawd, look at this fabric," a Great Neck matron shrieks at a Calvin Klein frock. "What a dog!" Back on the rack it goes, next to the crisp architectural linen of an Albert Nipon, a snip at $250. This is S & W Ladies Wear (165 West 26th Street), the largest in a series of major name discounters that dominates most of Seventh Avenue between 26th and 27th streets. It's where you'll find a rack of Calvin Klein separates at a constant 50% off, Bill Blass jackets for under $100, classy designs by Harvé Benard and Adrienne Vittadini, and a bargain basement with even greater reductions. The savings are available during the week, but the real floor show happens on Sundays, when bargain-crazed shoppers drag salesgirls to racks to confirm that extra 10% or 20% off.

Just next door there's petite-to-large lingerie by Natori, Oscar de la Renta, Givenchy, and Dior at 30% to 50% off (with an under-$30 rack), at S & W Lingerie (177 West 26th Street). Turn the corner and, *voila!* S & W Bags, Accessories and After 5 Boutique, featuring mind-boggling hand-painted leather purses (around $200), Chanel-y quilted leather handbags (around $80), garish metallic egg-shaped evening bags, and the likes of gold leather penny loafers ($70) from a range of the Italian shoes for sale there.

Next to that is the S & W Coat Boutique, the most famous and focused markdown mecca, stocked with heavy wool warmsters even in April, when next fall's coats arrive here before some department stores have put them on the racks. Flamboyant wetwear recently included Perry Ellis's pearly plastic trenchcoats ($250) and Blass's down-filled floral-trimmed parka ($140). On the second floor, just beyond a door that typically bears an ad from a major department store sale with a their price/our price nose-thumbing comparison, lurk fur-lined raincoats (over $1,000) and beautiful Perry Ellis overcoats, including beaver-lapeled melton wools for under $300.   — D.K.

S & W Ladies Wear, 165 West 26th Street, 924-6656; S & W Coats, 287 Seventh Avenue, 741-1065; S & W Lingerie, 177 West 26th Street, 255-7582; S & W Bags, Accessories, and After 5 Boutique, 283 Seventh Avenue, 675-1659. Open Monday to Friday, Sunday, 10 A.M. to 6 P.M. AE, MC, V, checks.

STYLE WORKSHOP

INFLUENCED by the funky fashion sensibilities of the FIT campus on which it's located and the cut-price merchants a block away, this young women's sportswear boutique succeeds in being both trend and cost conscious. Contemporary pacesetters like Freego, Soda, Malibu, and the Blanc Bleu line share rack space with some on-consignment student work and local designers who provide spectacular buys like $65 double-breasted linen duster coats and one-of-a-kind pastel suede patchwork dresses ($229).

Styles here vary from the soft romanticism of lace-trimmed viscose granny dresses ($65) and inexpensive preppy tartan skirts to body-baring nouveau primitive prints on knit crop top and tube skirt sets and de rigueur cotton leggings (all around $30). The Workshop styles its own line of pleated trousers ($59), mini and longer straight skirts ($49 and $59), and one-button short jackets ($99) year-round in goatskin leather. Large rhomboid carrier bags in phony pony and gold crocodile vinyl, with matching, massive, hip-slung belts (under $20), typify the flashy accents here, including a caseful of rhinestone jewelry from $10 to $30.   — D.K.

Style Workshop, 234 West 27th Street, 924-0705. Open Monday to Saturday, 10 A.M. to 7 P.M. Checks.

YESTERDAY'S YEARNINGS

Y E A R N no more, vintage hounds—through the metal gate of this vast, atticlike space that's dark, cozy, and cool even in summer, lies a serious collection of antique and military clothing. Hard-to-find nylon flight pants and jumpsuits (from $75) share a corner filled with flight, field, and cadet jackets (around $55) and gabardine band uniforms. Civilian menswear revolves around madras sports jackets ($30); 1950s and 1960s suits, with particularly good sharkskins ($75ish); baggy trousers and sporty shirts, with a swell sampling of World War II-era wingtip, buck, and spectator shoes from $25.

Tuxedo jackets, tails, and trousers are plentiful (from $55) and complement chic black crepe dresses (from $35) and a panorama of spangly tops, hand-sewn bugle-beaded sheaths, and floor-length sequined fantasies costing less than $200. Casual housefrocks, shifts, and flowing floral silks starting at $35 complete the strong range of dresses, and there are nearly 100 pairs of shoes for matching. Suits and blouses are less abundant, but owner Eve Jacquet designs fabulous skirts, including trumpet shapes in panne velvet ($150) and circles in patchwork vintage silk ($150) that sell for nearly twice the price uptown at tony Henri Bendel.

Antique bathing suits for both sexes, especially the Esther Williams type, are eye-catching, as are scarves, gloves, jewelry, and particularly pretty cotton handkerchiefs. Men can accessorize with silk ties (junior clip-on models for sons are $4), cummerbunds, evening scarves, and a caseful of military patches and gear including hand grenades!   — D.K.

Yesterday's Yearnings, 245 West 29th Street, 971-3205. Open Monday to Saturday, 11 A.M. to 7 P.M. MC, V, checks.

MODISTE FUR CHAPEAU

Y O U can prowl the fur-lined streets of West 28th to West 30th for the best deal on jackets and coats, but this is where you'll want to top it all off. Modiste will match your mink and custom-make a hat in one of hundreds of styles, from pillbox to beehive to their best-selling "floppy hats that can be worn a dozen different ways." All this at wholesale prices!

Luxurious minks, sables, foxes, opossums, raccoons, and lynxes perch on utilitarian wire racks, and yellowing photos of young Shelley Winters and Barbra Streisand smile benevolently from the walls in glamorous harmony with the hasn't-been-decorated-in-years workshop ambience. Men's hats occupy a small corner, with traditional styles including raccoon and mink trapper hats ($200 and $400, respectively) and Persian lamb, envelope-shaped ambassador caps ($125); unisex earmuffs at $30 are particularly fluffy and fetching in silver fox with a velvet band.

Ladies can choose from classic derby, bowler, and fedora variations ($220 and up) and kicky novelties like Persian lamb taxi driver hats and shaggy Tibetan lamb berets (around $150). Older models hanging discreetly above eye level may include incredible bargains. Velvet-backed scarves measure 3 feet and are priced from $175, flings are 6 feet with heads and tails at a cost of $250 and up. Oversized muffs, mostly $300, are lined in satin with zippered compartments; and $150 buys incredible mink pouch purses with expanding metal closures.   — D.K.

Modiste Fur Chapeau, 158 West 30th Street, 239-6541. Open Monday to Thursday, 9 A.M. to 5 P.M.; Friday till 2:30 P.M. Checks.

ANN TAYLOR

1293 Broadway, Herald Center, 695-4474. See index for main listing.

MACY'S HERALD SQUARE

I F a modern-day seven wonders of the world was compiled, Macy's Herald Square might well make the list. A New York shopping institution for over a hundred years, it covers the entire block of 34th to 35th streets, from Avenue of the Americas to Seventh Avenue. Even by the standards of jaded New Yorkers, that's big.

One of the last of a dying breed—the full-service (and full-price) department store—Macy's is a city unto itself, with its own branch of the U.S. Post Office, a pet shop, beauty salons, restaurants, and an apothecary. Surveying the first floor alone (and there are *ten* shopping floors at this branch of Macy's) can be awesome. Walk in on 34th Street and Avenue of the Americas. Stand right by the escalators. It's like looking at infinite lines of gleaming counters, stretching as far as the eye can see. But it's more than sheer size, of course; it's the astounding merchandise mix that makes Macy's so wondrous. It's an outpost for ritzy Louis Vuitton luggage and Gucci small leather goods and watches, but it also has a Swatch minishop for inexpensive, fun items in the same merchandise category.

In order to get a real feel for just how big each floor is, take a rest stop on the mezzanine at the Chocolatier Expresso café, decorated like a classic Italian ice-cream parlor with white marble flooring and pink marble bistro tables. It looks out on the accessories counters. From there it seems as if Macy's store buyers have acquired every pair of sunglasses, every belt, every handbag, every piece of gold and costume jewelry in the known world.

The fashion floors offer a similarly monumental array of clothes. Here you can spend $24 on an updated white cotton button-down work blouse from Chaus or else $225 on a superfashionable white linen number from Italy's Complice, designed by Claude Montana. You can pick up Jordache five-pocket floral-print denim jeans for $40 or a Charles Jourdan cotton miniskirt and big shirt outfit from France for $400. Men can spend hundreds on leather bomber jackets from Giorgio Armani or $15 on a cotton polo with Macy's private label.

In the last few years the store has aggressively gone after the upscale market, so virtually all top European talents from Claude Montana to Karl Lagerfeld are represented. And they've done an admirable job in exposing young designers from the East Village and London. Other major department stores haven't even tried. Yet Macy's is still where you can find the basics—cotton flannel pajamas or housedresses.

The housewares floors here are as extensive as all the other areas. The Cellar has everything from Beluga caviar to Conair blow-dryers and all you would ever need for cooking and personal care. Furniture and rugs are upstairs.

From maternity dresses to mattresses, a bakery to business machines; from the ground floor Arcade, which year-round, sells funky New York souvenirs, such as T-shirts of Lady Liberty done up in punky makeup, to the high-prep of the Ralph Lauren minishop—Macy's has it all.

Don't be ashamed if you get lost and can't find your way back to an elevator or escalator. It happens to the best of us at Macy's, the store that's as sprawling, diverse, funky, cosmopolitan, fun, exotic as New York City itself.

Because it's as much a tourist attraction as anything else, be prepared for crowds. At Christmastime you'd swear the entire population of the city had the same idea: "Let's go shop at Macy's." Usually, weekday mornings and after work are manageable.   — S.F.

Macy's Herald Square, 34th Street between Broadway and Seventh Avenue, 695-4400. Open Monday, Thursday, Friday, 9:45 A.M. to 8:30 P.M.; Tuesday and Wednesday till 6:45 P.M.; Saturday, 10 A.M. to 6 P.M.; Sunday, noon to 6 P.M. AE, Macy's, checks.

HERALD SQUARE BOOTERY

I F you can't afford the masters of witty shoe design like Maud Frizon, you can still put some flash on your feet with interpretations of their shoes from the Herald Square Bootery.

Of course, the quality of construction or the materials used are not nearly as fine as Frizon's or Charles Jourdan's, but then they don't cost $250 a pair, either. At the Herald Square Bootery, a leather-lined and leather-soled gold leather and black patent leather pointy-toed oxford Frizon clone is $68. Considering that, at these prices, most major shoe manufacturers offer manmade soles, you're already one leather-lined step ahead of the game.

The Bootery offers hundreds of shoes to choose from. Close to a third of their stock is made in Europe to the specifications of the owners. You'll find everything from conservative midheeled brown leather pumps for the office with the Italian "Amore" label (all leather construction) for $60, to a wild purple-and-black leather wedgie with metallic straps (with a made-in-Spain label) for $45—very Jourdan in feeling!

The rest of the Bootery's stock consists of moderately and upper-moderately priced name brands, all at approximately 10% to 15% off other shoe or department store prices. For example, a pair of Unisa loafers with gold studs at the toes sells for $42 regularly. Here, they're $38. Other widely recognizable brands include Liz Claiborne, Andrew Geller, Sasha of London, Josephine, Nickels, Zodiac, and Academia of London.

So whether you need a pair of sensible shoes for work, a warm pair of shearling knee-high boots for cold winter days, or sexy ankle-strap multicolor strippy sandals for hot nights out—and you don't want to spend a fortune for above-average-quality footwear—you should plan a visit to the Herald Square Bootery.

Even though the store can be packed on Saturdays and during lunch hours, the cool Art Deco pink-and-gray decor makes it almost bearable. Better times to avoid crowds are mornings, Sundays, and after 6 P.M.. — S.F.

Herald Square Bootery, 41 West 34th Street, 714-0320. Open Monday, Thursday, Friday, 10 A.M. to 9 P.M.; Tuesday, Wednesday, Saturday till 7:30 P.M.; Sunday noon to 6:30 P.M. AE, CB, DC, MC, V, checks.

COCO

AT first, Coco seems like all the other slightly schlocky women's and juniors' fashion emporiums on 34th Street. But venture to the back of the store and a surprise awaits.

You'll find very interesting imported French, Italian, and Spanish fashions and outerwear with updated styling, including suits, and separates for work and weekend. The prices are very reasonable for the fabrics and detailing of the garments. For example, a French cotton long-sleeved rhinestone-encrusted "cowboy" shirt goes for $35. Similar shirts in an inferior quality cotton sell for $60 in the better junior sections of many department stores.

And when it comes to office wear, you'll chance upon

goodies like a black linen pencil-slim knee-length skirt with brown linen insets that form a V to accentuate the waist, backbuttoned in brown and black linen-covered squares ($60). To match, there's a black linen 7/8-length jacket with a double-lapel treatment of black and brown and fashionable detailing like rounded (not square) padded shoulders and a fitted waist ($89). If you hanker after Italian designs, like Byblos's funky suits, you'll love these advanced styles.

During the fall/winter season, Coco stocks a very nice selection of well-priced, not-for-the-timid leather jackets and skin-tight skirts in bright colors and basic black. Some are more stylish than others, so know what you're looking for in the way of shape. The prices range from $59 to several hundred for a suit.

As with the other midtown shops, lunchtime isn't the right time to shop Coco. Evenings after 6 and mornings till 11:30 on weekdays are quiet.　　　　　　　　　　　　　　　　　— S.F.

Coco, 25 West 34th Street, 947-5505. Open Monday, Thursday, Friday, 10 A.M. to 9 P.M.; Tuesday, Wednesday, Saturday till 7:30 P.M.; Sunday, noon to 6:30 P.M. MC, V, checks.

MARTIN FREEDMAN

"I N the garment center we're well known as the store to come and knock off," says manager Sam Berman. But there's nothing to fear if you shop here, guys—"knocking off" is merely garmento parlance for copying designs. And the beautifully tailored fashion-forward clothes here, predominantly those of Italian masters like Ermengeildo Zegna and Punch and private-label creations, are certainly worthy of all the attention.

Snappy fashion execs and hip suit-and-tie guys swear by this quiet, unpretentious neighborhood shop, which boasts better prices than haute peers like Barneys and Charivari. This is where they'll find Kiton's hand-sewn suits (around $1,000), hand-knit wool and cotton sweaters in outrageous colors and innovative shapes ($125 to $750), Bill Kaiserman's rubber-look acetate-and-polymode trenchcoats, and hand-sewn Swiss voile shirts by Marol ($125 to $175). Then there's the house collection, styled by buyer Fred Kahn: a rainbow of linen shirts (around $85 to $225) in pastels and brights, doeskin blazers by Kiton, and uncommonly elegant, delicately draped cotton jersey knit jackets (from $650). Footwear ranges from $65 deck shoes to $500 alligator penny loafers, with nary a wing tip in sight, and ties are lustrous and loud ($20 for knits to $45 for silk Zegnas). Tuxedo shirts are a specialty, with back and front hand pleateds in cotton ($245) and silks (from $165), some with matching bow ties.

Martin Freedman II, the sportswear annex, is located one block south at 1370 Broadway, offering a younger, less-expensive collection of popular Italian and British designs, with an accent on bright colors, patterns, and natural fibers year-round, as well as leather pants and jackets in the fall.   — D.K.

Martin Freedman, 1372 Broadway, 921-1030. Martin Freedman II, 1370 Broadway, 563-1944. Open Monday to Friday, 8:30 A.M. to 6:30 P.M. AE, DC, MC, V, checks.

HYMAN HENDLER & SONS

C A L V I N Klein and Oscar de la Renta get things matched here; so do sew-it-yourselfers. Hyman Hendler is the blue-ribbon, tie-a-yellow-ribbon ribbon, you-name-it ribbon source, where 90¢ buys you a yard of 3/8-inch-wide satin strip in your choice of 250 colors.

A family business for almost 90 years, Hendler's is now presided over by the "& Sons," Aaron and Harold, who design everything exclusively for the store, from picot-edge ribbons to moire satins to grosgrains to made-in-France lacy florals priced $3 to $10 per yard. Embroidered tapestries run to $30 per yard, as does marvelously elegant reversible 10-inch-wide satin; square yardage of velvet starts at $35. The merchandise is displayed with a casually chaotic logic: display cases to peruse, spools stacked Tower of Pisa-like toward the ceiling, and lots of boxes set out on long tables to paw through. Stock dates all the way back to the 1930s, and there's a wonderful selection of denim-styled cotton ribbons from the 1960s that depict hunting, golfing, flower-power, and fruit motifs.

Hendler also stocks some sewing and trimming accessories, most notably frog closures and a large selection of decorative tassels from plain ones at $2.50 to $50 multicolored yarn minisculptures that resemble Ukrainian chandeliers.   — D.K.

Hyman Hendler & Sons, 67 West 38th Street, 840-8393. Open Monday to Friday, 9 A.M. to 5:30 P.M. Checks.

CINDERELLA BRIDAL AND TRIMMINGS

T H E Y don't sell glass slippers, but they do have tiaras, hat forms, crowns, veils, feathers, sequins, silk flowers, leaves, and fruits. "Everything for the bride-to-be," a savvy saleslady cracks, "except the groom." Cinderella's custom-order service for hats and bouquets offers a mind-boggling selection of wholesale-priced ornamentation that could provide hours of browsing and fulfill any bridal fantasy. Over 500 kinds of Korean silk flowers appear in virtually every color imaginable and range in price from $2.25 tiger lilies to $31 French carnations. Not good enough? Then bring in your own fabric and Cinderella will transform it into flowers. And for craftsier folk, Cinderella carries a complete range of sizing, glue, glitter, and other do-it-yourself supplies.

There's an exhaustive supply of parasols, gloves, garters, beautiful antique brooches, necklaces, and thirty different tiaras, which range in price from $13.50 to $200. For those ticklish moments after the big day, there's a huge range of decorative feathers, sold individually, by the yard or by whole skins (pheasant runs $10 to $25). Feather boas are a standard 72 inches, running from $5 marabou to $85 turkey; Harlowesque marabou capes are a mere $21.

Through an archway lies Cinderella Trimmings, which has more crafts supplies and notions, sequined and beaded appliqués, sequins, satin cord and "pearls" by the yard, and lace collars costing $4.25 to $20. In the mezzanine, the newly opened Matthew's Collection boutique carries trousseau items like crepe de chine dresses, suits, and beaded silk dresses at wholesale prices.   — D.K.

Cinderella Bridal and Trimmings, 60 West 38th Street, 840-0644. Open Monday to Friday, 9 A.M. to 5:30 P.M.; Saturday, 8:30 A.M. to 4:30 P.M. AE, MC, V.

SHERU

I F you're easily strung along, this is the place to shop for baubles, bangles, and beads, beads, beads. Costume jewelry designers and avid accessorizers fill its hectic environs, drawn by an enormous selection and wholesale prices. Famed for its beaded curtains, which hang around the entrance, Sheru is a clutter of display cases, steel shelves, file drawers, and sift-through-yourself wooden bins igniting that kid-in-a-candy-shop rush for jewelry freaks and serious scavengers. Piling your selections on a plastic divided dinner plate, you can choose from workaday plastic seed beads (75¢ a pack), brightly painted wooden beads, rhinestones, carved ceramics, glass, metal, seashell, and stone, plus all the supplies you'll need to string and glue them into your own creations.

Or you can simply choose from Sheru's under-$5 case filled with earrings, chains, and brooches and racks of plastic bangle bracelets, necklaces, and strands of beautiful European crystal ($11 and up), and semiprecious stones (from $4 for rose quartz to $20 for tiger eye). For the perfect sew-on ornamentation or an attention-getting accent—from folksy Americana to haute simplicity to tasteful tack—Sheru has it. Or it probably isn't made.   — D.K.

Sheru, 49 West 38th Street, 730-0766. Open Monday to Friday, 9 A.M. to 6 P.M.; Saturday, 9:30 A.M. to 5 P.M. AE, MC, V, checks.

TINSEL TRADING

Y O U ' R E in for an education here, if owner Arch Bergoffen has anything to say about it (and he usually does). Tinsel Trading is where you'll learn the difference between ribbons and galloons (the latter being a stiffer, patterned, woven ribbon) and marvel at the glistening array of metallic threaded trimmings, the largest in the United States. Many date back to the 1930s, when this business was founded.

Antique metallic threads—silvery, golden, coppery, and brassy—plus a host of lamé colors are sold by the spool ($3.50 to $35) and woven into ribbon ($4 per inch wide per yard). There are also ball fringes ($25 to $75 a yard), thirty different patterns of intricate galloon banding, fringes, braids, tassels, and cords, including gorgeous military antiques in purple, red, and real gold stripes (at $25 a yard), a Tinsel Trading specialty. Lamé, gauze, faille, early lurex, and brocade fabrics from the 1930s are sold by the yard from $20.

Indian bullion, which incorporates dazzlingly intricate sequin and bead work, is strongly featured in braided trimming ($2 to $25 per yard), crests, and over 100 types of appliqués. French ombré ribbons (75 cents to $2.50) with their delicate gradations of color on silk, diminutive sew-on rosebuds (a deal at $2.50 per dozen), and beaded and passementerie buttons (to $2.50 per dozen) also provide voguish embellishment, adding just as much flash as the truly extraordinary must-see metallics that have made Tinsel Trading famous. — D.K.

Tinsel Trading, 47 West 38th Street, 730-1030. Open Monday to Friday, 10:30 A.M. to 5 P.M.; Saturday, noon to 5 P.M. Closed Saturday in July and August. MC, V.

JAY LORD HATTERS

H A T S off to Burton Berinsky, who lords it over New York's finest chapeau chateau, where they *do* make 'em like they used to, and they'll even let you watch! Jay Lord specializes in fine fur felts and straw hats with enough classic styling to earn a Coty Fashion Award in 1982—all first quality, perfectly fitted, and extraordinarily reasonable. Celebrities such as Tom Wolfe, Miles Davis, Mick Jagger (who ordered a special 3-foot witch's hat for Halloween), and hat fanciers the world over visit regularly, enjoying the warm, no-nonsense clutter and Burt's genial and informed wit.

Customizing for size, shape, length and width of brims and crowns, and hatbands creates an infinite selection, including snappy two-tone porkpies with black crowns and gray brims (special-ordered at $150), but the most popular lids are well-worn classics from the past fifty years. Indiana Jones-type fedoras and jaunty trilbies are $80 ($70 for straw trilbies), 10-gallon hats start at $80, derbies are a C-note in straw and felt, and "John Foster Dulles" homburgs start at $100. For winter there're fine tweed caps ($30), while straw boaters ($55) and panamas ($60 to $80) add preppy dash and safari chic to summer wardrobes. Top hats, priced up to $300 for collapsible brocades or 12-inch-crowned models, are $150 in straw.

Jay Lord creates most hats in a 6½-to-8½ size range, and has enough women shoppers to inspire blue, red, and camel derbies, coachmen's hats, and a combination of a derby and gaucho hat, whimsically referred to as a "Groucho." Renovation is offered for felt hats, and $25 buys cleaning, blocking, a new band and lining. New bands, from a range of hundreds, are a mere $8.50. — D.K.

Jay Lord Hatters, 30 West 39th Street, 221-8941. Open Monday to Friday, 9:30 A.M. to 6 P.M.; Saturday, 10 A.M. to 5 P.M. AE, checks.

JOB LOT TRADING CORP./ PUSHCART STORES
412 Fifth Avenue, 398-9210. See index for main listing.

57TH STREET
AND MIDTOWN

INTRODUCTION BY
Elaine Louie

The WPA Guide to New York City wrote in 1939 that 57th Street was America's Rue de la Paix. It still ranks as the preeminent street for retailers, art dealers, shoppers, and gawkers. At 57th Street and Fifth Avenue, there are probably more well-dressed men and women per square inch than anywhere else in Manhattan. It's on the southwest corner that Bill Cunningham, the legendary fashion photographer, used to plant himself weekly to photograph the comings and goings of New York's most fashionable women—documenting, for *The New York Times,* the week that they sported polka dots, wore black leather trenchcoats, or cut their hair short like men.

Celebrities roam this street, owning it. Carmen the legendary model was glimpsed in a white fox coat with a gentleman also robed in fur. Robert Redford has stood on this corner looking blond and golden and clothed in a tan corduroy sports jacket, a

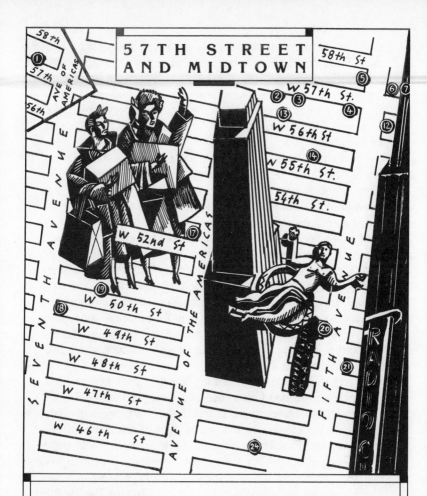

57TH STREET AND MIDTOWN

1	The Ritz Thrift Shop	16	Fogal
2	Charivari 57	17	Alcott & Andrews
3	Henri Bendel	18	Capezio Dance-Theatre Shop
4	I. Miller	19	Emotional Outlet
5	Bergdorf Goodman	20	Fil à Fil
6	Ann Taylor	21	Saks Fifth Avenue
7	Chanel Boutique	22	Emotional Outlet
8	Laura Ashley	23	J. McLaughlin
9	Maud Frizon	24	McCreedy & Schreiber
10	Matsuda	25	F. R. Tripler & Co.
11	Susan Bennis/Warren Edwards	26	Paul Stuart
12	La Lingerie	27	Brooks Brothers
13	Omo Norma Kamali	28	J. Press
14	Manolo Blahnik	29	Alcott & Andrews
15	To Boot	30	Chipp
		31	Dollar Bill's General Store

pink shirt, and brown slacks. Here on 57th Street and up and down Fifth and Madison avenues in this area are the stores that purvey the accoutrements of celebrity and glamour, the fabled Tiffany & Co., Bergdorf Goodman, Brooks Brothers, Cartier. Status is implicit when you carry a shopping bag emblazoned with one of these names. Quality is assumed. Yet bargains can be found here, too.

Tiffany has elaborate wedding rings and some perfectly plain ones—the latter no different than what a local jeweler may carry—though somehow a wedding band that comes in the famous blue Tiffany's box has an extra-special aura. Some of the fanciest jewelers in the world vie for your attention along this stretch. Cartier fills its windows with literally millions of dollars' worth of emeralds the size of quail eggs, while Van Cleef & Arpels displays a tiara that belonged to Empress Josephine. Right upstairs, in the salons at Bergdorf Goodman, are furs more extravagant than even Josephine could have imagined— the largest and best collection of Fendis, the most innovative furs created today. For more quotidian outerwear, there's Burberry's, creators of the ultimate English raincoat, which has its flagship store at 9 East 57th.

Amid the prestige shops are tourist attractions, bringing the regular middle-class tourists nose-to-nose with socialites. Slightly north of 57th Street, there is F.A.O. Schwarz, the legendary children's toy store, which features such outlandishly priced items as $400 rocking elephants. Children and adults gape alike. Proceed down Fifth Avenue and there is the Trump Tower with its vertigo-inducing escalators, its waterfall cascading down roseate marble walls, and a pianist playing "Tea for Two" in the lobby. Here you can buy hand-dipped Belgian chocolates, or enter the discreet confines of Bonwit Teller. Farther south on Fifth Avenue is St. Patrick's Cathedral, which can awe the heathen purely by force of its architecture, and beside it Saks Fifth Avenue. Rockefeller Center, with its gilded statues, and in the winter, ice sculptures, giant Christmas tree, and swirling skaters, is across the street.

Going south along Madison Avenue to the 40s, men will find the bastions of conservative American clothing—Paul Stuart and Brooks Brothers. The look is classic, and the prices sometimes surprising—basic oxford cloth shirts are $34 at Brooks Brothers, not the $75 (or more) charged these days for designer shirts.

This area also stimulates the intellect. Tucked away in the buildings that rise above 57th Street are dozens upon dozens of art galleries. There is Pace at 32 East 57th Street, where paintings by Jim Dine, photographic self-portraits by Lucas Samaras, and the sketchbooks of Pablo Picasso are shown. At 20 West 57th Street, there's the Blum Helman Gallery, home to painter Ellsworth Kelly and sculptor Bryan Hunt, among others.

The street also boasts the Rizzoli International Bookstore and Gallery at 31 West 57th. Paneled in mahogany, it is stocked with the best fiction and nonfiction, along with books on art and design and magazines from around the world. While you pore over a book, the music of Bach or Mozart filters through the air. If you really need an escape, try the Travelers' Bookstore at 22 West 52nd. Here there are both fiction and nonfiction books, along with standard guides, about nearly every country in the world.

The greatest cultural bastion of the neighborhood is, of course, Carnegie Hall. With its perfect acoustics, it was host to the Philharmonic in 1892, the Kool Jazz Festival in the 1980s, and virtually every major artist in between. Built above and around the hall are the famous Carnegie Hall studios, where architects, fashion designers, musicians, and dancers rent space to live and work.

For eating in the neighborhood, try 56th Street heading west from Fifth Avenue, a "restaurant row" of Italian, French, Japanese, and Korean food. But three good restaurants are on 57th Street proper. Pasta & Cheese has a restaurant in Bergdorf Goodman serving light lunch fare. Wolf's Sixth Avenue Delicatessen, on the corner of 57th and Avenue of the Americas, has the best mushroom barley soup in town, along with slippery, silken kasha varnishkes cooked in golden chicken fat, and juicy pastrami sandwiches. At the Russian Tea Room, 150 West 57th Street, favorite lunch spot for deal-making literary and movie agents where you must plan on spending about $30 per person for lunch, you might find Diane Keaton or Dustin Hoffman nibbling pelmeny, but only if you are seated on the celebrity-studded main floor, and not upstairs, which is Siberia.

The 57th Street midtown area is bounded by 57th Street on the north, 42nd Street on the south, Third Avenue on the east, and Seventh Avenue on the west. Begin in front of the Plaza, where Central Park ends, at the corner of 59th Street and Fifth Avenue.

To reach 57th Street by subway: Take the IND A, B, C, D, or K or the IRT 1 to Columbus Circle and head east; the IND B to 57th Street; or the BMT N or R to Fifth Avenue. By bus: Take the M104 up or down Broadway; the M10 up Eighth Avenue or down Central Park West; the M5 or M7 up Sixth Avenue or the M7 down Columbus Avenue; the M1, M2, M3, or M4 down Fifth Avenue or up Madison; or the M28 across 57th Street.

■   ■   ■

THE RITZ THRIFT SHOP

THE best-established place in New York for "gently used" furs is the fifty-year-old Ritz Thrift Shop, where you can get a used mink, fox, or raccoon coat in good condition for a third to half the price of a new one. Classic designs are the norm here. On a given day, the only high-style fur in stock was a very, very tired sheared-fox Fendi jacket ($1,950). The best-looking coat was a luxurious and voluminous silver-fox coat that reached the ankles and was in near-mint condition. The fox had life and didn't yawn and droop ($3,995). The most common fur here, among the hundreds of coats and jackets secreted in the downstairs vaults, is clearly mink, with most mink coats priced between $1,600 and $2,000.   —E.L.

The Ritz Thrift Shop, 105-7 West 57th Street, 265-4559. Open Monday to Saturday, 9 A.M. to 6 P.M. AE, MC, V, checks.

CHARIVARI 57

THE biggest and starkest of all the six chic Charivari shops, this one demands serious legwork from the consumer. The clothes for men and women are scattered on four floors and there are no escalators—which is to say that shopping here is like climbing up to your fourth-floor walk-up apartment. Or think of it as an aerobic workout. In any case, this store groups together Charivari's favorite designers, nearly all of them European or Japanese. Where some of Charivari's Upper West Side stores are either strictly for men or for women, are either sporty or for work and evening, this one is high fashion, aimed at both men and women, and encompasses styles from swimsuits to evening clothes and fur coats.

At the bottom, beneath the street floor, are the very casual clothes—T-shirts, swimsuits, and sweaters from designers like Irie. A sporty oversized bright orange knit polo shirt was around $115. A cocoonlike hand-knit wood sweater was a near steal at $150.

On the street floor, where the customers cluster, there are beautifully chosen clothes for women that are primarily high-style. A few are avant-garde. Max Mara and Matsuda tumble into the high-fashion category. A Max Mara linen dress may have broad shoulders, be snug at the fanny, and flare out at the hem, and what will make it exceptional is its fabric. If it's printed linen, it may have eighteen colors. If it's a blazer, it will have a softer line than an Armani blazer, but be made of an exquisite Italian linen. Matsuda's clothes are more subtle: A plainish black jersey sleeveless dress with a bias-cut skirt might look thoroughly dull on a hanger. But put it on and the dress will come to life—faintly see-through, therefore sexy, and swirling at the slightest breeze. Other designers here include Jean-Paul Gaultier, represented last season by a remarkable pleated black silk organza shirt that billowed from the shoulders ($375).

Men's clothes are on the second floor, and include sports jackets, slacks, shirts, and suits by Giorgio Armani, Jean-Paul Gaultier, and Byblos. What's coveted in these clothes are the fabrics. The usually Italian linens and wools incorporate odd colors, like chartreuse, lavender, or magenta, woven into black and white tweeds. A fabric may have a subtle iridescence, a surprising but not flashy sheen. A sports jacket might run $300 to $500.

Yohji Yamamoto's clothes for men and women take up the third, topmost level. While these clothes are found at other stores, Charivari has the most extensive collection. His styles used to be strictly for the avant-garde, but have become more wearable (say, for work) lately. Still, Yamamoto is for a special customer. He has made impossible skirts where the waistband was twice as wide as the actual waist of the wearer and so had to be wrapped double to stay on. A jacket may be extremely oversized with shoulder pads extending 2 inches beyond the shoulders, and the length closer to the knees than to the hips. He may also espouse unusual proportions such as a short waist-length jacket worn over a very long shirt with the shirttails dangling over slacks. On the other hand, he may design an oversized shirt to be worn over skinny black or white pants, where the great appeal is not just its big voluminous silhouette, but the fact that it's made in crisp white cotton piqué, the best possible summer fabric ($190)—it's hard to wrinkle, stands away from the body, yet is soft and pleasing to the touch. What's interesting about Yamamoto is not just his silhouettes but his fabrics, which are considered absolutely extraordinary.

All Charivari stores participate in the twilight sale held from 6:30 P.M. to midnight one day each July, with markdowns up to 80%. —E.L.

Charivari 57, 18 West 57th Street, 333-4040. Open Monday to Friday, 10 A.M. to 7 P.M.; Thursday till 8 P.M.; Saturday till 6:30 P.M. AE, MC, V, checks.

Other branches: See index for other Charivari stores, each of which carries different merchandise.

HENRI BENDEL

HENRI Bendel is a specialty store, with 99% of the merchandise devoted to women's clothing and the remainder divided among children's clothes, cosmetics, and accessories for the home. Bendel's was originally designed in the likeness of its long-time president, Geraldine Stutz, who is a small woman (about 5'4"), slim, and extremely stylish. She decided that the store should cater to women like herself, presenting a well-edited collection of very chic but very wearable items. Her other major innovation was to turn the store into a collection of boutiques, rather than permanent departments.

At this writing, however, the store has just been purchased by Leslie Wexner, owner of The Limited, a chain of specialty shops aimed at the young market. The new management intends to keep Bendel's sophisticated, upscale image, and make it "the most forward store in Manhattan." The visual and merchandise changes contemplated now will be evident by the time this book is published, but many of the current departments will remain.

New designers will doubtless still be welcomed. It has been a Bendel's tradition that on most Friday mornings, any designer in the world can stand in line and show the buyers his wares. It is through this audition process that Carlos Falchi and Mira de Moss were discovered, and it has helped Bendel's earn its reputation for selling new, chic, upscale, and usually elegant, clothing.

The first floor is famous for its Street of Shops. Tiny stalls offering aromatic scents for the home, stockings, jewelry, linen, and shoes fill the floor. Begin with Bendel's own private-label stockings, which are considered especially nice for texture and fit ($3.50 per pair of panty hose), and come sheer or opaque in colors like basic black, charcoal, birthday suit (a nude), and ivory, along with whatever colors are au courant. One year, stockings might be forest green and cobalt. For another year, they may be orange and deep crimson. The stocking sales here are so popular that savvy customers list the dates on their calendars, so they can buy dozens of pairs at a time. Bendel's knee-high stockings stay *up* on the leg, and the store inevitably has the funniest socks in town, adorned with palm trees and flamingos, polka dots, or Scotch plaids—a whimsical departure from their usual upscale look.

Kidz is the shop's tiny but impeccable children's department. Each item is displayed on a brightly colored board. Pure cotton T-shirts, camp shirts, pants, skirts, and one dress per season (inevitably a very full, unfitted dress with a dazzling floral or plaid from France or Sweden) are the basis of the collection. Adorableness is the keynote here. A hand-crocheted white cotton pullover is edged in red, and smack in the middle there is a red pocket holding a real teddy bear ($38).

Shoe Biz has terrific shoes that are pretty without being deadly classic or totally outrageous. You can wear them to work. For example, a city huarache may come in basic colors of brown, black, and navy, but also in the odd silver or magenta.

One floor is devoted to the big-time designers, and it's here that Bendel's features many of its exclusives. Jean Muir has a boutique here filled with her soft, elegant knits, while a section of the floor is reserved for another designer exclusive to the store, Holly Harp. Her beaded, floaty chiffon gowns are around $1,100. There is a fur boutique, which includes some Fendis, and tucked behind the furs there is a bridal boutique. Enter a cream-colored salon, pick up a bell with clapper, and ring it. A saleswoman materializes, ushers you into a spacious dressing room, and brings you gowns both long and short, tailored or Victorian.

The fourth floor is the least expensive, and has had the wonderful characteristic of always having something on sale. One day it may be sundresses, and another, sweaters. This is the place to find basic everyday clothes, including lots of oversized sweaters by designers like Joan Vass, raincoats, and inexpensive shoes (a good $100 less than those sold on the first floor)—for instance, $60 plain black flats and $175 silver-toned leather cowboy boots. The new owners are promising to make it a very hot floor for lower priced merchandise.   —E.L.

Henri Bendel, 10 West 57th Street, CI7-1100. Open Monday to Saturday, 10 A.M. to 6 P.M.; Thursday till 8 P.M. AE, MC, V.

I. MILLER

T H E shoes are stylish but hardly on the cutting edge, yet I. Miller distinguishes itself on three counts. Along with plenty of customers, it has plenty of sales help. It's also one of the few places carrying a number of styles in narrow widths. Plus, you can smoke while you shop.

This is the place to shop for basics. Year after year, I. Miller has an extensive and handsome collection of winter boots, including fleece-lined suede ones from England, along with sleeker ones from Anne Klein and Golo.

As for evening shoes, you can always find pretty jewel-encrusted black or white peau de soie pumps or sandals. It is in daytime wear that the store goes quite safe, specializing in shoes by Salvatore Ferragamo, Bruno Magli, Pancaldi, and Yves Saint Laurent. Shoes range from Chanel-type sedate to whimsical, but are never outré. Here, a shoe that's left of center would be a loafer studded with fake jewels.

Major sales are held in February and late May, with markdowns of 30% to 50% and more. — E.L.

I. Miller, 734 Fifth Avenue, 581-0062. Open Monday to Saturday, 9:30 A.M. to 6 P.M.; Thursday till 7 P.M. AE, CB, DC, MC, V, checks.

BERGDORF GOODMAN

ALL AROUND, Bergdorf Goodman may be the best specialty store for men and women in New York City because the taste level of the clothes, from cotton polo shirts to fur coats, is consistently elegant.

This was the first store in the city that really promoted Italian designers such as Giorgio Armani and Gianni Versace. It has the most breathtaking collection of Fendi furs. It is also the only store in the city to carry Turnbull & Asser's shirts and ties for men. If its exclusive hold on some designers makes the store exceptional, the range of its merchandise is also impressive. While some of its clothing is clearly expensive ($100 for a Turnbull & Asser shirt, and $20,000 for a Fendi fur), Bergdorf's is far more accessible than its reputation would suggest. Not only does it carry a selection of moderately priced lines, but it also has amazing and constant sales. On a blissfully lucky day, you might find an Issey Miyake khaki-colored shoulder bag reduced from $100 to $50.

Start on the fifth floor, the floor for the working woman. Here are clothes from Anne Klein II, Joseph Tricot, and Roberta Freymann for Cilantro that are relaxed but can be worn to work. Anne Klein II has the silhouettes of Anne Klein at two-thirds the price. You can find an easy, unstructured long blazer and matching skirt or pants for around $250 to $300 for the whole outfit—clothes that move easily and make you feel unconstrained but impeccably groomed. Both Joseph Tricot and Cilantro specialize in oversized knit tops along with knit skirts or pants that are durable, chic, youthful, and hip. They go easily to the office and on to a dinner party. A knit skirt is around $80 to $150, a top $120 to $180.

Going down to the fourth and third floors, you must pick your way through the haute-couture shops, where you can admire a Tiktiner silk suit at $1,500 or a Thierry Mugler sundress for $1,300. Then head straight for the sale racks, where you'll find elegant, haute-couture basics marked down. One day there might be a Fendi heavy black silk-crepe gored skirt for $150, originally $300. You might find an Anne Klein blazer reduced from $350 to $200, or her black wool slacks, slashed from $225 to $125. A major treasure hunt might yield an $800 Jean-Paul Gaultier wool coat marked down to $500—while not cheap, this could be the coat you will wear all winter and enjoy more than anything in your closet, so perhaps it *is* a fashion investment.

The second floor is where you find Turnbull & Asser's distinctive men's shirts and ties. Prince Charles wears these shirts, and the male fashion maven can recognize one on another man at a hundred paces. The colors and patterns are bold. Classics include their large-scale emerald-green or chrome-yellow checks. A delightfully unusual pattern has green checks shadowed in crimson on a pink ground. The most popular tie features bright white medium-sized polka dots on a ground of brilliant chrome yellow or jade green—because the colors are so beautiful, it isn't vulgar. There are also suits, topcoats, sports jackets, and trousers from more conservative houses such as Hickey Freeman and Oxxford (doctors, lawyers, and investment bankers like these clothes) as well as more au courant clothes from Gianfranco Ferré. You can top off your choice with a Burberry trenchcoat.

Also on this floor are the Fendi furs, designed by Karl Lagerfeld. These are the most inventive furs in the world. There have been coats of black net strewn with gigantic polka dots of black fox, coats of taupe mole with the fur cascading down the front in one lavish ruffle, as well as a 1930s-inspired silver-fox cocoon with an enormous collar ($12,500). You don't have to own a Fendi to appreciate these state-of-the-art designs.

The first floor houses Bergdorf's superb handbag department. These handsome bags are usually free of too much metal in the way of clasps or chains. The silhouettes can be amusing—for example, a bright pink leather shoulder bag in the shape of a Chinese coolie hat. And the markdowns are spectacular—one day, a quilted taupe leather clutch, made of the softest leather possible, was reduced from $125 to $75.

The hat department is one of the few places in the city where you can find the amazing creations of Patricia Underwood. Her specialty is taking a classic shape and inventing on it, usually by enlarging it and making it more dramatic. She has rescaled a beret to the size of those worn by Flemish painters in the sixteenth century and produced it in beaver ($500).

For men, there are the oversized, tightly knit sweaters of Jean-Paul Gaultier ($300), which are collectible because of their classic, strong shape and very relaxed but rugged look. Polo shirts here achieve distinction through their exquisite cotton fabric and soft, appealing colors—shades of palest yellow or celadon ($60).

Bergdorf Goodman is a surprising place to shop. Because it does have fancy, high-priced merchandise in large quantities, it also has to have lots of sales, so paradoxically it is a bargain hunter's paradise. Yet it also has fairly priced clothes for the working man or woman. But what unites its less-expensive clothes and its haute couture is the high level of design elegance.   — E.L.

Bergdorf Goodman, 754 Fifth Avenue, PL 3-7300. Open Monday to Saturday, 10 A.M. to 6 P.M.; Thursday till 8 P.M. AE, Bergdorf Goodman, Neiman-Marcus.

ANN TAYLOR

T H I S is a store for the working woman who doesn't think that dressing for success means dressing like a man. Ann Taylor has relaxed clothes, so that a woman can put together an unconstructed long blazer with a bias-cut or stylishly long stitched-down pleated linen skirt for around $300 an outfit. When Ann Taylor carries a basic, such as a good-looking white shirt, it stocks a variety of fabrics and prices: a cotton shirt for $60, a linen one for $80, and a silk charmeuse one for $140. Most likely, the shirt will come with small shoulder pads, so the woman can look a little more authoritative.

Since sweater dressing has been in vogue for the past few years, the store has sweater dresses and long, oversized knit tops to go with slender pull-on knit skirts. Joan Vass's cotton sweaters in white or pale yellow run about $100. A top price point may be Perry Ellis's linens, with pants priced from about $160 to $250 and coats around $400. If there's one criterion that unites the clothes here, it's that they are easy to take: stylish without being cutting-edge. The same goes for their shoes.

Joan & David monopolize the shoe department here, and you will find the graceful, slender silhouette that has made them famous at affordable prices. Many shoes suitable for work are around $125, and a great many have easy-to-walk-in low heels.

Ann Taylor is a store where you can never go wrong about taste. Even better, it is one of the city's friendliest stores. The sales help is unfailingly amiable. You can even call them by phone and ask them to hold an item for you from overnight to three days. They hear you, and they hold it. Remarkable.

Major sales are held in January and July. — E.L.

Ann Taylor, 3 East 57th Street, 832-2010. Open Monday to Saturday, 10 A.M. to 6 P.M.; Thursday till 8 P.M. AE, Ann Taylor, MC, V, checks.

Other branches: 25 Fulton Street, South Street Seaport, 608-5612. Open Monday to Saturday, 10 A.M. to 9 P.M.; Sunday, noon to 8 P.M. 1293 Broadway, Herald Center, 695-4474. Open Monday to Saturday, 10 A.M. to 7 P.M.; Sunday, noon to 6 P.M. 308 Third Avenue, 308-5333. Open Monday to Friday, 10 A.M. to 7 P.M.; Thursday till 8 P.M.; Saturday till 6 P.M.

CHANEL BOUTIQUE

THE punk fashion victims of the early to mid-1980s have found a new image: They wear black velvet bows in their now-smoothed-back hair, quilted tote bags are slung over their shoulders, and their white-collared necks are decked with numerous fake gold chains and strands of pearls. The accoutrements are knockoffs, their primal source umistakably Chanel—firmly back in style, as influential as when the peasant-born designer was lionized by Paris in the 1920s and 1930s.

Those who wish to reconnoiter the genuine articles can do so at the Chanel Boutique, which sells the entire range of Chanel-made goods, from $14 lipsticks (in great colors, with excellent staying power) to the crucially important accessories (gold chains, though fake, start at $180) and black satin ribbon evening dresses ($4,740). If you can't buy, at least you can ogle these wares in surroundings said to approximate those of Coco Chanel's Rue Cambon salon, with its cream and black lacquer appointments and its famous mirrored staircase with wrought-iron handrail.

The recent resurgence of the House of Chanel has come about not only because of the designer's androgynous approach to dressing (Dali said she took the English masculine and made it feminine) and the way she made practicality chic (she introduced wool jersey and rayon, made pants acceptable for women, and put pleats into skirts), but also because of the genius of Karl Lagerfeld in projecting Chanel's spirit into the late twentieth century. In his versions of her suits, the collarless, boxy jackets are cut with exaggerated space-age proportions.

If you're budget-minded, the rakish houndstooth check pants suits and the little black crepe maid's-type dresses trimmed in white satin will be well out of your price range. But maybe, if you're feeling lavishly self-indulgent, you could possibly spring for a classic long black pleated wool crepe skirt ($730). — L.D.

Chanel Boutique, 5 East 57th Street, 355-5050. Open Monday to Saturday, 10 A.M. to 6 P.M. AE, MC, V, checks.

LAURA ASHLEY

H A D Lady Di never met Prince Charles, she might have typified the Laura Ashley customer's sweet romantic English country look. The clothes, all made of 100% natural fibers (namely, cotton and linen), are demure and usually flower-sprigged. They are clothes for *jeune filles*.

While the clothes were originally limited to dresses, blouses, and skirts, today you can wear Laura Ashley from birth on — at the beach, at school, for working, or for getting married.

The clothes for newborns to preteens include pastel cotton pinafores, lace-edged white blouses, and plaid wool jumpers. Once a girl edges toward womanhood, she can choose from swimsuits, sundresses, bathrobes, cotton corduroy long-sleeved dresses, and Fair Isle sweaters. A cotton sundress with white carnations on a blue ground is around $70, and a white cotton petticoat that can be worn as a summer skirt is $40.

Bridal dresses are antebellum in feeling. A high-necked Victorian gown of white dotted voile runs about $375.   — E.L.

Laura Ashley, 21 East 57th Street, 735-1010. Open Monday to Saturday, 10 A.M. to 6 P.M.; Thursday till 8 P.M.; Sunday, noon to 5 P.M. Closed Sunday during the summer. AE, MC, V, checks.

Other branches: 4 Fulton Street, South Street Seaport, 809-3555. Open Monday to Saturday, 10 A.M. to 9 P.M.; Sunday, noon to 8 P.M. 398 Columbus Avenue, 496-5151. Open Monday to Wednesday, Friday and Saturday, 10 A.M. to 7 P.M.; Thursday, 11 A.M. to 8 P.M.; Sunday, noon to 6 P.M.

MAUD FRIZON

K N O C K · O U T, wildly inventive shoes are the specialty of this store. They are expensive, but they are outrageously stylish and a favorite in fashion editorials.

Attention grabbers have included a bronze evening sandal that wraps around the ankle with what appears to be a bronze leather serpent, which actually hides a spring coil that can be tightened to fit ($350). Another stunning evening shoe was a frivolous mass of burgundy and gold suede leaves ($265) that fluttered in the breeze. On a slightly more conservative note were beautifully proportioned suede pumps with gold-studded heels ($220). Frizon is the mistress of decoration and embellishment. Leathers inset with lizard look rich rather than pointlessly flashy. Net frills and purple metallic piping on black suede or combinations such as pony and crocodile are not overkill but inspiration.

Men who would be happy here would be rock-and-roll musicians or other extroverts. For example, loafers come in stenciled pony fur ($265).

June and December are the sale times here. — E.L.

Maud Frizon, 49 East 57th Street, 980-1460. Open Monday to Saturday, 10 A.M. to 6 P.M. AE, MC, V, checks.

MATSUDA
461 Park Avenue, 935-6969. See index for main listing.

SUSAN BENNIS/
WARREN EDWARDS

I F Imelda Marcos didn't shop here, she should have. This is the store for some of the snazziest (and most conspicuously expensive) shoes for women and men in town. Some people swear that the last, a medium width with a narrow AAAA heel (for women), is extremely comfortable. But at the prices charged (shoes *start* at $275 and soar to the thousands of dollars), you shouldn't get blisters. You probably shouldn't even have to walk.

The shoes here are of astonishing colors, fabrics, and exotic skins. While there are loafers and pumps, the specialty is high glamour shoes, some of which have three-inch stiletto heels. Says a saleswoman, "The stiletto heels are for ladies who go to lunch in limousines."

In the store, the shoes bear no prices—probably on the theory that if you are distracted by the cost (your heart stops beating), you won't notice the design of the shoe.

There is a fairly wide range of styles. Last season, $265 got you floral-printed cotton shoes perched on platforms. A low-heeled shoe had a net toe appliquéd with poppy red leather; the heel was a gleaming patent leather ($425). Less flashy classics are the loafers of ostrich ($550) and crocodile ($695).

For a slightly dressier look, there are baby alligator pumps, which come in your choice of three different heel heights. You can also choose any of ten different colors, including black, purple, and forest green. For this privilege (you get the shoes in six weeks), you pay $1,595.

Men can wallow in the same luxury. There are plain loafers for $365 or crocodile ones for $895. For night, men may choose from dance pumps of patent leather, satin, or suede that come with or without a bow.   — E.L.

Susan Bennis/Warren Edwards, 440 Park Avenue, 755-4197; (800) 634-9884 for out of state. Open Monday to Friday, 10 A.M. to 6:30 P.M.; Saturday till 6 P.M. AE, MC, V checks.

LA LINGERIE
725 Fifth Avenue in the Trump Tower, 980-8811. See index for main listing.

OMO NORMA KAMALI

N O R M A Kamali is one of the most popular and inventive American designers—it was she who created the sleeping-bag coat, sweat-fabric designer sportswear, and dresses with enormous shoulder pads. Kamali is also considered the most avant-garde swimsuit designer. Her suits were the first to be cut up past the thigh to the waist, and when that palled, to be lengthened down over the tops of the legs again. In her multilevel gray concrete store, you will continue to find exceptional swimsuits—from maillots to minimal bikinis—and their colors and patterns are always amusing.

Kamali's dresses and suits are reminiscent of the 1940s, emphasizing the female figure and flattering nearly all shapes and sizes. One standard is continuous variations on her long-sleeved, snug-at-the-waist, full-skirted dress in fabrics like denim, or pristine white cotton, or printed rayon (under $150). A wool crepe suit might run around $400.

The cheapest buy is a pair of her famous big shoulder pads ($10). The most extravagant items are her one-of-a-kind evening dresses. A breathtaking gown, perfect for a summer wedding, was of hand-embroidered white-on-white linen ($3,100). Most of her clothes are priced affordably in between.   — E.L.

Omo Norma Kamali, 11 West 56th Street, 957-9797. Open Monday to Saturday, 10 A.M. to 6 P.M. AE, MC, V.
   Other branches: 113 Spring Street, 334-9696.

MANOLO BLAHNIK

M A N O L O Blahnik is considered by the fashion cognoscenti—editors, designers, and shoe mavens—to be maybe the best shoe designer in the world. His shoes are inventive without being trendy, unique yet with a fit and silhouette that won't date. One woman retailer has collected his shoes for over twenty years. What makes Blahnik so appealing to women is that he makes the best of three different kinds of shoes—daytime, evening, and purely whimsical. While they are clearly pricey, they are investment shoes: They don't fall apart, and you never tire of them.

For day-in-day-out wear, there have been black suede shoes with 2-inch heels and straps that crisscross gracefully in front ($250), or cream-colored closed-toe summer shoes with open backs and the skinniest straps to tie around the ankle ($240). These shoes can pound the pavements or the corridors of power. For pure whimsy, he has designed elvish shoes that envelop the feet in six triangles of soft buttery suede and come in red, black, or purple ($300). For evening, there might be low-heeled gold lamé shoes; the front of the shoe has been knotted at the vamp and rises in a fan shape ($300). The perfect, flawless wedding shoes are floral-embroidered ecru cotton low-heeled pumps ($325).

For men, there are elegant loafers ($250 in calfskin, $425 in lizard) and boots. But the stars of Blahnik's collection are clearly the women's shoes—for this is where he can be his most dazzling.

Sales are held here in January and July, with markdowns of 30% to 50%. — E.L.

Manolo Blahnik, 15 West 55th Street, 582-3007. Open Monday to Saturday, 10:30 A.M. to 6 P.M. AE, MC, V, checks.

TO BOOT
520 Madison Avenue, 644-5661. See index for main listing.

FOGAL
510 Madison Avenue, 355-3254. See index for main listing.

ALCOTT & ANDREWS
1301 Avenue of the Americas, 315-2796. See index for main listing.

CAPEZIO DANCE-THEATRE SHOP
755 Seventh Avenue, 245-2130. See index for main listing.

EMOTIONAL OUTLET
135 West 50th Street, 957-9340. See index for main listing.

FIL Á FIL
610 Fifth Avenue, 247-4290. See index for main listing.

SAKS FIFTH AVENUE

S A K S Fifth Avenue tries to run a close second to Bergdorf Goodman, which most would rank as the city's top fashion specialty store. While Bergdorf's is clearly more sophisticated when it comes to women's and men's clothes, not to mention home furnishings, Saks has great depth in all departments— and especially, it has service. Saks may be the last store in the city where you may be in the middle of a purchase and suddenly need to call home—to tell the babysitter you're going to be late or to find out the exact shirt size of your spouse—and have the salespeople immediately offer you a phone, a chair, and a desk. At another store they'd point you to the nearest pay phone, often two floors away.

Saks also has a clever design that makes it one of the least fatiguing stores to shop in. Except for the first, eighth, and ninth, the floors are laid out in a circle. You walk down an aisle; clothes are displayed on either side, and within moments, assuming you haven't stopped to fondle a piece of merchandise, you have traveled the entire floor. There are no secret nooks or crannies.

The first floor features men's furnishings and the Louis Vuitton shop, where the well-heeled can order trunks to accompany them on safari, as well as handbags, hose, cosmetics, jewelry—the usual contents of a department store's ground floor.

The second and third floors harbor the priciest women's departments. The second has designer sportswear from Calvin Klein, Donna Karan, and Perry Ellis, while the third has couture, as well as a taste of the avant-garde. On the third floor are clothes by Adolfo, the sweetheart of Nancy Reagan and her cohort. For those whose politics or at least personal style leans to the far left of Mrs. Reagan's, there are also clothes by Patricia Clyne, Norbury & Osuna, and Premonville et Dewavrin. Here you will find suits of chartreuse, with skinny legs.

The fourth floor is given over to lingerie and women's shoes, while the fifth is working girl's heaven. Here are affordable clothes by designers such as Liz Claiborne, Rebecca Moses, and Andrea Jovine that can be worn to the office. There are oversized sweaters priced around $100 to be paired with matching knit skirts for $60 to $80. The bridal shop is here, too, but a word of caution: All the dresses have a virginal look.

The sixth floor is devoted to men, and the depth of merchandise is excellent. A man can dress himself here from the age of eighteen unto death and never have to go anywhere else. The designers featured range from ubiquitous Ralph Lauren, with his Polo shop, to Gianfranco Ferré, Gianni Versace, and Giorgio Armani. And for those who are hard to fit or simply fussy, Saks offers made-to-measure suits, shirts, coats, and jackets. There are also basics galore: khaki pants, cashmere sweaters, oxford cloth shirts, swim trunks, windbreakers, and sweatshirts. A handsome oversized black and white houndstooth sports jacket was $350.

The seventh floor has moderate-priced sportswear and dresses from manufacturers like Evan Picone and Spitalnik, and Saks' own private label, Real Clothes.

The eighth floor is for children from infancy through pre-teen. All the clothes are beautifully chosen, ranging from dressy to sporty-casual and from Italian imports to Esprit or Guess. Occasionally, the sales are splendid. On one visit a $50 Italian wool knit sweater with a bodice of red, collar of green, one sleeve pink, and the other blue was marked down to $20. The ninth floor, finally, is given over to the home.

But wherever you shop in this store, the saleshelp are particularly courteous. The shopping here is easy.　　— E.L.

Saks Fifth Avenue, 611 Fifth Avenue, 753-4000. Open Monday to Saturday, 10 A.M. to 6 P.M.; Thursday till 8 P.M. AE, CB, DC, Saks.

EMOTIONAL OUTLET
242 East 51st Street, 838-0707. See index for main listing.

J. MCLAUGHLIN

976 Second Avenue, 308-4100. See index for main listing.

McCREEDY & SCHREIBER

RANCHERS, city slickers, and just plain Joes put their best feet forward toward this renowned men's shoe establishment, which has fit the best since 1922. The *Pirates of Penzance* and Metropolitan Opera stars get their $250 just-below-the-knee buccaneer boots here, and urban (and otherwise) cowboys stampede the place, which is the exclusive Manhattan dealer for San Antonio's famed Lucchese boots. "They're the standard of excellence, the Rolls-Royce of western boots," owner Frank Schreiber glows, "from $300 for Italian goatskin to $2,500 for full crocodile."

Boots are a specialty—stock includes Tony Lamas and Dan Posts along with Italian dress zip boots and British classics—but there're also handsome hand-stitched low slip-ons by Lorenzo Banfi from $145 to fancy $395 crocodile models. The "Country Gentleman Collection" is styled by Schreiber and manufactured in England with styles that include crepe-soled lace-ups ($79) and classic ankle boots ($175).

Yankee patriots walk tall with Americana traditionals like Cole•Haans, Bass Weejuns, Sperry Topsiders, and Frye boots. Serious belt lovers will marvel at a selection of leather models with stitching that matches Lucchese cowboy boots, and western buckles ($75 to $300) in scrimshaw, gold, and silver.   — D.K.

McCreedy & Schreiber, 37 West 46th Street, 719-1552. Open Monday to Saturday, 9 A.M. to 7 P.M. AE, DC, MC, V, checks.

Other branches: 213 East 59th Street, 759-9241. Open Monday and Thursday, 9 A.M. to 9 P.M.; Tuesday, Wednesday, Friday, and Saturday till 7 P.M.; Sunday, noon to 6 P.M.

F. R. TRIPLER & CO.

T H I S Madison Avenue haberdashery is a gentlemanly tradition. Though not as status conscious as its neighbors Brooks Brothers and Paul Stuart, F.R. Tripler specializes in Ivy League basics for men and women. The clubroom ground-floor interior—woodsy and gleaming with perfectly arranged cases—is presided over by knowledgeable, slightly stodgy professionals with the demeanor of trustworthy tailors.

There is nothing too trendy and form-fitting among Tripler's formidable furnishings, but fabric and workmanship are terrific. Sporty polos in pima and luxe Sea Island knits ($37.50 to $55) exemplify the fine cottons; and dress shirt fabrics add an Edwardian flavor to made-in-England nightshirts, pajamas, and robes ($85 to $175). Tripler's own matching hand-intarsiaed pullovers seem downright reasonable at $120.

Outerwear, dress slacks, sport jackets, suits, and tuxedos occupy the equally hushed second floor, with a special emphasis on two-button suits by Hickey Freeman, Oxxford ($900 plus), and Graham & Gunn, a line produced by Hart, Schaffner & Marx. Made-to-measure suits begin at $700. Womenswear is on the third floor.   — D.K.

F. R. Tripler, 366 Madison Avenue, 922-1090. Open Monday to Saturday, 9 A.M. to 5:45 P.M. AE, MC, V, checks.

PAUL STUART

P A U L Stuart shoppers, they say, are "the most cosmopolitan customers in New York, if not the world; movers and shakers who are not afraid of style." Once known as "the poor man's Brooks Brothers," Paul Stuart has blossomed into Trad Avenue's least stuffy purveyor of "classic clothing with personality," with an eye for luxurious, colorful fabrics and sophisticated tailoring.

Prices, not surprisingly, reflect the high quality of their mostly European private-label production but are not astronomical. Men's suits dominate the second floor, varying in cut from the Ivy League to continental, running as high as $600 for double-breasted glen plaids in linen and $450 for basic winter wools. Dress shirts begin at $35, climbing to around $90 for fine Sea Island cotton. Long-sleeve linen sports shirts in lustrous colors are as little as $76. Cotton madras ties are $12.50 in spring and hand-knit Fair Isle cravats for winter are under $50. Sweater styles number nearly 200, from basic cotton crewnecks at $22.50 to reversible cashmere "sweatshirts" costing $415. English and Italian shoes can be as casual as under-$100 white bucks or as spiffy as alligator loafers for $475.

Furnishings are fanciful, from embroidered ribbon suspenders to cotton boxer shorts ($10 to $30) to a large selection of hosiery from a sock bar that sports vivid cotton argyles ($8.50 and up) and cushy cashmeres ($35). Jewelry is exquisite, created by a former Tiffany's designer, mixing contemporary elements and classic styling in Edwardian-flavored vermeil cuff links (around $300) and a beautiful hunting watch with galloping horses on the face and a spring-action dome in 14K gold ($1,250) and 18K gold plate ($500).

Paul Stuart's women's line is neatly displayed on the mezzanine and boasts the same high quality as the men's line, resulting in costlier prices than other conference room couturiers. Suits are languorously tailored and less conservative than those of most corporate outfitters, starting at just under $500 for linens, gabardines, and saxonies. They also feature a fine collection of antique jewelry and handmade Italian shoes ($200 and up) that accent their chic business womenswear perfectly.   — D.K.

Paul Stuart, Madison Avenue at 45th Street, 682-0320. Open Monday to Friday, 8 A.M. to 6 P.M.; Saturday, 9 A.M. to 6 P.M. AE, DC, MC, V, checks.

BROOKS BROTHERS

"W E ' R E a fuddy-duddy old place," a dapper old salesclerk admits cagily, "but profitable!" And then some. Like Kleenex tissues and Xerox copiers, Brooks Brothers has come to stand for a product—a complete range of menswear that adds up to the identifiably generic look of collegiate/corporate middle America. The man in the gray flannel suit buys it here, and hip downtowners shop for reverse chic items like the classic French-back boxer shorts (around $20) and velvet slippers with fox crests ($95). Brooks Brothers is an institution.

The ground floor of this flagship store is a dizzying labyrinth of counters filled with furnishings: sports shirts, sweaters ($35 and up), pajamas ($36 or less for fine cottons), socks, sunglasses, underwear, jewelry (including their rather smart watch line, $130 to $165), backgammon sets, picture frames, and grooming and desk accessories. Everywhere you look there are neatly arranged rows of ties and stacks of button-down shirts, including the "fun" model that pieces together five different colors of bold-striped cotton for around $40.

The second, third, and sixth floors are devoted to their own-label classic jackets, dress trousers, and suits (including special-order tailoring, with suits starting around $500), and a luggage department that's noteworthy for the handsome leather attaché cases by Peal & Co. (around $500). The fourth floor carries pint-size versions of Brooks' classics—boardroom suits (around $150), rugby shirts and khakis, and horribly garish golf pants (around $36)—for lads; as well as surprisingly pretty and colorful women's suits ($200 for linen, $250 and up for corporate tweeds) and go-togethers. Brooksgate, the trimmer-cut suits and furnishings line, is housed on the fifth floor and boasts a sportier look (for example madras plaid shirts and paisleys!) for the generally younger customer.

Sales are held here in January, June, and August.   — D.K.

Brooks Brothers, 346 Madison Avenue, 682-8800. Open Monday to Saturday, 9:15 A.M.to 6 P.M. AE, Brooks Brothers, DC, checks.
   Other branches: 1 Liberty Plaza, 267-2400.

J. PRESS

PRESIDED over by a large portrait of Mr. J. Press, a serious-looking gent who founded the business in New Haven, Connecticut, in 1902, this cool, slightly cluttered haberdashery is, according to grandson Richard Press, "the quintessential purveyor of quote-unquote Ivy League conservative clothing." J. Press boasts the largest selection of two- and three-button, natural-shoulder suits ($275 to $450) and jackets ($175 to $350), all cut specifically for the store in fabrics as jaunty as madras tartan and as sober as gray flannel. A hefty 90% of their own-label dress shirts are button-downs in pin-striped cotton and broadcloth ($37 to $50), and their fancy striped polo shirts run $25 to $30. Custom-tailored suits cost $1,200 and up and usually require three fittings.

On the more whimsical side, J. Press is notable for their truly hideous shorts and trousers in calico patchwork, 1960s floral, and embroidered lobster fabrics. Club ties sport an amusing menagerie of grasshoppers, hippos, owls, pheasants, and wine bottles and glasses. Leather tab suspenders ($30) and pungently colored Indian silk ties ($18.50) sport traditional rep stripes, checks, and plaids. For a touch of reverse-chic label snobbery, try their regulation sweatshirts, handsomely printed with the marvelously old-fashioned J. Press logo.

Sales are held here in January and July.   —D.K.

J. Press, 16 East 44th Street, 687-7642. Open Monday to Saturday, 9:15 A.M. to 5:30 P.M. AE, MC, V, checks.

ALCOTT & ANDREWS

WHERE do Brooks Brothers' sisters shop for their corporate couture? Right this way, ma'am, where classical music and whitened wood floors set the tone for clothing that's businesslike without sacrificing femininity. Designed specifically for the executive woman (sizes 4 to 14) who tends to shop for complete outfits, Alcott & Andrews arranges their private-label suits and dresses with coordinating blouses by color stories, heavy on spring pastels/neutrals and navies, grays, and burgundies for fall. Thus, you're likely to find the same embroidered cotton, silk, or pleated linen blouses ($36 and up) racked with a variety of blazers ($350 to $500), jackets ($100 to $350), and tweedy suits all over the spaciously laid-out career department that also offers shirt- and coat-styled dresses (from $150) on the main floor.

On the lower level resides the Casuals Department, stocked with easy separates and signature sweaters that feature angora duckies and 3-D sailboats (around $100). Across the aisle is an area dedicated to red, white, and black officewear and The Shirt Shop, which sports button-downs and round collars in pinstripes, oxfords, and broadcloths. Coordinating silk bow ties, scarves, and fabric flowers are around $16. For the brand-conscious there's a small but well-stocked Ralph Lauren shop, offering styles and colors that mix perfectly with A&A's own designs.

Sales are held twice yearly, after Christmas and early in the summer.   — D.K.

Alcott & Andrews, 335 Madison Avenue, 818-0606. Open Monday to Friday, 10 A.M. to 8 P.M.; Thursday till 9 P.M.; Saturday till 6 P.M.; Sunday, noon to 5 P.M. AE, MC, V, checks.

Other branches: 1301 Avenue of the Americas, 315-2796.

CHIPP

A MAN'S best friend is his *tie?* Well, not exactly, but this is the place where dog lovers can find over ninety breeds of pooch on a classic polyester club tie ($17) by Chipp, along with skunks, balls-and-chains, and racket-toting gophers ("I Go For Tennis," get it?). New dads can boast with a stork tie with the name and date of the new family member inscribed for an additional $3.50, and granddads can plump for a silk cravat with two hand-painted grandchild names for a mere $20 ($2.50 for each additional name). Rah-rah alumni and jacket embellishers alike cheer for Chipp's selection of $25 school blazer crests and button sets from simple brass ($20) to monogrammed ($28) to cloisonné ($35) and pewter doggies on a brass base ($100).

Naturally, there's a host of jackets and suits, from $175 Haspel seersuckers to $2,500 customized cashmere "million-aire's suits" to give all these accoutrements a reason for being. Chip specializes in Ivy League/Wall Street flannels and tweeds, with some tastefully loud madras and silk jackets for spring. Custom tailoring begins at just under a grand per suit, but men who fancy themselves stylists can design their own "special, ready-cut" suits, which are produced one at a time at Chipp's factory. A choice of nearly 1,000 fabrics and the ability to specify the number of buttons—two or three—and location of vents allows the fashionable gent the freedom to be individual without paying any more than the off-the-rack prices, starting at $400; physically fit fellas can exercise this option to split sizes on jackets and trousers and avoid alterations.

Look for seasonal sales here in January and July.   —D.K.

Chipp, 342 Madison (on the second floor, entrance on 43rd Street), 687-0850. Open Monday to Friday, 9 A.M. to 5 P.M.; other times by appointment. MC, V, checks

DOLLAR BILL'S GENERAL STORE

"WE cannot advertise designer's names," the signs at this discount dream declare. But that's exactly the reason to be there—the big names are all over the place, on hangtags, packages, and not-so-carefully inked-over labels, like the ones on an ultra-famous Italian designer's dress shirts that sell for a flat $39.99. Located in a storefront of Grand Central Station, Dollar Bill's has all the ambience of a modern drugstore (the clothes share space with cut-price beauty products, candy, and cigarettes) and all of the merchandising panache of a small-town Woolworth's, but the prices and consistently high-fashion names outweigh such cosmetic considerations.

European menswear is the highlight. Very well-known, hard-to-pronounce name-brand shirts run from $14.99 to $19.99; dress trousers are $59.99; jackets and suits from award-winning couturiers range from $149.99 to $349.99. Belts from Bill's Belt Bar and Italian silk ties from the Cravateria cost $14.99. Snazzy rubber raincoats with corduroy collars and tartan linings prove fair-weather friends at a mere $79.99, and spiffy leathers are a snap at just under $150 (you guessed it, they're $149.99). Even staples like socks and undies are relentlessly reduced to $3.99. Through an archway there's an annex with further reductions and gracious signs offering, "Take another 20% off!" Here you'll find trousers (around $20) and inexpensive American and Italian sportswear as well as extremely inexpensive women's sportswear separates.   —D.K.

Dollar Bill's General Store, 99 East 42nd Street, 867-0212. Open Monday to Wednesday, 8 A.M. to 6:30 P.M.; Thursday and Friday till 7 P.M.; Saturday, 10 A.M. to 6 P.M. AE, DC, MC, V, checks (during banking hours).

THE UPPER EAST SIDE

INTRODUCTION BY
By Linda Dyett

A hundred years ago, the terrain that's now the poshest piece of real estate on earth was strictly exurbia—a maze of shanties and squatters' towns hemmed in by marshland. Hardly had it pushed its way out of the primeval ooze when multitudes of Italianate palazzi and Beaux Arts mansions sprang up. Normally, it takes centuries of nurture and inbreeding to create millionaires' turf, but the property developers were diligent and did it in a matter of decades. Upstart neighborhoods (notably the Upper West Side) aspire to compete, but the Upper East Side staunchly remains the wealthiest, most elegant sector of New York.

You can still see uniformed nannies pushing high-wheeled baby carriages into Central Park. You can spot Garbo flitting by, and Jackie Onassis, Calvin Klein, Henry Kissinger, the Ten Best Dressed of any year, Brooke Astor, Cornelia Guest, and most of

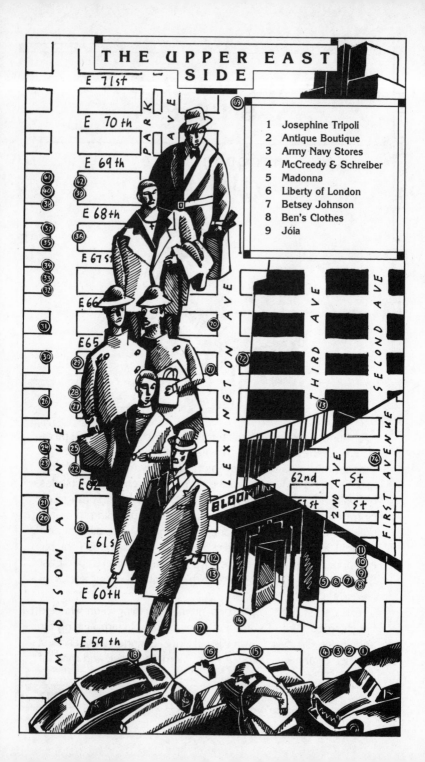

THE UPPER EAST SIDE

1 Josephine Tripoli
2 Antique Boutique
3 Army Navy Stores
4 McCreedy & Schreiber
5 Madonna
6 Liberty of London
7 Betsey Johnson
8 Ben's Clothes
9 Jóia

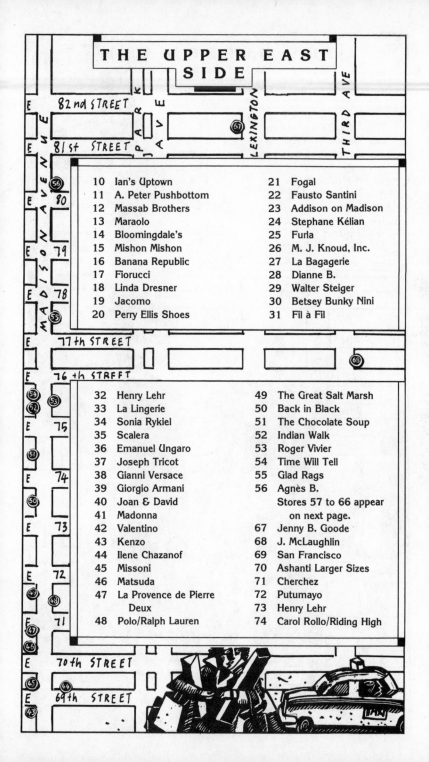

THE UPPER EAST SIDE

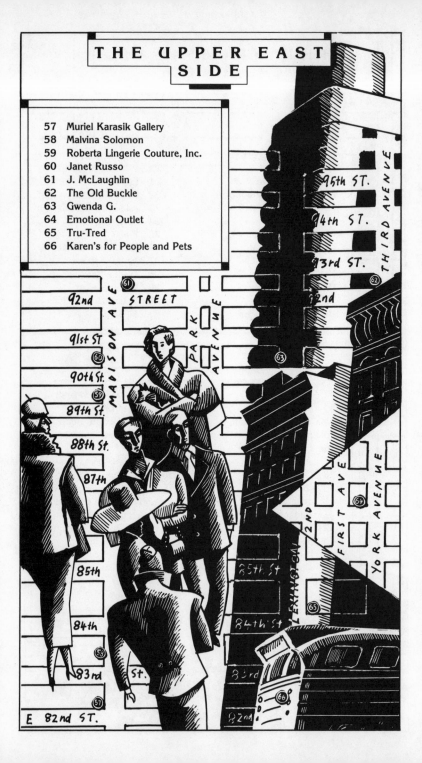

THE UPPER EAST SIDE

the other aristocrats, tycoons, and nouveaux riches who make New York their home.

Not surprisingly, the best shops on this side of the Atlantic are on the upper stretch of Madison Avenue, sandwiched between Fifth and Park, certainly the two most sumptuous residential streets in the Americas. No department stores here. This is the place to go for the one-of-a-kind, the handmade, the blowout splurge of a lifetime. Nearly all the European couturiers have outpost salons on Madison, and there are a number of small shops selling everything from antique toy soldiers to luxury juice squeezers. This is prime shopping turf for New York bluebloods, the Concorde tourists, the wives of friendly despots, and anyone else who wants to be outfitted by the upper echelons of mainstream and couture fashion.

Clothing prices are usually high. A couple of hundred is the least you'd be likely to pay for a typical dress or turnout. But it is definitely possible to find bargains on Madison Avenue if you know when and where to go and if your taste is not exclusively bohemian. Even the most chichi of these stores holds grand-slam end-of-the-season sales (though they're often unannounced). A number of shops—branches of foreign and out-of-town retailers like Joseph Tricot and Janet Russo—sell in the upper-moderate price range. And the major designers tend to have "second" and "third" lines of sportswear that are almost inexpensive.

There are several high-caliber men's shops here and men's departments in the couture salons, but basically this is women's territory, with dozens and dozens of clothing boutiques (far too many to include in our reviews—we've limited ourselves to the best and most specialized) and accessories marts. It is a particularly strong area for shoes and handbags—not necessarily more expensive than Soho or the Upper West Side.

If you're a connoisseur of shops *qua* shops, you'll find paragons here, like Linda Dresner and Dianne B.—with decor so exquisite you'll want to give parties on the premises, and with a mix of wares so gorgeous you'll be tempted to forfeit your next year's salary to own a sampling of each.

Lately, the commercial rents on Madison have zoomed astronomically, and a lot of the small specialty shops have been forced to close—or, if they're fortunate, to move to side streets and upstairs locations. They're being replaced by major chain stores like Benetton and The Limited, which can afford the rent. Pundits predict that Madison Avenue will soon head into an unstoppable downward slide and will turn into another 34th Street by the millenium. But dozens of good little shops remain to tantalize, offering maybe not the utterly sumptuous goods you find in Paris or Florence, but the best in America. Naturally, this makes for browsing territory that can be both exciting and intimidating. As if to enhance the offputting atmosphere, security guards, who sometimes deign to double as doormen at the expensive boutiques, act like maîtres d' and inspect your shoes as you enter for confirmation of your wealth or poverty. Disregard them. Unless you're inebriated, shrieking obscenities, or brandishing a .45, you can browse anywhere on Madison Avenue. In fact, few of these shops are *truly* distingué. And don't be scared of the sales help. Think of the snobbish ones as pathetic creatures. Actually, many of them—especially the ones with the biggest smirks—are young and often ignorant of their wares.

You'll also find some of New York's best hairdressers here, such as Bruno Dessange at 760 Madison and David Daines at 833 Madison. If you're seeking cosmetics, try Boyd Chemists, 655 Madison, for a total makeup experience or Cambridge Chemists at 21 East 65th Street for the best in men's toiletries. Several other outstanding shops on and around Madison Avenue are: Books & Co., 939 Madison; Krön Chocolatier, 884 Madison; and Wallis Mayers Needlework, for luxury knitting yarns and needlepoint supplies, 33 East 68th Street.

This western ridge of the Upper East Side sprang to life in the late nineteenth century when a number of Murray Hill millionaires began migrating north to be close to the open spaces of the newly completed Central Park. They built their mansions and townhouses shamelessly, setting lavish new standards for homes as status symbols. You can still see these edifices, long ago converted to apartment dwellings or institutional headquarters, lining Fifth Avenue from 60th to 96th streets.

The side streets between Fifth and Madison are also filled with chic rowhouses and brownstones. In the 1920s and 1930s,

Park Avenue succumbed to wealth, too, becoming one of the world's grand boulevards, solidly crammed with immense, fortresslike apartment houses designed in a dizzying variety of styles—Georgian, Romanesque, Italian Renaissance, and Deco—often all in the same structure. These buildings, among the most desirable in Manhattan, all come equipped with doormen who whistle for cabs, hold back the riffraff, and doze when they can in ornate lobbies the size of the Taj Mahal. Upstairs, the cavernous apartments are still inhabited by the oldest money, as well as by the new, and it is the domains of the arrivistes that are regularly photographed by *Better Homes and Gardens* and the ever-faithful Sunday *Times* magazine section.

Blessed by the patronage of its wealthy settlers, the neighborhood has the highest concentration of museums in the city—including the Metropolitan Museum of Art, the Guggenheim and the Whitney (modern art), the Cooper-Hewitt (design), and the Frick Collection. The Frick is particularly recommended, not just for its Old Masters, but as a serene, Beaux Arts resting spot when you're all shopped out.

In the high 50s and low 60s, you'll also find most of the luxury hotels, beginning with the Plaza at the southeast corner of Central Park, and the nearby Pierre and Sherry-Netherland—classical, slender structures with high-peaked roofs that add grace to the skyline. On the quiet and charming side streets, you'll pass the city's most selective establishments—the private clubs (The Metropolitan Club and Harmonie Club, both designed by McKim, Mead & White, are on 60th Street at Fifth Avenue), private schools, and doctors' offices as posh as the Plaza.

East of Park Avenue, the ambience changes. There are small patches of elegance, such as Carl Schurz Park, East End Avenue, and the area around the Beekman Theater (a little gem of a movie house on Second Avenue and 66th Street). But on the whole, Lexington Avenue and points eastward are basically unattractive, filled with cheaply built high rises and renovated tenements occupied by an astonishing number of New Yorkers (and out-of-towners who claim to be New Yorkers) who think anything below 59th Street is bansheeland.

The highest concentration of singles bars in New York is on

First and Second avenues in the 60s and 70s, while further north is a former German-Czech-Hungarian quarter called Yorktown. A number of beer halls and ethnic food markets remain on and around 86th Street.

Most of the stores on the eastern cusp of the Upper East Side are disappointingly bland, selling the kind of wares you get in shopping malls. But there are delightful exceptions. In addition to a sprinkling of good clothing shops on Lexington Avenue and east of Bloomingdale's, check out Silk Surplus, an outlet for Scalamandre Silks, at 223 East 58th Street in the midst of the home-decorating market; and Katagiri, a Japanese 5 & 10, and Plaza Furniture and Mirror Co., a wonderfully inexpensive used-furniture store, side by side at 224 and 226 East 59th Street. Tender Buttons at 143 East 62nd has an impressive array of new and vintage buttons. And walking north on Lexington, you'll find the Phone Boutique at 828, for aesthetically pleasing new and vintage telephones; Ad Hoc Housewares at 842, selling well-conceived kitchen and bath goods in a wide price range; Garnet Liquors at 929 for the best prices on fine wines; Il Papiro, an exquisite Florentine paper goods shop, at 1021; and Kitchen Arts and Letters, a culinary bookstore at 1435. And if you have a tooth for marzipan, you'll find an enormous supply at the Marzipan Store at 240 East 86th Street.

Speaking of nourishment: Though New York's luncheonettes have become an endangered species, there are a couple of good ones in prime shopping turf, such as O'John's East at 864 Madison Avenue, and Eat Here Now at 839 Lexington. Or for a somewhat more formal but modestly priced lunch, try the Right Bank at 822 Madison Avenue. Madame Romaine de Lyon serves lovely traditional omelettes at 29 East 61st Street. Or if you want to picnic in Central Park, you can pick up excellent take-out food at Kalinka Café, a Russian restaurant at 1067 Madison, or Country Host, 1457 Lexington, specializing in Scottish meat pies, sausage rolls, and Cornish pasties.

For drinks, there is Manhattan's most elegant bar, the Polo Lounge, in the Westbury Hotel at Madison and 69th or, a close second, the Bemelmans Bar in the Carlyle, 35 East 76th Street.

As regards dinner, uptown restaurants, though often visually stunning, are generally expensive and unadventurous. If price is no object, try the super-elegant Le Cirque, 58 East 65th, a beautiful-people favorite, or the more serene Devon House, 1316 Madison. Other good places are La Goulue, a French bistro at 28 East 70th Street; Uzie's, for Italian food, 1442 Third Avenue; the New Arcadia, 21 East 62nd, for nouvelle American; and Arizona at 206 East 60th Street for southwestern fare. If your budget is modest, try the Ideal at 238 East 86th for bratwurst and sauerkraut.

The quickest entry to the Upper East Side is by subway: Take the IRT 4, 5, or 6 or the BMT N or R to 59th Street (Bloomingdale's). By bus: Take the M1, M2, M3, or M4 down Fifth Avenue or up Madison; the M101 or M102 down Lexington Avenue or up Third to 59th Street; or the M103 across 59th to Third Avenue. Fifty-ninth Street itself is a strange thoroughfare filled with honking traffic inching onto the Queensboro Bridge and a weird assortment of stores, including high-tech design showrooms, a repertory movie house, a Meatland Butcher Shop, and a couple of special wearables shops, which is where we'll start.

(If you'd rather construct your own tour, you might want to begin at 96th Street and Lexington. There, on the northwest corner, you'll find the Danish Palae, a sleazy-looking, styrofoam-coffee-dispensing bakery that happens to make the greatest Danish pastry this side of the North Sea—well worth a side trip. With your bag of Danish, just head west to Madison Avenue and head downward.)

■ ■ ■

JOSEPHINE TRIPOLI

S T A C K S of gold and floral hatboxes seem ready to careen from their perches. Little cloches are piled on larger berets nesting on fedoras and tilted Watteau brims. The very cluttered Josephine Tripoli, founded in 1937, may well be the last of New York's millinery shops, a holdover from the era when ladies' hats were *de rigueur*. All the wares have been designed by the octogenarian Tripoli herself and Suzanne Newman, her former apprentice, who now owns the business.

Trends aren't catered to here. Instead, the shop is a virtual repository of traditional hat shapes. Some styles, like the Princess Di flying saucer or the straw sunhat with a colossal 14-inch brim, may be whimsies, but nothing's silly or outlandish. The bretons, turbans, and cartwheels—to name a few Tripoli confections—are timeless classics.

Service is highly personalized. Each customer's head shape, hairstyle, earlobes, jaw, nose, and neck are scrutinized. Then the perfect hat is suggested. The advice can be blunt but it's always sound, and Tripoli insists that there is a suitable hat for *every* head. Some models are ready to buy. Others may need a quick, on-premises size or style alteration. Special orders, say, for hats copied from pictures (and probably improved on) or for the creation of fantasy chapeaux, may take up to three weeks.

Prices range from $90 to $300. The superb materials include straws, fur felts and velours, furs, and a plentitude of trimmings—even hand-pleated ribbon *cocardes* (little curlicues that look delicious on the killer veiled cocktail hats). — L.D.

Josephine Tripoli, 237 East 59th Street, 421-5667. Open Monday to Saturday, 10 A.M. to 5:45 P.M. AE, MC, V, checks.

ANTIQUE BOUTIQUE

227 East 59th Street, 752-1680. See index for main listing.

ARMY NAVY STORES

I N the old days, you could always rely on army and navy suppliers for military surplus that cost almost nothing and lasted forever. Now that the authentic, classically styled, natural-fiber goods are no longer available, the shops that've kept the name tend to specialize in budget-priced jeans and work clothes. Designers haunt them in search of sportswear ideas. The best of these marts in Manhattan—with the steepest discounts—are Army Navy Stores, in business since 1933, with their main branch on East 59th Street. They're the leading local outlet of Levi's classic 501 button-fly jeans, which they discount at about $17—up to $10 less than most places sell them.

There are other stylish items here—cotton tanks that sell for about $6; Wallace Beery jersey shirts, $13 to $15; and leather jackets, ranging from basic and distressed bombers to fringed suedes and Rocky jackets, most well under $200.

The pants department includes suspender styles, about $30; many fatigues, about $20 to $30; and comfortable painters' pants with hammer loops and ruler pockets, under $20.

Here you can also buy chic accoutrements like $1.50 bandanas and $6 Swiss canvas army bags. If you want a larger container, carry your purchases away in a handsome canvas duffel, $20.

Sales are held in midsummer and midwinter.   —L.D.

Army Navy Stores, 221 East 59th Street, 755-1855. Open Monday and Thursday, 10 A.M. to 8 P.M.; Tuesday, Wednesday, and Friday till 7 P.M.; Saturday till 6 P.M.; and Sunday, 1 P.M. to 6 P.M. AE, MC, V, checks.

Other branches: 110 Eighth Avenue, 645-7420. Open the same hours. 328 Bleecker, 242-6665. Open Monday to Wednesday, 10 A.M. to 8 P.M.; Thursday to Saturday till 9 P.M.; and Sunday, 1 P.M. to 6 P.M.

MCCREEDY & SCHREIBER

213 East 59th Street, 759-9241. See index for main listing.

MADONNA

T H E brownstone location is idyllic. A Deco burled walnut desk is up front, and a slightly overgrown garden opens out from the main floor rear. Upstairs beyond the suit and coat department lies a quiet terrace. The clothes are exquisite, too, so the tendency is to linger at Madonna.

This store bears absolutely no relation to the rock star. Its name is an off-the-cuff joke about flamboyant Italian males who spend hours preening and fussing over their wardrobes. Madonna opened in 1968, a pioneer in Italian men's boutique clothes. It was the first to import beautiful linen chambray suits, wrinkled jackets, and sumptuous sweaters. Its owner, Robert Mitrotti, was the style consultant for *American Gigolo* and *Miami Vice* in its premier season. The clothes continue to be chic—not as avant-garde as Gaultier's or Yohji Yamamoto's, but racier than Armani's. Their look has been described as subtly exotic. You'll find similar lines at Barneys and Charivari, but Madonna's stock is smaller and more rarified. The little wholesalers Mitrotti locates may lack cachet, but they're appreciated by men who understand raffish elegance.

The jackets have broad shoulders, but they're boxy and likely to be very long or very short—or whatever shape is about to be in mainstream fashion. The best of them—Manuel Ritz Pipo's—are cut from reproductions of sumptuous 1950s Chanel tweed and stripe fabrics, and they're lined in jazzy viscose checks. Their price range is $200 to $350. Yoko Ono buys stuff like this here and has it altered to size.

The suits sell for $450 to $700, shirts for $65 to $150, pants for $90 to $160, and sweaters for $100 to $150.

The very wide or very thin ties are especially wonderful in odd-colored prints—like black and gold stylized paisleys. Some of them are made from antique silk kimonos found in Japanese flea markets. Their prices range from $40 to $50.

Madonna is too provocative for bankers, real estate brokers, and matrimonial lawyers. But for movie moguls or entertainment lawyers seeking appropriate business attire, this is definitely the place.

During January and August, the merchandise is reduced by at least 50%. —L.D.

Madonna, 223 East 60th Street, 832-0268. Open Monday to Saturday, 11:30 A.M. to 7 P.M. AE, DC, checks.
Other branches: 822 Madison Avenue, 879-3748. Open the same hours.

LIBERTY OF LONDON

I N 1875, Arthur Lasenby Liberty opened a department store in London. He specialized in fabrics imported from the Orient. They grew wildly popular, so Liberty soon began manufacturing them in England, using Eastern dyeing, weaving, and printing techniques. The company's still producing its sumptuous silks, wool challis, and Egyptian cottons in the original floral and paisley designs taken from Japanese woodcuts and Indian shawls. But new prints have been added over the years, based, for instance, on costumes for the Ballets Russes, Art Nouveau and Deco motifs, and psychedelia.

In addition to dress and upholstery fabrics, Liberty's New York store sells a small range of ready-made clothes and accessories produced in England from its fabric lines. Traditional puff-sleeve, tie-back smock dresses for children sized 2 to 10 make perfect use of the small-print cottons, $55 to $100. These prints also work nicely on the adult bikinis with bows, $40 to $60; and the men's ties and suspenders, $15 to $27.50.

The womenswear consists mostly of disappointingly drab tuck-front and safari dresses and shirts with pointed collars, $50 to $250. But for under $60 you can find some ready-to-sew classic smock-top sundresses (that double as long skirts) and dirndl skirts that've already got smocked waistbands. All you do is stitch one seam and a hem—or Liberty's will do it for you for an extra $10.

Always desirable and gorgeous are the silk scarves in squares and oblongs—perfect gifts at $25 to $55.

Sales are held in January and late June, with markdowns of 25% to 50% and up to 80% on older merchandise.   —L.D.

Liberty of London, 229 East 60th Street, 888-1057. Open Monday to Friday, 11 A.M. to 7 P.M.; Saturday, 10 A.M. to 6 P.M. AE, MC, V, checks.

BETSEY JOHNSON
251 East 60th Street, 319-7699. See index for main listing.

BEN'S CLOTHES

B E N ' S Clothes looks like an old-time general store. Pants are piled high on counters, shirts and dresses lie folded on shelves along the walls, and coats and dresses get hung wherever there's room. Every bit of merchandise is out on display. But this is not your typical dry goods mart. The premise here is advanced sportswear, in the manner of Georges Marciano's Guess line—though this stuff is more exclusive. It's worn by Manhattan's most excruciatingly posh high school students as well as forever-young types like David Brenner, Frank Langella, and Armand Assante.

The mix of hard-to-find labels (many imports from southern Europe and the Third World) makes this place a good spot to buy moderately priced but fashionable sportswear basics. One of the leading men's brands is Shang-Hai, which specializes in broad-shouldered, viscose-blend jackets and 1930s-style textured baggy pants. Prices go from $50 to $120. Also available here are Longue Distance's exquisite cotton print shirts, cut for men, in the $50 range; and new-wave teenwear from a promising West German company called S. Oliver—sweats, T-shirts, cardigans, and sweaters in good jerseys and satin blends, $25 to $65.

The dresses are from CP Shades. They're basic jersey knits in pullover, button-front, and ballerina styles, and they sell for $40 to $60.   —L.D.

Ben's Clothes, 1149 Second Avenue, 753-4792. Open Monday to Wednesday, 10 A.M. to 7 P.M.; Thursday and Friday till 8 P.M.; Saturday, 11 A.M. to 6 P.M.; Sunday, noon to 5 P.M. AE, MC, V, checks.
  Other branches: Ben's Village, 7 Greenwich Avenue, 924-8145. Open Monday to Wednesday, 11 A.M. to 7 P.M.; Thursday and Friday till 9 P.M.; Saturday till 7 P.M.; and Sunday, noon to 6 P.M.

JÓIA

" A F T E R the 1950s," sighs Carol Caver, "all you have are conglomerations of previous styles. You need to go back to the 1930s and 1940s for innovative design and great fabrics and construction." She does, at Jóia, her little vintage clothing shop that's truly vintage. No "I Love Lucy" shirtwaists here, not even early Courrêges. Jóia's goods are the sort the young Bette Davis, Gene Tierney, and Rita Hayworth wore.

There's a beautiful selection of 1930s and 1940s day dresses with cunning sweetheart and jewel necklines, and some have peplums. These tend to be in small floral and geometric rayon prints—from the days when rayon was silky and drapey—and they sell for $65 to $85. Bias-cut satin, silk crepe, and lace evening gowns of the same era go for $120 to $200.

Other staples are 1940s and better 1950s Hawaiian shirts with real coconut-shell buttons, costing $45 to $150; good Western shirts and skirts, $65 to $120; and hand-embroidered silk piano shawls, $175 to $900.

In the showcase is a large selection of pre-1950s costume jewelry and Mexican and Indian silver, $35 and up.

The decor is supplied by numerous *objets d'art*—also for sale. Caver's specialty is Clarice Cliff's hand-painted pottery, dating from the 1920s to the 1940s. A jam jar or dish is about $150. Tea sets go up to $2,500.   —L.D.

Jóia, 1151 Second Avenue, 754-9017. Open Monday to Saturday, 10:30 A.M. to 6:30 P.M. AE, MC, V, checks.

IAN's UPTOWN
1151 Second Avenue, 838-3969. See Enz listing in index.

A. PETER PUSHBOTTOM

C O T T O N sweaters with a handknit look used to be hard to find. Now you can get them everywhere, strewn with knitted-in koala families or *trompe l'oeil* Vasarely-type graphics that cause immediate migraine. What's hard to find are solid-color classics in quality yarns.

A. Peter Pushbottom specializes in them. Its bookcase-lined walls are filled with cardigans and pullovers in several essential styles. The traditional long-sleeved crew neck comes in twenty-five colors, including a couple of rare and gorgeous bronzes and jade green. Especially nice are the V-neck cardigan with cables continued on the pockets, and the short-sleeved boat-neck pullover. A couple of oversized styles in stockinette and Shaker knits are offered in bulky yarn and look great over billowy floral print skirts.

With its subdued club ambience, Pushbottom is no doubt targeting the yuppies, but never mind. The sweaters will adjust to any personality. They're all hand-loomed out of domestic cotton that's guaranteed machine-washable and tumble-dry-able. Sizes range from women's small to men's extra-large. Prices are $40 to $100; most styles are about $60. A children's branch, Pushbottom for Kids, at 252 East 62nd Street, 888-3336, sells basic styles in sizes 2 to 7 for $30 to $45.   —L.D.

A. Peter Pushbottom, 1157 Second Avenue, 879-2600. Open Monday to Saturday, 11 A.M. to 7 P.M. AE, MC, V.

MASSAB BROTHERS

W H E N George Massab and his three brothers arrived from Syria in 1928, they opened a business selling rare Oriental carvings and a smattering of antique jewelry from around the world. Some of the *objets d'art* are still being stocked in dusty showcases along the wall, but today Massab Brothers, run by George's children, specializes in jewelry—a staggering amount of it.

The inventory is almost a library of precious and semiprecious pieces from the Georgian period through the Victorian, Art Nouveau, and Deco eras, and into 1950s cocktail baubles. There's a profusion in every conceivable category—fashionable and hopelessly outdated, delicate and garish, commonplace and arcane.

Diamond watches from the 1920s, including some Cartiers, go for $1,250 to $1,850. Diamond wedding and engagement

---

bands in dozens of settings are $770 and up—way up. But if you have the time and patience to look through the dozens of trays, you're bound to find some very special baubles in unique ethnic settings that are not inexpensive but are certainly Massab's strongest values for the money. There's a varied selection of ivory bangles, including an ongoing supply of large fossilized cuffs carved by a contemporary sculptor ($250 to $400). From China: clunky link bracelets with goldwork filigree, enamel, and tiger's eye (about $250). And handmade silver and gold earrings dating mainly from the 1920s. Most captivating among them are occasional silver Yemenite hearts traced with embossed silver dots. These come in several sizes ($75 to $150).

Also well stocked, and currently popular, are marquisite and paste jewelry from the 1920s and 1930s ($75 to $400). —L.D.

Massab Brothers, 782 Lexington Avenue, PL2-7139. Open Monday to Saturday, 10 A.M. to 6 P.M. AE, MC, V, checks.

MARAOLO

T H E Italian family shoe store reeking of good leathers at affordable prices is a dream that nearly comes true at Maraolo, a large shop with cozy sofas and subdued high-tech decor—the early 1960s variety as seen in vintage Antonioni movies.

Maraolo carries Giorgio Armani footwear and bags, bearing the casual but austere look of the designer's clothes, at surprisingly reasonable prices. His most expensive men's shoes are tie bucks with rubber soles, about $210. The women's shoes, priced at $90 to $180, have rounded toes, sensible heels, and uppers frequently made of offbeat materials like batik-printed suede and clear Lucite (Cinderella's glass slippers). Armani handbags come in leather and velour and include the occasional wacky plaid. They cost around $180 to $300.

Several other brands produced at Armani's hallowed shoe factory are also sold here. The most chic is the least expensive (under $100)—the Coca line for women, with low platform heels and wide toes, perfect for wearing with jazzy socks. The house brand includes basic pumps in several heights for $130; skimmer flats with bows, $80; cute summer boots in cowboy and moccasin styles, $185 to $285; lovely, clunky clogs, $45 to $75; and fur-lined winter boots, $180 to $300.

There's a children's line, too, if you'd like to see your kids in black patent tuxedo pumps and loafers with low vamps. They're priced about $75.

Sales with up to 60% reductions are held every year around Christmas and the Fourth of July.   —L.D.

Maraolo, 782 Lexington Avenue, 832-8182. Open Monday to Saturday, 10 A.M. to 7 P.M.; Thursday till 8 P.M.; Sunday, noon to 5 P.M. AE, DC, MC, V, checks.

BLOOMINGDALE'S

A jazz combo, seated precariously on a platform above the Lancôme cosmetics counter, performs a beautiful rendition of Duke Ellington's "Don't Get Around Much Anymore." No one listens. The perfume spray girls positioned at the escalators smile vacuously and hawk their wares in bored, shrill voices. Bloomingdale's, the legendary block-long department store that anchors the Upper East Side business district, has grown dull and raucous. Its ground floor, redecorated in 1970s disco style, has chiaroscuro lighting—more a drawback than a draw for sensitive shoppers.

It used to be "reliable"—a place to buy quality sewing notions and sensible shoes for toddlers. In the 1960s, when it started importing European boutique items, Bloomingdale's got hot. The shopping was good, and being seen there became a social necessity. It was great cruise and score turf, with never a minimum or a cover charge. But by the mid 1970s, the magic fire had cooled.

It's still a mob scene on late nights and a circus on weekends, only now it's jammed with new, nontrendy customers who buy late model Cuisinarts and Tahari suits. The clothing departments are flooded with homogenized goods.

But maybe Bloomingdale's has a right to survive. It's one of the few *real* department stores remaining in New York. It still sells curtains and rugs. It still has small appliances. And some of the clothing choices can actually be good. You have to admire the Paradox department for women, which features such forward designers as David Cameron, Premonville et Dewavrin, Romeo Gigli, and Patricia Clyne. You have to admit they were smart to set up satellite boutiques for both Agnès B. and the Girbauds in the contemporary sportswear department. And as for the expensive clothes, no other major store in New York offers quite the selection of major designers that Bloomingdale's does. Here you get an overview of Lagerfeld and Armani, Montana and Mugler, and nearly all the other notables of Paris and Milan. And during the semiannual sales, you can have your pick at this pantheon of European heavies in one go.

The best items on the main floor are the food department's smoked salmon, the vast range of cosmetics and perfumes, and the long-suffering makeup artists who offer their services (courtesy of various cosmetics companies) in virtual darkness. But don't come looking for them on a Saturday afternoon unless you like stampedes. —L.D.

Bloomingdale's, 1000 Third Avenue, 705-2000. Open Monday and Thursday, 10 A.M. to 9 P.M.; Tuesday, Wednesday, Friday, and Saturday till 6:30 P.M.; Sunday, noon to 6 P.M. AE, Bloomingdale's, DC, checks.

MISHON MISHON

R I G H T next to a hot dog depot on the corner of Lexington and 59th, the Upper East Side's most honky-tonk corner, is a large, busy jewelry store. No carpeting or suited sales help here.

In fact, no ambience at all. Mishon Mishon feels as if it were rented for an afternoon, which might lead you to expect low prices. Wrong. Few of the baubles cost under three figures.

The premise at work here is jewelry as fashion. Eddie Mishon, the owner, chooses avidly (too avidly) from a wide variety of successful and promising commercial designers. Most of them are derivative, their prices out of proportion with the workmanship and the quality of the metals and stones, but it's all here for those who would like to see an overview of contemporary "designer" jewelry, and occasionally there are oddball treasures.

The shop also stocks a wide range from interesting designers like Steve Vaubel, who does some understated matte-finish sterling pieces in the $250-to-$300 range. Debora Fine Yohai shows clean, slick chokers for about $150. And Stephen Dweck, who's in all the department stores and fashion magazines, has a selection of his black onyx, dyed ivory, and mother-of-pearl necklaces and earrings in organic-looking, free-form settings for $200 to $250.

Otherwise, the best items in the store are the sunglasses, particularly L.A. Eyeworks' chic nerd shades with heavy top rims that turn to wire at the bottom. These are $75 to $100.

It was delightful to see hat pins among the hair ornaments. But $25 is too high a price for colored glass stones pasted to a metal pin.

Fortunately, sales are frequent. There's usually a case or two with items going for half price.   —L.D.

Mishon, Mishon, 140 East 59th Street, 688-1886. Open Monday to Saturday, 10 A.M. to 7 P.M.; Thursday till 9 P.M.; Sunday, noon to 6 P.M. AE, DC, MC, V, checks.

Other branches: 410 Columbus Avenue, 769-2277. Open Monday to Saturday, 11 A.M. to 10 P.M.; Sunday, noon to 10 P.M.

BANANA REPUBLIC
130 East 59th Street, 751-5570. See index for main listing.

FIORUCCI

T H E ambience is calculated high-tech, aimed both at the preteen fashion victims who swoop down on the sweatshirts with the store's logo (curly-haired cherub twins in sunglasses) and at their mothers, who try on the rhinestone-studded sneakers.

The fashion intelligentsia love to hate Fiorucci. This warehouse-size Italian chain store (which manufactures most of its goods) specializes in marketing cutting-edge clothes and accessories that its intrepid trendspotters usually have little difficulty discovering in England. Some of the merchandise seems unutterably silly, but it's produced with élan and expertise, and this is the only shop in America that consistently offers us the very latest accoutrements of Eurotrash. In fact, a lot of the stuff is underrated.

The graphics are dazzling—as in the jungle-print bikinis and the cartoon beach towels. The totebags are gorgeously designed and come in rakish colors. A pick hit is the dresses. Usually every year there's an updated chambray or denim day dress made with classic Italian flair.

Despite the presence of Barry Hendrickson's wig salon (he does Cher's); a makeup department with an artiste on hand to help apply the green lipstick and yellow mascara; and a basement concession that offers the latest in downtown designer clothing—an accommodation for those who fear Manhattan below 59th Street—there are signs that Fiorucci is heading into the mainstream. It's now got a children's department selling $30 rompers, and Classic Nouveau, a line for men offering retro 1950s styling—code, perhaps, for 1980s clothing conservatism.

Clothing is priced from $15 for T-shirts to over $100 for dresses. The Maripolitan jewelry (as worn by Madonna) is 50 cents to $100. Bags are about $25 to $85.

Watch for end-of-season markdowns, to 50%.   —L.D.

Fiorucci, 127 East 59th Street, 751-5638. Open Monday and Thursday, 10 A.M. to 8 P.M.; Tuesday, Wednesday, and Friday till 6:30 P.M.; Saturday till 6 P.M.; and Sunday, noon to 5 P.M. Closed Sundays mid-July to mid-August. AE, MC, V, checks.

LINDA DRESNER

I N 1984, with less than six years' experience running a tony clothing boutique in a Michigan shopping mall, Linda Dresner decided to conquer New York. Passing on Madison Avenue (too commercial), she had the impudence to choose a cavernous Park Avenue location within the somewhat fusty but elegant ambit of Sarah Fredericks and Martha, purveyors of dowager couture.

No clothes are displayed in the massive front window. All you see is a handsome, casually dressed guard. The minimalist space inside is extraordinarily designed, with sight lines like a gallery's. Beyond a black cube the size of a kitchen (that hides a stockroom), you discover an inner sanctum with a huge, square marble table and wood-and-leather benches—spare but inviting and perfect for civilized rumination over the Gaultiers and Azzedines.

Dresner's designer roster also includes Vicky Tiel, Derek May, Premonville et Dewavrin, Rifit Ozbek, Romeo Gigli, and Soprani, among others. But it's not so much these formidable choices that have made her business the most directional, pacesetting ladies' shop in New York. It's her zealous editing of such disparate designers down to their most classical and lyrical. It's the way the clothes are displayed in recessed wall cabins that hold only one sample of each style, so that detail and cut stand out. And it's also Dresner's sales staff—enthusiastic about the merchandise, eager to explain its subtleties. There's a lot of personalized service here, regardless of your budget. This is not a boutique. Though the fashions are contemporary and the decor is distinctly post-tech, this is an updated frock salon. In spirit it is kin to all those overembellished couture salons that formed the backdrops for pivotal scenes in 1930s movies.

In an era when clothing design isn't at its most scintillating, Dresner shrewdly goes in for label mixing and eclectic buying. With several thousand dollars, it would be a cinch (and a delirious joy) to buy a closetful of clothes here and know you've tuned in to the most beautiful fashion being made today. But if your funds are limited, you could wind up with a sweater, skirt, and earring outfit for $400 to $500. The less-expensive items are private label—not best-seller knockoffs but basic shapes, some of them derived from Dresner's own treasured classics. They're priced from $150 to $800 or so and could become the basis of a wardrobe.

There are two relatively new but spectacular designers here. One is Martine Sitbon, who does modern tailored dresses and dinner suits with retro details like split peplums, $450 and up—worth saving for if you lust after exquisite cocktail-hour gear. The other is Tom Binns, a jeweler-genius who makes Dadaist cutlery pins, savage but elegant brooches from found objects, and, for Dresner alone, an astonishing line of Lucite faces with sterling backs. His prices are $150 to $1,200.

The January and June sales, with prices reduced by a third and more, offer a nice selection of leftovers. And here even the leftovers are incredible. —L.D.

Linda Dresner, 484 Park Avenue, 308-3177. Open Monday to Saturday, 10 A.M. to 6 P.M. AE, DC, MC, V, checks.

JACOMO

MANHATTAN'S most chic handbag mart is a little French-style boutique hidden away on a side street. No chrome. No counters. Just Louis XVI furnishings and exquisite goods lit by a crystal chandelier.

Jacomo's usual customers are the carriage trade, as befits the high-priced evening bags that have become the house specialties. They cost $600 to $2,500, but it's not the rare leathers like African anteater and shark that make them so expensive. It's their one-of-a-kind metal or antique Bakelite frames molded with totally fabulous Deco and Egyptian Revival motifs.

But actually, even more exciting because they are frequently affordable and beautifully designed, are the day bags. Many are the creations of Jim Kaplan, the owner, and reflect his Deco sensibility in shape and details. He does softest baby-calf shoulder bags, textured totes, and an absolutely marvelous briefcase clutch in waterproof gabardine. His rectangular version of the Chanel bag has a Lagerfeld sort of insouciance. The calf and kidskin bags go for $150 to $350. All the white leathers are washable.

Also available are reptile belts with 1930s buckles at $250 and up, and a small but can't-live-without selection of Deco jewelry, $45 to $300.

There's always a 30% to 50% sale on selected bags, including some vintage beauties.   —L.D.

Jacomo, 25 East 61st Street, 832-9038. Open Monday to Friday, 9:45 A.M. to 5:30 P.M.; Saturday, 10 A.M. to 5 P.M. Closed Saturday in July and August. AE, MC, V, checks.

PERRY ELLIS SHOES

E V E R Y self-respecting fashion house with licensing clout has produced a footwear line. In most cases, the shoes bear little connection to the clothes. Perry Ellis women's shoes are different. They exude the clean-cut but slightly antiquated style and the typical muted colors of the Ellis collections. They really do work perfectly with these clothes, as well as with many others.

The shoes are made in Italy, but they're moderately priced. Nothing's over $150. They're also comfortable.

This shop, the company's first freestanding boutique, resembles the Seventh Avenue showroom with an uncomplicated, updated Deco ambience—grainy sycamore wood, smoked glass, and luggage-leather couches.

There are several basic shoe styles: classic low-heeled perforated oxfords, sometimes with mesh, sometimes as two-tone spectator shoes; unembellished high heels in several different heights; and mid-heel Victorian-looking pumps with a strap across the arch.

Also in the line are canvas espadrilles, slender penny loafers, strappy metallic evening sandals, and flat winter boots (these sell for $220 to $360).

All the shoes have an oval toe and a fairly high vamp. They're available in 7 to 9 narrow and 5 to 10B, although 11s can sometimes be special-ordered.

End-of-season sales offer markdowns of 30% to 50%. —L.D.

Perry Ellis Shoes, 680 Madison Avenue, 980-7012. Open Monday to Friday, 10 A.M. to 7 P.M.; Saturday till 6 P.M. AE, MC, V, checks.

FOGAL

T H E world's greatest hosiery store has an image problem. Unspeakably gorgeous and luxurious as Fogal's Swiss-made stockings, panty hose, and socks are, they're basically perishables. Nylons always run and socks get holes. Yet the old-money ambience—Deco chandelier, pearwood cabinets, marble floor—is calculated to convince us that these dry goods are fine, expensive lingerie.

It doesn't take much persuasion. The basic sheer and opaque panty hose may cost just under $10, but they come in 105 colors, most of which you'll never find anywhere else, and, like all Fogal nylons, they last several times longer than other brands. Many styles are sized extra small to extra, extra large. There's a dressing room for trying samples.

Particularly heartstopping is the bodystocking with camisole top and spaghetti straps. It comes in sheer, opaque, various laces, and cotton and cashmere blends, and it cries out to be exhibited under a transparent dress or on its own for nonchalant evenings at home.

If you want texture, Fogal has polka dots, fans, op art patterns, tweeds, seams, glitter, and the best texture of all—silk.

If you seek to drive your sexual partner wild with desire, try the garterless stockings with elastic tops, the high-cut lace bikini panty hose, or the ones with cutouts that mimic a garter belt. Or, to send a hint, buy the panty hose decorated with red kisses all the way up the legs and thighs.

The men's selection seems conservative after this—only thirty colors of plain ankle and over-the-calf socks. There are, however, silks, cashmere-silk blends, and semiopaque tuxedo socks with baguettes.

Prices start at $7.50 for stretch sheers and ascend to $185 for cashmere tights. Be prepared to spend *minimally* $20 for the fancy indulgences.   —L.D.

Fogal, 680 Madison Avenue, 759-9782. Open Monday to Saturday, 10 A.M. to 6 P.M. AE, DC, JCB, MC, V, checks.
Other branches: 510 Madison Avenue, 355-3254. Open the same hours.

FAUSTO SANTINI

F R O M the all-glass exterior, it looks like a swank fish tank. Inside, surrounded by white tiles, you'll feel as if you're in a high-tech bathhouse. The hard marble floor isn't just for show, explains the manager. It's an ideal surface for fitting the shoes.

Fausto Santini, the only American branch of an Italian retailing and manufacturing chain, sells footwear as cleverly crafted as its decor. The shoes here are certifiably fashionable. They can accommodate all manner of expensive and avant-garde clothes. Those who lust after Manolo Blahnik but can't afford him often find these shoes acceptable substitutes. Their prices are reasonable enough for you to feel like Imelda Marcos on a half-hour shopping spree. The shoes go for $60 to $120, the boots for $150 to $220.

Styles change, of course, but for example last season's look was basically plain, with long, pointy toes, broad, curved heels, and stately high vamps. Its jazziness came from the materials.

Summer flats and heels—and some of the men's tie oxfords and loafers—were covered in silk and linen fabric with large jungle florals and abstract prints that gave the shoes a zany, asymmetrical look.

The sandals are often clunky platform affairs with a lot of multicolored straps. The boots may have rolltops with print fabric inside. Like everything else here, they're immensely comfortable even if they don't last as long as expensive shoes.

—L.D.

Fausto Santini, 697 Madison Avenue, 838-1835. Open Monday to Friday, 10:30 A.M. to 6:30 P.M.; Saturday till 6 P.M. AE, MC, V, checks.

ADDISON ON MADISON

A L L you get at Addison on Madison are men's pure cotton poplin dress shirts and their accoutrements—silk neckwear and pocket squares.

The long, narrow shop, with suitable pinstripe wallpaper and a settee and stripped-pine hutch positioned at the entrance, reeks of preppiness—Gallic variety. All the shirts are manu-factured at Addison's own factories in France, and they display the strange and uncanny French expertise at rendering the minutiae of orthodox preppiness—from tattersall plaids and bold Bengal stripes to mother-of-pearl buttons, single-needle tailoring, and full American cut.

Elsewhere, good poplin shirts cost upwards of $75. Most of Addison's shirts are $49 to $55. They come in five basic styles, all named for presidents who wore them. The Adams has a 3-inch straight-point collar and French double cuffs. The Madison has a 2¾-inch spread collar and single-button cuffs. The Hoover's a button-down Madison. The Coolidge is a button-down with a white collar, and the Garfield is a Madison with a white spread collar. The tuxedo shirt with forward wing-tip collar and double French cuffs (about $80) is named after John F.

Kennedy. Your basic, standard shantung and crepe de chine ties are $22 to $24. Bow ties, some pretied, are $14, and the solid silk pocket squares go for $12.

If you want to browse in peace, come early in the week. The shop gets busy Thursdays through Saturdays. —L.D.

Addison on Madison, 698 Madison Avenue, 308-2660. Open Monday to Saturday, 10 A.M. to 6:30 P.M. MC, V, checks.

STEPHANE KÉLIAN

N O cozy sofas, plush carpets, or the other living room amenities you have come to expect at Madison Avenue shoe salons. The decor at Stephane Kélian is slick white marble—expensive, but otherwise out of sync with the basically casual, funky footwear this Armenian in Paris designs.

Kélian produces four shoe lines—his own, Gaultier's, Montana's, and sneakers for American Eagle. They're all sold at the New York flagship boutique, and they range in style from traditional business pumps with his trademark woven leather vamps to raucous takes on classics. He built his signature-line reputation on men's leather slip-ons that are more like sophisticated moccasins. They're so soft, they bend in half. His typical women's shoes tend toward Olive Oyl clunky retro styling in outré materials. Last season he did sling-back wedgies and ballerina flats in pony skin.

In the Gaultier collection, odd materials like quilted satin, iridescent taffeta, and boot elastic turn up. Toes are squared off, soles extended. The look is high kitsch.

The Montana line has a tailored but offbeat elegance. Heels take on thickish comma shapes and slingbacks may display wide straps, like Bette Davis's in *The Letter.*

Men's shoes average about $225; women's, about $175. The American Eagle high-top sneakers come in prints and plaids and often lack tongues. They're about $30.

Woven leather belts and bags to match some of the shoes are $75 to $150.

Watch for the end-of-season sales here, with markdowns of 30% to 40%.   —L.D.

Stephane Kélian, 702 Madison Avenue, 980-1919. Open Monday to Friday, 10 A.M. to 6 P.M.; Saturday, 11 A.M. to 6 P.M. AE, MC, V, checks.
   Other branches: 100 West 72nd Street, 769-3344. Open Monday to Friday, noon to 8 P.M.; Saturday, 11 A.M. to 7 P.M.; Sunday, 1 P.M. to 6 P.M.

FURLA

FURLA is a very intelligent Bolognese operation, manufacturing, retailing, and wholesaling women's accessories. It applies postmodernism to its production of knockoff handbags. They're not slavish, smarmy department store-type imitations, but witty, charming, unabashedly fake-looking retakes on classics.

The Vuitton satchel, for instance. Furla removed its execrable trademark print and redid it in trendy colors. The Kelly bag comes not in costly, silken Hermès kid (though God knows *that* would be desirable), but in an ersatz imaginary-animal hide that looks simultaneously phony and elegant. There are some comely looking string, feed, camera, and tote bags, too, most in pressed calf—not the greatest leather in the world, but respectable enough to last a couple of seasons. Favorites here are the extra-wide doctor's bag and the pretty clutches with gathered tops.

All the bags are canvas lined and given zippered inner compartments. Many styles come in several sizes—to accommodate varying heights. Best of all are the prices, ranging from $35 for a tiny Chanel-style bag to $250 for a large briefcase. Most are $80 to $160.

Also good: wallets, from $15 to $55; cowboy belts and belts

encrusted with jewels, $25 to $80; and generously sized wool challis shawls, $60 to $80.

Watch for end-of-season sales here around February and July. —L.D.

Furla, 705 Madison Avenue, 755-8986. Open Monday to Saturday, 10 A.M. to 6 P.M. AE, CB, Discover, DC, JCB, MC, V.

Other branches: 159 Columbus Avenue, 874-6119. Open Monday to Saturday, noon to 7:30 P.M.; Sunday, 1 P.M. to 7 P.M.

M. J. KNOUD, INC.

T H E shop is long and narrow, with a coffered ceiling and milk glass lights. The dark wooden display fixtures with glass doors haven't changed since 1926, when Knoud's opened on Madison Avenue. One of the last of the specialty houses that's managed to survive in this neighborhood, Knoud has first-quality English-style riding equipment as its stock-in-trade.

The clothes never vary. Many of them, like the frock coats and britches, are desirably chic in nonequestrian circumstances and have been imitated by numerous designers (especially Ralph Lauren, who used to come in to study the goods). You can buy knockoffs all over, but the originals may be less expensive.

Ready-made hacking jackets go for $200 to $650 here. See them, and you'll know the meaning of a tailored, constructed jacket. Britches and jodhpurs are $80 to $140; and rubberized Egyptian cotton riding raincoats, split from the waist, cost under $285.

The boot department carries all the traditional riding styles, from elastic-sided jodhpur shoes to lace-front and closed-front dress boots. They're priced at $265 to $550. Wooden boot trees cost a mind-boggling $300.

Fortunately, certain of the lower-priced items are fetching,

---

too, like the plain leather bridle belts with brass horseshoe buckle for under $35, and the Guernsey wool riding sweaters with a garter stitch border where you usually find ribbing, about $125.   —L.D.

M. J. Knoud, Inc., 716 Madison Avenue, 838-1434. Open Monday to Saturday, 9 A.M. to 5 P.M. Closed Saturday from June to August. AE, Discover, MC, V, checks.

LA BAGAGERIE

HANDBAGS, pullmans, duffels, vanity cases, and attachés are neatly lined up everywhere you look in La Bagagerie. Somehow this store, the only American branch of a French manufacturing and retailing chain, always manages to look orderly and elegant. Yet here in this shrine of the Western world's most touted handbags, the most vaunted store of its kind in New York, you falter and question their meaning. La Bagagerie specializes in handbags as fashion concepts. They produce their versions of all the current styles—Chanel and Kelly, hobo, knapsack, doctor's satchel—each in at least eight colors. But the spark of innovation is lacking—they begin to look like dowdy appendages. Still, their quality and workmanship are far above average and some are rather special, like the long, strapped hunting bags and the legal-size briefcase totes with detachable clutch bags. Both of these are produced in Madras kid, the house specialty leather that's tight-grained, absorbent, and gives good mileage.

Prices range from $45 for an envelope clutch to $2,000 for crocodile and lizard. Most of the large totes and shoulder bags are between $150 and $300.

There are wide selections of men's bags; classic and magnificent briefcases and attachés, $120 to $750; and excellent basic belts, $25 to $100.

Half-price clearances are held every January and July. It's worth calling in advance to get the opening date and arrive that morning. —L.D.

La Bagagerie, 727 Madison Avenue, 758-6570. Open Monday to Saturday, 10 A.M. to 6:30 P.M. AE, MC, V, checks.

DIANNE B.

D I A N N E B.'s Madison Avenue shop was the first of her New York stores, setting a standard of innovative, serious design for its progeny, although each store has a different character. This one, exclusively for women, has carried Issey Miyake and Dorothée Bis since it opened in 1976, and they're still available on the main floor, along with Gaultier, Castelbajac, and other advanced Europeans. The store also has a secluded mezzanine that's become a sort of long-term swing shop for individual designers of favor. It's an austere, minimalist space. The only decor on the gray tile ceramic floor is a black leather chaise that looks as if it's awaiting a tryst. Fitting. The mezzanine is currently consecrated to Azzedine Alaïa, the cultish but misunderstood Tunisian who's brought sex back to fashion.

In the midst of the oversized-clothing era, this dressmaker-turned-ready-to-wear-magnate resuscitated the hourglass silhouette. His snug knits and tights revealed bulges even on the emaciated. The American verdict: Azzedine may be glamorous and influential, but he's cruel to anyone who isn't super-skinny or Raquel Welch.

We're such prudes. Azzedine celebrates North African voluptuousness. Unexercised curves and residual baby fat are intended to show. If you run in expensive fashion circles and you can mold his size large (about a 10 or 12) or smaller around your flesh without straining the fabric, wear it. And if you can't or won't, he's been designing looser things of late.

The only problems are that his turnouts—the peplum jackets and skirts with low fishtails and the body-hugging denim dresses with diagonal zippers—are getting instantly recognizable, and his prices hover around $600. But if you buy his basic, lush acetate bodysuit, you'll have the best bodysuit ever. It costs about $150 and comes in truly divine colors like indigo, deepest lavender, and mustard.

End-of-season sales are held in July and December, with markdowns of 30% to 50%.   —L.D.

Dianne B., 729 Madison Avenue, 759-0988. Open Monday to Saturday, 10 A.M. to 6 P.M. AE, DC, MC, V, checks.

Other branches: See index for other Dianne B. stores, each of which carries different merchandise.

WALTER STEIGER

T H E maroon lacquer exterior and tiny recessed windows prepare you for indescribable treasures inside. The interior is an exquisite parlor with mirrored walls and brass lamps. You would wish to have intellectual discussions on the leather settees. But the terra-cotta carpeting, adorned with a single Oriental rug, is for trying on the designer shoes.

They're all by Walter Steiger, son of a Swiss shoemaker, who's well established in the pantheon of world-acclaimed footwear couturiers. Steiger concentrates on classic, formal styles, but always with contemporary quirks. His men's shoes are known for their minimalist vamps; his women's, for their innovative heels, some of which look like delicate sway-back commas, while others are pyramids with bumps and knifebacks. Scores of imitators mimic them but don't capture Steiger's clean, sculpted flow through the rest of the shoe.

His toes tend to be pointy, toplines frequently curved or curlicued. His d'orsay slip-ons, with sides that dip in the middle, are the most elegant business-to-dress shoes imaginable—

particularly in two-tone dyed snakeskin or crocodile. These could probably see you through several years of frequent wear.

Boots and evening shoes are similarly minimalist but elegant.

Though prices can climb above $500, most styles cost slightly over $200. There's a handsome sale at the end of each season.   —L.D.

Walter Steiger, 739 Madison Avenue, 570-1212. Open Monday to Saturday, 10 A.M. to 6 P.M. AE, MC, V, checks.

BETSEY BUNKY NINI

B A C K in the 1960s, Betsey Bunky Nini was a cute shop on East 53rd Street. One of its owners was Betsey Johnson, and the wares were offbeat but pretty, like the clothes she's continued designing. But the store's since moved to Madison Avenue, changed owners, matured, and streamlined its name. Its prices are higher, the goods more subdued. In contrast to Dianne B. just down the street, nothing's extreme, iconoclastic, or Japanese here. The emphasis is on classic things. But the store retains vestiges of its demure past. It carries European high flyers like Montana and Byblos, but they're edited down to their daintiest looks.

Shelved at the front is New York's prettiest selection of wool and cotton hand- and machine-knit sweaters, made by British knit geniuses like Artwork, Marion Foale, and Christopher Fisher. They're priced from $150 to $500.

The designerware includes smart, understated separates, suits, and dresses from not-yet-well-known Americans. For example, the store might feature Bosha Johnson, who does elegant knits and gorgeous lace and chiffon flapper dresses. Her prices are $200 to $1,200. Patricia Clyne, who used to work at the shop, has a line of tailored, feminine classics that go from $125 to $300. The sportswear might include Nancy Heller's jerseys and Go Silk's soft silks and linens, $80 to $300.

The accessories are as fastidiously chosen as the clothes and include Navarro's trinket-trimmed pins, $200 to $350, and Montana's quirky takes on classic belts, $150 to $300.

Every January and July, the stock goes on sale at 30% to 75% reductions. —L.D.

Betsey Bunky Nini, 746 Madison Avenue, 744-6716. Open Monday to Friday, 10:30 A.M. to 6 P.M.; Saturday, 11 A.M. to 6 P.M. AE, Discover, MC, V, checks.

FIL À FIL

FIL À FIL, a French manufacturer-retailer, is threatening to mushroom all over America. It already has more than forty boutiques in Europe—clone stores with a Scandinavian pine supermarket atmosphere. The Madison Avenue branch was its first here, soon joined by a sister store in Rockefeller Center.

The major goods are full-cut men's and women's shirts (the shop's name refers to a common French shirting weave), all folded neatly and displayed on racks. Men's double-seam styles come in solids and stripes with tape, spread, wide button-down, classic, tuxedo, and Madison collars. They're around $60.

Women's styles range from good and plain white pique drop-shoulder classics with rounded Claudine collars to novelties the French are clever at concocting. The most appealing is a V-neck style with button-down collar. Prices go from $60 to $75.

The accessories, which seem aimed for career professionals at work and play, include women's bow and men's insignia ties (about $35), silk scarves ($45 to $60), wool V-neck sweaters (about $60 to $70), printed cotton scuffs with foam padding inside (under $25), and argyle socks (about $12). —L.D.

Fil à Fil, 758 Madison Avenue, 772-2023. Open Monday to Saturday, 10 A.M. to 6:30 P.M. AE, CB, DC, MC, V, checks.
Other branches: 610 Fifth Avenue, 247-4290. Open the same hours.

HENRY LEHR

772 Madison Avenue, 535-1021. See index for main listing.

LA LINGERIE

T H E furnishings are a cinnabar Chinese secretary overflowing with garter belts, a very good Oriental rug, and black lacquer accents. This is not a shop for picking up foundation garments. "We sell to the couture customer," explains Diane Tucker, the manager. "Our goods are meant to be worn before she puts on her Ungaro and after she takes it off." There are many who reckon La Lingerie has the finest selection of night finery and frilly underwear in the country.

Now here's the truth: The smalls—the lacy Perla bras from Italy that start at $60, the high-cut silk bikinis (about $135), and the perfect British-made silk G-strings that customers collect in every color at $60 each—are exquisite and definitely worth splurging on. Also perfection in their way are the sluttish high-heeled French bedroom mules ($150) and the long cashmere V-neck cardigan and indoor jogging suits (about $1,600).

But the shop's hideously expensive forte items—its $1,500 to $8,000 handmade gown and peignoir sets from Italy—are strewn with so much lace and intricate needlework that they end up being frumpy and fussy, like Lily Tomlin's nightgowns in *All of Me.* Maybe sexy underwear simply has got to be cheap.

—L.D.

La Lingerie, 792 Madison Avenue, 772-9797. Open Monday to Saturday, 9:30 A.M. to 6:30 P.M.; Thursday till 7:30 P.M. AE, CB, DC, MC, V.

Other branches: 725 Fifth Avenue in the Trump Tower, 980-8811; also features European bed linens. Open Monday to Saturday, 10 A.M. to 6 P.M.

SONIA RYKIEL

S O N I A Rykiel started out in the 1960s as a Parisian boutique owner and became one of the first ready-to-wear designers to topple the reign of the couture. Like Chanel, who some regard as her guiding spirit, she favors comfortable, practical clothes.

Rykiel's cut is essentially stark and untailored—soft knits and velours, often in black (truly a basic in her case) juxtaposed with ivory or peach. These combinations often appear in broad or narrow stripes. Individual pieces, like her U-neck sweaters, narrow V-neck jackets, and full-leg trousers with big, deep pockets frequently in unexpected places, are terrific wardrobe classics. Prices for these collection items go from $300 for a little sweater to over $1,000 for cashmere.

But, despite the excellent fabrications, a fully orchestrated Rykiel ensemble can be clownish, overwhelmed by the bows and ties that are her trademark gimmicks. Oddly enough, Rykiel's two less-expensive lines escape the occasional garishness of her higher-priced clothes while echoing their shapes, colors, and her signature outside seams. Some of the gorgeous at-home and lingerie pieces, $100 to $300, could also go public as eveningwear. The T-shirt jersey separates and dresses ($60 to $100) can be absolutely marvelous, well worth a stop at this generally pricey boutique. Also for sale here are Rykiel's wonderful shoulder bags and totes, $300 to $400.   —L.D.

Sonia Rykiel, 792 Madison Avenue, 744-0880. Open Monday to Saturday, 9:30 A.M. to 6:30 P.M.; Thursday till 7:30 P.M. AE, CB, DC, MC, V, checks.

SCALERA

M O S T of the clientele here is carriage trade, and trendy New Yorkers blindly pass Scalera by on their appointed rounds of

Sonia Rykiel and Joseph Tricot. But this little Italian shop specializes in the sort of knitwear that provides the basics in truly classic wardrobes.

Piled everywhere in crinkly plastic bags are sweaters—a huge selection in sizes 6 to 20 in numerous styles: plain and frilled, collared, cowled, V-necked, or zipped at the back. Some (the sort of lightweight tops you put on under vintage gabardine suits) are body-hugging with small shoulder pads. Others are oversized. Many come textured with diamonds and cables.

But the allure of these sweaters is not only their styling but their outrageously sensual yarns—cotton jersey that feels like silk, almost liquidy silk with cashmere, and sinuous pure silk.

Scalera sells suits, too, the best of them unadorned styles with Chanelish jackets. Other finds here are the silk knit skirts with delicate panel pleats below the hipline, as well as basic slim pull-ons.

Considering the luxurious materials, prices are relatively reasonable. Cotton knits go from $70 to $250 (for shirtdresses). Silk sweaters start at $110 for a sleeveless suit shell and go to about $235. Skirts are about $155, and suits cost $225 and up.

An annex in a nearby office building carries out-of-season stock and mostly drab markdowns. But the cashmere clearances could be interesting. —L.D.

Scalera, 796 Madison Avenue, 988-3344. Open Monday to Saturday, 10 A.M. to 6 P.M. Scalera Annex, 790 Madison Avenue, 517-7417. Open Monday to Saturday, 10 A.M. to 5:30 P.M. AE, DC, MC, V, checks.

EMANUEL UNGARO

UNGARO has been known to design bankers' striped suits, but they'll be cut in pink or fuschia jacquard and have an ultra-sexy feminine line. Having trained as a tailor with Balenciaga, he's adept at devising drapery ploys that reveal the body even when it's all covered up.

He's the prototypical party-dress designer, brilliant at creating a sexy going-out look that manages to reek of high style, quite possibly because he's so liberal in his use of luscious—truly beautiful—silk prints in a myriad of jewel colors. His clothes are wild celebrations of a woman's body. Ungaro is also famous for his chemises and saucy peplum suits, his tunic-length jackets over tight skirts, his turbans and floppy berets. These are indeed uniforms for ladies who lunch and, lately, also for business-women at the pinnacle of their careers who've tired of Armani. But Ungaro is enormously influential and, every season, sets the standard for old-fashioned finery that runs the gamut from tasteful to tarty. It's no doubt he who inspires the wardrobe for *Dynasty.* (And as if in rebellion, he's recently been doing some almost simple sportswear separates.)

The Ungaro boutique is the place to scout the genuine article, though if you are not expensively turned out, you risk the sales staff's disdain. Collection dresses, bearing Ungaro's Parallele label, go from $850 to $2,700; the simplest blouses are over $400; and sexy little skirts start at $250. But even if you can afford these prices, be forewarned that a lot of this stuff seems to be cut for the big-chested and slim-hipped (think Joan Collins and Linda Evans), and major alterations—costly if they're well done—may be needed. Also, to look truly devastating in Ungaro, a woman needs a great sense of restraint. Hair and makeup shouldn't be overdone. With clothes like his that speak a universal language of lust, adding to the allure might be distasteful.

Still, in every woman's life there are occasions—for example, reviving an old love affair—when, to be utterly blunt, appearance is all. For times like these, Ungaro could well be your best ally, and you'd feel secure knowing he was waiting in your closet. So maybe you should consider a blouse or a skirt, or, in a pinch, one of his silk or challis scarves priced at $250 to $400.

Recently, Ungaro began manufacturing second and third lines, labeled Solo Donna and Prima Donna, that sell for a half to a quarter of the prices of his Parallele collection. Though they lack the sumptuous fabrications, they're sexy and elegant and can be worn on a daily basis by real people. Their functionalism is woefully missing from his expensive clothes. Department stores sell these lines, but they *aren't* available at the Madison Avenue boutique—a privately owned venture that's chosen not to sully Ungaro's haute image with poor-girl dresses for a couple of hundred bucks.

The multitudinous mirrors and gold showcases make for a surprisingly drab, moneyed decor—the most charmless of all the designer boutiques in New York. It's out of whack with all those lush clothes. And the mirrors aim straight for the narcissism that is undoubtedly part of—though hardly all of—Ungaro's appeal.

January and July sales offer 30% to 50% markdowns. —L.D.

Emanuel Ungaro, 803 Madison Avenue, 249-4090. Open Monday to Saturday, 9:30 A.M. to 6:30 P.M.; Thursday till 7:30 P.M. AE, DC, MC, V, checks.

JOSEPH TRICOT

WHENEVER a trend hits London, you can count on Joseph Ettedgui to market it. He's a clothing tycoon, speculating not quite at the leading edge but very, very close to it. Joseph Tricot, his first freestanding New York venture, sells only a smattering of his knits—not the wildest stuff but representative of his precise, minimalist sensibility.

Joseph tops are oversized, usually with polo neck collars or off-the-shoulder necklines, with sleeves that are sometimes so long they must be pushed to the elbow. Typical bottoms are cuffed leggings and narrow tube skirts. Lately, some of his skirts have been showing below-the-knee flares. Only the very thin can wear such items with impunity. But the unisized polo collar dresses give everyone, regardless of size, the correct Dickensian poor-girl look.

Yarns and colors are gorgeous. Joseph's summer stretch rayon-acrylic blend has a raffish sheen. His bulky wool and cotton yarns give a handmade look to his sweaters and leggings. His navy is a lush, purpled indigo, his yellow an acidic chrome. But mostly he sticks to basic cream and black. These are the colors of his minimalist post-tech shop with plain, sanded wood floors. The only decor is supplied by the pretty, waiflike English salesgirls.

There's also a line of lightweight French cotton jersey separates with prices starting at $45. Most sweaters and skirts are between $100 and $200, and sweater coats are about $250.

Accessories here are sublime, particularly the large doctor's satchel, under $250, and the French leather belts with silver trim, $65 to $150.

Sales are in January and July; markdowns start at 30%. —L.D.

Joseph Tricot, 804 Madison Avenue, 570-0077. Open Monday to Saturday, 10 A.M. to 6:30 P.M.; Thursday, 10:30 A.M. to 7 P.M. AE, MC, V, checks.

Other branches: 320 Columbus Avenue, 787-0036. Open Monday to Saturday, 11 A.M. to 7 P.M.; Sunday, noon to 6 P.M.

GIANNI VERSACE

V E R S A C E is the deviate among the Milanese tailor-designers. He does a lot of complex layering, toga draping, and asymmetrical cuts, and he sells his clothes to rock stars who aim for the sexy ragamuffin look but want it in the exquisite silks and wool crepes Versace is known for.

In his somberly appointed New York boutique with gray and steel surfaces and marble floors, prices range from $25 for a pleated silk scarf to $5,000 for a metal mesh dress. Separates, suits, dresses, and coats are mostly in the $450-to-$1,000 range, for which you get a lot of fine detailing and subtle draping.

If $600 suddenly blows your way, you wouldn't regret springing for his perennial collarless wool crepe jacket in traditional navy but with exaggerated dolman sleeves, deep side vents, and low-slung gargantuan pockets—all Versace trademarks. This is a refreshing take on the blazer that could probably see you through the 1980s and 1990s.

Versace's most recent men's line—with crinkly shirtings and textured suits with baggy pants—seems based on an oversized Japanese aesthetic. Ten years ago, it was shocking. Today, his menswear is looking vaguely conservative. Hip businessmen should be able to carry off the Versace look with no trouble. Suits go for $900 to $1,200; shirts for $120 to $400; and sweaters from $500 to $2,000.

But you can also buy the look for less. Men's dress shirts with all those outrageous pockets (as if the wearer couldn't afford a wallet) start at $100. Bias-cut T-shirts go for slightly more. And for about the same price, you can buy a stretchy 17½-inch viscose tube to wear as a hip sash, miniskirt, neck cowl, or strapless top.

That is, if you haven't been ambushed by the handbags. Versace's beautiful silken suede pouches and little envelopes with fan spoke motifs exude his funky grace. They go for $200 to $400.

Sales are held at the end of each season, with 50% markdowns on women's clothes and 40% on men's.   —L.D.

Gianni Versace, 816 Madison Avenue, 744-5572. Open Monday to Saturday, 10:30 A.M. to 6:30 P.M. AE, DC, MC, V, checks.

GIORGIO ARMANI

A L L the other Italian designers went for marble decor. Armani the spartan chose indoor tennis court materials for his black and taupe interior. Admittedly, his Madison Avenue townhouse is no hovel. But the austere ambience is unmistakable. Sales help are instructed to wear tame hairdos and identical Armani suits.

Primarily, Armani is a haberdasher who's changed the look of menswear. It's said that his business clothes have a built-in slouch that's blurred the distinction between tailored and casual attire. His men's suits have an unconstructed cut, wide lapels, and sometimes slightly raffish stripes to juxtapose with the stripes of his narrow-collared shirts. While it's no longer avant-garde, this line is constantly imitated, but the genuine articles have a perfection. They'd better, at $900 per suit, $500 per jacket, and over $200 for a shirt.

In tune with the direction of late twentieth-century social custom, Armani women look like sexy men. His women's cuts are based on men's proportions, with strong shoulders and side tapering. His $1,000 blazer is the ultimate dress-for-success item, luxurious without being obviously rich. He also does some wonderful V-neck and mandarin-collar jackets.

Lately, Armani's been designing silk and chiffon eveningwear, as tailored as his day pieces but laminated with thin plastic paillettes—his version of sequins. They sell for $500 to $8,000. He's also doing men's and women's sleepwear and lingerie. The underwear, particularly, captures his sensual-but-pure look and sells for $25 to $75.

Armani's moderately priced men's and women's Emporio department lacks his lush fabrics and styling details. Most of its wares have an advanced L. L. Bean aura, but not the wonderful open-back cotton shirts, about $100.

The children's line is a telling tour-de-force triumph of American-inspired sobriety and sells for $35 to $100.

End-of-season sales are held in early January and late July.

—L.D.

Giorgio Armani, 815 Madison Avenue, 988-9191. Open Monday to Saturday, 10 A.M. to 6 P.M. AE, MC, V.

JOAN & DAVID

J O A N and David Helpern sell their graceful, never clunky shoes for men and women all over town, but only here can you find their whole line—including luggage, belts, umbrellas, bathrobes, and shawls—all together. But the best buys are the shoes—especially those for women that go from work to party.

All the shoes have that supple, light silhouette that is clearly Joan and David. Leathers are glove soft. Toes have a graceful, slightly elongated curve. These shoes are for those who like an understated au courant look. Recently, for example, there have been patent leather low-heeled shoes cut out on the sides that doubled for both day and evening, as well as taffeta ones with lace inserts around the toe, both in the $110 range. While the top price for shoes here is around $250 (and for boots $325), there are always shoes for a nonscary average of $125.

Men's shoes are limited, with a calfskin loafer at $140 and a crocodile one at $525.

Girls' party shoes—variations of basic pumps colored in black, white, or perhaps the more fanciful gold and silver—are highly overpriced at $75 to $85, but after all, this is one of the few sources in the city for golden slippers.

End-of-season sales here offer 20% to 50% markdowns.

—E.L.

Joan & David, 816 Madison Avenue, 772-3970. Open Monday to Saturday, 10 A.M. to 6 P.M. AE, CB, DC, MC, V, checks.

MADONNA
822 Madison Avenue, 879-3748. See index for main listing.

VALENTINO

"VALENTINO, live a hundred years," willed Jackie Onassis, who wore him to her second wedding. The Farah Diba chose him, too, in her last official appearance before making her getaway from Iran. He's the perfect answer when you need to look inviolable and self-possessed under questionable circumstances. The rich and famous don't want to be photographed in anything else.

It's easy to dismiss the Sheik of Chic as an inaccessible society designer whose prices can climb into the five figures. But Valentino is cunning and skilled. He knows how to combine precise Italian tailoring with sassy French couture. He doesn't mind giving a woman her best shot at looking gorgeous, mainstream-style.

His trademark turnout, a broad-shouldered, slim-hipped jacket coat or blouson over a jewel-neckline blouse and a short sexy skirt, is being bought by businesswomen who no longer need to dress for success—they've arrived. Prices start at $175 for a simple suit shell, $250 for skirts, and $350 for blouses.

Valentino's menswear is known for its classic jackets with wide, peaked lapels and lush fabric blends. His suits are absolutely gorgeous, a splendid personal reward for hard work, for those who can afford to pay $600 to $1,200 per suit.

The New York salon, modeled on home base in Rome, is decorated as an impersonal palazzo—with black marble tables with inlaid Vs (a little tacky, no?) in a series of small rooms where you could bump into Catherine Deneuve.

If you're a poor person who wants to exude Valentino's aura, those slim skirts are occasionally on sale at the end of the season, and his $60 men's ties in subtle prints could add allure to a Mernsmart suit. —L.D.

Valentino, 825 Madison Avenue, 744-0200. Open Monday to Saturday, 10 A.M. to 6 P.M. AE, CB, DC, MC, V, checks.

K E N Z O

K E N Z O is a true cross-cultural hybrid. He was the first major Japanese designer to settle in Paris—in 1965. His original designs were influenced by French street fashions, and from the start he knew in his fingertips how to combine austere Orientalia with Parisian frills.

Though his clothes can be expensive—up to $600 for a silk suit—his image remains casual and irreverent. It's conveyed even in the wood scaffolding furnishings of his New York store. But the renegade charm of his early collections has given way to commercialism. Some of his kimono tops now seem like cheap ethnic effects. His construction and fabrications can be poor.

Although his silhouettes aren't innovative, Kenzo's colors—especially his color combinations—have a master's touch. Nobody does cabbage-rose prints and antique stripes like Kenzo does. He still offers some oversized dresses, $200 to $300, that are particular favorites of expectant mothers. His wool tunics and asymmetrical coats are standouts every winter.

For his excellent menswear line, he designs conservative suits in colorful, racy glen plaids and leopardskin prints, $200 to $300. They're shown with flamboyant floral print ties (about $40), contrasting print shirts (over $100), and canvas shoes with houndstooth checks (about $60).

The women's shoes, also great buys, range from classic ballerinas to elf boots and clunky Commes des Garçons-type wedgies ($50 to $150). Other accessories that convey his look are T-shirt turbans (under $50) and well-constructed leather bags ($100 to $200) that prove how Frenchified Kenzo's become.   —L.D.

Kenzo, 824 Madison Avenue, 737-8640. Open Monday to Saturday, 10 A.M. to 6:30 P.M. AE, DC, MC, V, checks.

ILENE CHAZANOF

F O R jewelry lovers, Ilene Chazanof's secret shop, three floors above Madison Avenue, may be the best store in town. Chazanof, a young Elsa Lanchester look-alike, has collected treasures upon treasures of antique jewelry for over sixteen years and sells them at prices that can seem like wholesale compared with those of many other dealers. Her shop is filled with Mission oak furniture, on which sit teddy bears bedecked with brooches and silver necklaces, and there are glass-front cabinets and floor-to-ceiling wood cabinets crammed with jewelry from the 1880s to the 1950s.

One case is filled with Georg Jensen silver, one of her specialties, with pins ranging from $49 to $125. Another has pins and earrings shaped as dogs and cats. Dachshunds, Scotties, and cocker spaniels abound. A carefully detailed silver owl buckle is $120. There is also a display of Mexican sterling silver, including pieces by William Spratling, the American professor of architecture who encouraged the Mexicans to refine their silver jewelry. A Spratling butterfly pin is $130. A third case holds pricier Art Nouveau designs with opals and diamonds in delicate gold settings.

The recesses of her wood cabinet drawers, each organized by category (silver earrings, insect pins, Bakelite bracelets), yield a wide, etched Victorian 18K gold wedding band, which is priced at a startlingly affordable $68. A delicate 14K gold chain, strung with a half dozen jade beads, is $185. In costume jewelry, there are the coveted crown-shaped pins by Trifari that our mothers wore on suits in the 1940s, $8 to $65.   —E.L.

Ilene Chazanof, by appointment only, 737-9668. Open Monday to Friday, 10 A.M. to 5:30 P.M.; Saturday, 11 A.M. to 5:30 P.M. Closed Saturday in July and August. Checks accepted.

MISSONI

THIS sleek shop sells Missoni's suits and cotton shirts for men, along with wool and silk skirts and dresses for women. While these clothes are elegant, they are not as striking as the knits, for Tai and Rosita Missoni design the most sophisticated knits in Italy—and maybe even in the world. Their colors are extremely subtle, with purple arrayed next to black, teal, and rust. Patterns are complex, and in some of their best designs, the Missonis have made sweaters and coats with abstract patterns or tweedy effects that *seem* to be one-of-a-kind. Because Missoni knits are so elegant, they are coveted and are also extravagantly priced. The sole reason to come here, if you are not well heeled, is to begin a Missoni collection with the moderately priced accessories. In this sleek glass box of a shop, sweaters cost upward of $300 and coats more than $1,500. So think socks and ties—or plan on a glorious splurge.

Men's socks may come in unusual blends of colors such as a chevron pattern in teal, green, and turquoise. In cotton, a pair is $22. Pure wool socks are $22 to $30. Men's silk or cotton ties come in muted plaids of purple, cream, scarlet, and teal ($45 to $50). Long knit scarves of cotton and wool are woven in stripes of lavender/olive/rust/black/white ($105) for men or women.

Should you begin to covet a Missoni sweater, you can haunt the shop for its sales (January and July), when a $300 sweater might cost around $200. In the other months, there is a rare, occasional markdown. —E.L.

Missoni, 836 Madison Avenue, 517-9339. Open Monday to Saturday, 10 A.M. to 6 P.M. Closed Saturdays in July and August. AE, MC, V.

MATSUDA

MATSUDA'S clothing delights because his fabrics are exceptionally tactile and his detailing is so intricate and surprising. His overall silhouette is gently avant-garde tailored, sometimes with slightly oversized blazers, coats, or trousers for men and women. But to get the sense of his clothes, you have to try them on. They do not possess what is known in the trade as "hanger appeal."

For example, what seems like a simple, oversized white cotton shirt might have a "puffed-sleeve" collar—a tube of cotton that billows around the neckline—and sleeves of white silk ($150). These clothes are never loud and shocking. The artfulness is quiet. They move with great fluidity. Even socks are subtle. Women's might come in black with wide stripes of rust and narrow stripes of beige ($15).

In menswear, pleated oatmeal linen pants are flecked in black ($220). A pure silk tie has irregularly sized black and gray polka dots on a beige ground ($40).

Sales are held twice a year, in January and July, with 50% markdowns.   —E.L.

Matsuda, 854 Madison Avenue, 988-9514. Open Monday to Saturday, 10 A.M. to 6 P.M. AE, DC, MC, V, checks.

Other branches: 461 Park Avenue, 935-6969. Open Monday to Saturday, 11 A.M. to 7 P.M.

LA PROVENCE
DE PIERRE DEUX

T H E two Peters, Pierre Le Vec and Pierre Moulin, import fabrics from the Provence area of France—the richly colored floral and paisley challis and cottons printed with eighteenth-century woodblocks by Charles Demery. The fabric may be bought by the yard, or as clothing or accessories for the home.

The most irresistible items in the two-story shop, even for people who cannot abide prints, are the enormous 52-inch-square wool challis shawls. The fabric is silken and never wrinkles. The prints are luxuriant: teal wool emblazoned with crimson chrysanthemums or purple printed with clusters of grapes and deep pink peonies ($125).

For little girls, there are sundresses each spring and long-sleeved dresses each fall that billow from the yoke, leaving the body happily unfettered. A dress may be crimson splashed with pink carnations, or have blue cornflowers on a white ground. In cotton, they are $35 to $95.

The women's dresses are extremely genteel and speak of country clubs and lawn parties. A typical long-sleeved, high-necked wool challis paisley chemise runs upwards of $300.

The best buys for men are the ties in emerald green paisleys on pink or blue grounds ($10 a bow tie, $20 for a regular tie).

—E.L.

La Provence de Pierre Deux, 870 Madison Avenue, 570-9343. Open Monday to Saturday, 10 A.M. to 6 P.M. AE, MC, V.
   Other branches: 381 Bleecker, 675-4054. Open the same hours.

POLO / RALPH LAUREN

I N this store that reportedly cost him $14 million to build, Ralph Lauren has created an environment that bespeaks old money. There is a monumental staircase, as well as Oriental rugs, and oil paintings of men riding to the hounds, young boys in bucolic English countrysides, and women in white lawn dresses, none of whom are Mr. Lauren's relatives. Even the sales staff reflects this blue-blooded image, albeit with a more casual gentility. One girl had short blond hair that shone like the hair of the 1950s Breck girls, a white polo shirt (collar turned up), white slacks, and a white sweater tied oh, so casually around her waist. Yet, while Lauren has touched the souls and pocketbooks of many Americans in his deification of the WASP, the store is *packed* with every hue and kind of person imaginable.

On the first floor, there are hundreds upon hundreds of ties, shirts, and handkerchiefs, all enticingly displayed, and all of flawless color and proportion. Shirts range from $42.50 for a button-down oxford cloth to $125 for Sea Island cotton. One day, there was even a rare item of kitsch—a souvenir handkerchief from Jamaica featuring muscular young men surfing.

On the second floor are sports jackets, suits, and slacks for men, along with a panoply of leather chairs and sofas. A handsome brown-and-white silk herringbone sports jacket was $430. Here, too, there was an understated whimsy, evident in the men's shorts decorated with celadon cabbage roses. Boys' clothes are also on this floor—the Young Gentlemen's Club.

The third floor is the women's domain, with potpourris and bouquets of fragrant flowers like freesia and lilacs perfuming the air. Two rooms are devoted to "rough wear," which includes country white clothes, with flounced white cotton skirts and ingenuous white cotton nightgowns. Others are for "classics," "executive dressing," and the women's Collection, which is filled with luxurious silks, including a bias-cut circle "Hampton" skirt of spindly brown flowers on a cream ground ($298). On this floor there are also shoes, including crocodile city sandals.

Home furnishings fill the fourth floor. There are quilts, lace-edged pillow shams, shower curtains (including ones of madras), and sheets. A snow-white wool throw was $100.

For those who like the Lauren look—and you cannot fault the man's unerring eye for beautiful fabrics—this store is nothing short of paradise. It is entirely possible to live and die, swaddled in his clothes.   —E.L.

Polo/Ralph Lauren, 867 Madison Avenue, 606-2100. Open Monday to Saturday, 10 A.M. to 6 P.M.; Thursday till 7 P.M.; Sunday, 1 P.M. to 5 P.M. AE, DC, MC, V, checks.

THE GREAT SALT MARSH

T H E R E seem to be two schools of thought about jewelry: sculptural and ornate. The Great Salt Marsh belongs to the latter school, which is immediately evident from its decor. Walls are covered in floral fabric. The white and pickled-hardwood floor has been painted with the occasional turtle, snail, or butterfly. The interior remains perpetual twilight, the better to spotlight the whimsical and baroque jewelry and accessories.

Lillianne Muller makes jewelry of found objects such as

beads, plastic buttons, and artificial flowers. A quartz bracelet watch is encrusted with black jet beads ($100).

Irene Reed crochets handbags, necklaces, and pins that are also soft sculpture. On one side of a black crochet evening bag there is an antique photo carefully framed in crochet. You can replace the photo with one of your own ($220).

From Wendy Gell, there are lushly ornamented bracelets with tiny dolls' heads surrounded by enormous cobalt crystals or translucent crystal dragonflies set amid a cluster of big jet-colored stones, along with earrings, necklaces, and pins. Prices run $60 to $450 for production pieces and up to $2,000 for one-of-a-kind creations.

While there is an occasional inexpensive pair of anodyzed aluminum earrings ($8), this is not a shop for minimalists. The specialty here is ornamentation.

Two major sales are held here, in early January and late July, with the entire inventory marked down 25% to 60%.   —E.L.

The Great Salt Marsh, 888 Madison Avenue, 517-2888. Open Monday to Friday, 10 A.M. to 6 P.M.; Saturday till 5 P.M. Closed Saturday in July and August. AE, DC, MC, V.

BACK IN BLACK
928 Madison Avenue, 737-4896. See index for main listing.

THE CHOCOLATE SOUP

O N the theory that children like to look at pictures of recognizable objects and not at plain, boring blocks of colors, nearly every item of clothing here, from T-shirts to raincoats, has flowers, hearts, a house, a hippopotamus, or Mickey Mouse, printed, embroidered, or hand painted on it. The effect is relentlessly winsome for adults, but lots of kids love it.

For newborns to ten-year-olds, there are T-shirts hand painted with zebras, bears, or stars and stripes; hand-knit sweaters depicting Gene Kelly singing in the rain; Mickey Mouse suspenders; and Hawaiian shirts. (There are also basic overalls, pajamas, raincoats, and swimsuits.) Prices range from affordable ($20 for denims) to pricey ($125 for snowsuits and jackets).

For adults, this is the home of that ubiquitous carryall, the Danish schoolbag, in black, gray, royal and navy blue, brown, green, purple, and red ($60).   —E.L.

The Chocolate Soup, 946 Madison Avenue, 861-2210. Open Monday to Saturday, 10 A.M. to 6 P.M.; Sunday 1 P.M. to 6 P.M. AE, MC, V, checks.

INDIAN WALK

T H E R E are two places where most Upper East Siders have their children's feet shod—Tru-Tred at 1241 Lexington Avenue and here. The smart parents shop during the week rather than on weekends, when there are often forty-five-minute waits. What makes these two shops more satisfying than department stores is not only the extensive range of styles and sizes they offer but the fact that their salesmen actually seem to like kids.

Here, there are sneakers from Nike, Adidas, and Keds; cowboy boots, school shoes, and party shoes from Capezio or Baby Botte. If your child is fidgety, give him a quarter to put into the Polyphon, a six-foot-high old-fashioned wood music box. He can press his face to the glass case and watch the carousel go round, the horses prancing up and down.   —E.L.

Indian Walk, 956 Madison Avenue, 288-1941. Open Monday to Saturday, 9 A.M. to 5:30 P.M. AE, MC, V, checks.
 Other branches: 2315 Broadway, 877-5260. Open the same hours.

ROGER VIVIER

ROGER Vivier approaches shoes as sculpture, and the museums treat his designs as art. This year, the Louvre's new fashion museum will mount an exclusive exhibit of his designs, along with shows featuring Christian Dior and other French notables. One of his classic creations is the "ball" heel, which starts like any other heel but an inch from the floor becomes a ball, perhaps of gold-colored metal or rhinestones. An evening shoe of black peau de soie with a rhinestone ball is $270. Vivier also conceived the comma heel, which curves deeply inward toward the instep and then juts out, just like a comma. A black suede pump with a gold comma heel is $350.

Among his less extravagant designs is the "turtleneck" sandal, available in black or white satin. The shoe stays on the foot because a wide band of satin wraps around the ankle and zips tight ($245). Another recent sandal is secured by an ankle bracelet that is a wide band of suede cut out in intricate curlicues. In magenta or emerald green, it is priced around $210.

Although he is seventy-six years old, Vivier invents anew, creating visionary wearable art.

Sales are held here twice a year, in January and July. —E.L.

Roger Vivier, 965 Madison Avenue, 249-4866. Open Monday to Saturday, 10 A.M. to 6 P.M. Closed Saturday in July and August. AE, DC, MC, V, checks.

TIME WILL TELL

FOR wristwatch aficionados, this tiny gray shop is one of the most satisfying of stores. Stewart Unger, the amiable and knowledgeable owner, has a stock of more than 700 working watches dating from 1915 to 1970. If the emphasis is on the classics—Patek Philippe, Bulova, Vacheron, Audemars, and Cartier—he also has less-expensive ones, notable for their charm if not for their rare workmanship.

For $175, there is a stainless steel Benrus with an embossed sunburst dial. For $2,500, there's a Patek Philippe with an oval platinum face paved in diamonds. He also has great flashy costume wristwatches around $150 to $200 that are almost more like bracelets, as well as Mickey Mouse watches from the 1950s. Each watch comes with a one-year guarantee.   —E.L.

Time Will Tell, 962 Madison Avenue, 861-2663. Open Monday to Saturday, 10 A.M. to 6 P.M. AE, MC, V, checks.

GLAD RAGS

F A C T : This is the friendliest, most helpful, and one of the best-stocked children's stores in the city. The owners, Gordy Woodhouse and her daughter Katie, and their staff perform a service that is nearly passé in New York: If you want something that is not yet in the store, they will actually telephone you when the item comes in, whether it's a week or three months later. Asked why they still bother, Katie laughs and says, "Fifteen years ago when my mother opened, she wanted a store that would be the kind she liked to shop in."

Where there is courtesy, there is also cheerful chaos. All shelves are open, so customers can pull down merchandise themselves. Jeans tumble helter-skelter. Children are blissfully happy here. Family dogs come in, tied to toddlers' strollers. Mothers nurse and change infants here.

The merchandise is excellent. This is the one store that carries all the basic outerwear—slickers, raincoats, coats, snowsuits, blazers, sweaters, and jeans—refreshingly unadorned, and in solid colors. Glad Rags leaves the animal prints, the cars, trucks, and fish for party dresses, shirts, and sweatshirts. They outfit newborns to twelve-year-olds in clothing from Levi's, Lee, Pacific Trail, Jean Le Bourget, Obermeyer, and Absorba. In the summer, count on finding Absorba's tank suits for toddlers in shades of pearl pink, cobalt blue, or crimson ($20). In winter, there are Jean Le Bourget's sturdy bright-red snowsuits as well as Pacific Trail's down-filled jackets and Obermeyer skiwear. This is a store that warms the heart.

Sales are held in January and June, with 30% to 40% markdowns. —E.L.

Glad Rags, 1007 Madison Avenue, 988-1880. Open Monday to Friday, 9 A.M. to 6 P.M.; Saturday, 10 A.M. to 6 P.M. AE, DC, MC, V, checks.

AGNÈS B.
1063 Madison Avenue, 570-9333. See index for main listing.

MURIEL KARASIK GALLERY

W H I L E this spacious gallery sells Pierro Fornasetti screens from the 1950s as well as Deco armoires, it also carries literally thousands of pieces of rather expensive but very handsome and well-chosen jewelry from the 1930s through the 1960s for the fashion cognoscenti.

There is sterling silver from Mexico, including a remarkable sterling cuff shaped as two twisting fish ($600) and William Spratling's earrings designed as blossoms ($125). Bakelite bracelets in ivory or moss green colors start at $50, and a compact in the shape of a French sailor's hat is $95. Chunky, geometric Lucite from the 1960s—clear and in colors like chartreuse—is less expensive. —E.L.

MALVINA SOLOMON

T H E windows are dimly lit, but press your face to them and you will see strands upon strands of Deco beads, dozens of Bakelite pins and bracelets, and a vast array of marcasite pins and rings. While Malvina Solomon tends to cater to the customer to whom these vintage styles were contemporary, this jewelry is just what a lot of younger people are looking for, too.

In Bakelite, Solomon has amusing pins shaped as flowers, as well as incised bracelets in cream, mottled greens, and rust. A three-and-a-half-inch-long bar pin with incised and painted flowers is $58, while an incised Bakelite bow is $38. From the collection of marcasite, a small brooch runs $85 and up, while an elaborate necklace is $395. And for the necklace fancier, she has over 300 strands of Deco beads alone. —E.L.

ROBERTA LINGERIE COUTURE, INC.

R O B E R T A calls itself a mini-department store, and indeed, it carries every conceivable kind of underwear needed by the female species—for the small or large, young or old, sexpot or dowager. Along with a wide array of flirtatious lingerie in pure silk, there might be a pink cotton nightgown with a smidgen of white lace ($34) or a Belgian linen gown ($140). Swiss silk-knit long johns are $76, but plain cotton Hanro bikinis are $11 each. There are also swimsuits, bathrobes, brassieres, socks, and stockings—right down to such banal necessities as nursing bras. Sales are held in January and July.   —E.L.

Roberta Lingerie Couture, Inc., 1252 Madison Avenue, 860-8366. Open Monday to Saturday, 10 A.M. to 6 P.M. Closed Saturday during July and August. AE, MC, V, checks.

JANET RUSSO

J A N E T Russo is a Nantucket-based designer whose forte is distinctly feminine, snug-at-the-waist clothing, best suited for women who have that ephemeral, wispy-tendrils-about-the-face, Pre-Raphaelite look. Hard-edged women should skip this place.

On the first floor, Russo has eveningwear that is aimed at youth in its prime, with wasp waists that can bear to be accentuated. For proms and debutante balls, she has strapless taffeta dresses with tulle skirts in black, white, or blush pink ($278). For the dewy-eyed bride, there are white polyester satin dresses with lace sleeves ($292) or without.

Upstairs, there are sportier clothes, including some offerings from other designers. But while there are simple oversized sweatshirts and hand-knit sweaters, the look is still feminine and genteel. Displayed next to the oversized black sweatshirt are the shoes Russo believes complete her special look—black ballet slippers by Mary Beth, hand-decorated with pink satin rosebuds ($72 to $106). This is a shop for the classic romanticist. —E.L.

Janet Russo, 1270 Madison Avenue, 427-8770. Open Monday to Saturday, 10 A.M. to 6 P.M.; Thursday till 7 P.M.; Sunday, noon to 5 P.M. Closed Sunday in July and August. AE, MC, V, checks.

J. MCLAUGHLIN

I S it possible to be hip and classic at the same time? The buyers at J. McLaughlin try. The shop was formerly a bastion of sporty conservatism (dirndl skirts that ended 2 inches below the knee and argyle sweaters that stopped precisely at the hips). Now the store is pushing a slouchier, more relaxed version of a traditional look, both for men and women.

In women's sweaters, the specialty is hand-knits that are oversized and nicely detailed. A beige linen sweater featuring a beach scene runs around $170. Others start around $130.

What makes their women's pants and skirts different from, say, Brooks Brothers', are the silhouette and the fabrics. Skirts are traditionally pleated or dirndl-styled, but they are cut long, nearly grazing the ankles, and have a luxurious swoop to them; prices are $50 to $150. Pants are cut more fully, and all the clothes come in unexpected fabrics, such as jacquards.

For men, the gamut ranges from the omnipresent khaki pants ($50) to linen slacks that may have subtle flecks of black on a gray or wheat-colored ground ($130). Lest preppies think the shop has gone too far left, there are also classic cable-knit sweaters and sets of silk braces ($80).   —E.L.

J. McLaughlin, 1311 Madison Avenue, 369-4830. Open Monday to Friday, 10 A.M. to 6 P.M.; Thursday till 7 P.M.; Saturday, 11 A.M. to 6 P.M.; Sunday, 1 P.M. to 5 P.M. Closed Sunday during the summer. AE, MC, V, checks.

Other branches: 1343 Third Avenue, 879-9565. Open Monday to Friday, 11 A.M. to 9 P.M.; Saturday till 6 P.M. 976 Second Avenue, 308-4100. Open the same hours.

THE OLD BUCKLE

B E C A U S E of its out-of-the-way location, this is an almost unknown "secret" shop of antique clothing, where prices are so reasonable (by New York standards) as to boggle the mind. The few items that are expensive are deservedly so.

For over five years, Adelaide Sena and Oscar Livrati have kept this shop, where they pore over their clothes, keep the steam iron in perpetual use, and lovingly explain their favorite pieces.

One spring day, the buy of the moment was a to-the-floor size 10 fitted beige linen coat, hand-embroidered down the front in pale tendrils of pink, cream, and green ($95). Another full-length fitted coat, moss-green with mother-of-pearl buttons and a swooping, curving hem, dated from the 1920s ($200).

Less ornate were a black rayon circle skirt striped in navy blue, magenta, and yellow ($35), and a long-sleeved black silk chiffon shirtwaist ($45). As they say in the *Guide Michelin,* this place is worth a detour.   —E.L.

The Old Buckle, 1658 Third Avenue, 860-2161. Open Monday to Friday, noon to 7 P.M.; Saturday till 6 P.M. Discover, MC, V, checks.

GWENDA G.

O N the corner, up three steps, is this shop filled with charming antique clothes for women, with a few treasures for lucky little girls and boys.

The windows are decorated with antique perfume flacons and silver-gilt hand mirrors, and hung with fragile silk chiffon evening dresses and infant frocks. Inside, there are 1930s upholstered chairs for easy browsing.

A 1920s red silk chiffon beaded flapper dress in mint condition was $380, while a white cotton slip that a small child could wear as a summer dress was fairly priced at $20. Victorian blouses lavishly trimmed with lace may start at $72.   —E.L.

Gwenda G., 1364 Lexington Avenue, 427-9672. Open Monday to Friday, 11 A.M. to 7 P.M.; Saturday till 6 P.M. Closed Saturdays in July and August. No credit cards. Checks (accepted only from neighborhood residents with ID).

TRU·TRED

C H I L D R E N like to buy their shoes here for two reasons. First, there is a vast collection of basic, party, and especially silly shoes (moccasins with colored stones, winter boots that look fit for walking on the moon). Second, at the rear of the store, sitting on the carpet, there is a barrel of pretzels, free for the taking, as well as a free nickelodeon and a big, stuffed elephant wearing tennis shoes.

The store carries domestic and imported shoes and boots, so you can pay $18 up to $40 for a pair of sneakers. For boys, there are plain sneakers of canvas or leather, loafers, lace-ups, and coveted cowboy boots. For girls, there are assorted variations on the Mary Jane, including plain ones, ones with scalloped edges, and ones with bows. The staff is completely at ease with children and measure not just the length of the child's foot but also the width. Every three months, the store will send you a reminder that Johnny's feet have grown and that you're due in for more shoes and more pretzels.

To avoid forty-five minute waits or more, shop on weekdays and never on weekends. Sign your name on a ledger at the door and wait for your name to be called. During that wait, a huge number of pretzels will be eaten.

Sales are held in late December and late June, markdowns up to 50%. —E.L.

Tru-Tred, 1241 Lexington Avenue, 249-0551. Open Monday to Wednesday, 9:30 A.M. to 5 P.M.; Thursday till 7 P.M.; Friday till 6 P.M.; Saturday till 4:45 P.M. Call to find out extended hours during the back-to-school rush. AE, MC, V, checks.

KAREN'S FOR PEOPLE
AND PETS

I N the lobby of this black-lacquered pet-grooming salon, Pekingese with pink satin bows in their hair wait patiently for their owners. But few doting pet parents can simply collect their charges and leave without at least browsing through the animal fashions. This is where you'll find the city's most extensive collection of hand-knit dog sweaters. One sweater comes in red and black checks, while another is pink on one side and gray on the other, with a cable stitch running down the middle. For the dog who likes costume, there is even a sweater designed as a tuxedo, complete with a snappy bow tie. Most sweaters run about $50.   —E.L.

Karen's for People and Pets, 1220 Lexington Avenue, 472-9440. Open Monday to Saturday, 8 A.M. to 6 P.M. AE, MC, V, checks.

JENNY B. GOODE

I T is rare to find a shop that sells toys, clothes, dish towels, jewelry, and French china, but Jeannette Gavaris's has flourished for thirteen years. The formula for her success is that whimsy pervades the teapots, toys, and dish towels, but in clothing, good taste prevails.

The jewelry she features is both new and antique, but the latter is the more appealing. At one visit, there was a carnelian Deco choker for $195, the same price as a Victorian bar pin with a bird and three stars. The most curious pieces here are the muff chains. At the turn of the century, the era of furry muffs, a woman hung a delicate 60-inch-long chain around her neck and looped the chain through the muff so she could have her hands free. These silver chains start at $195, depending on how many crystal beads embellish them.

For clothing, count on terry cloth or European cotton robes; a Belgian robe of waffle cotton is $60. A plain denim child's apron is $17.50. Capacious bags are a specialty. In summer, there are linen totes, and in winter, fat leather pouches to hold notebooks and running shoes. There is also a small collection of evening bags.   —E.L.

Jenny B. Goode, 1194 Lexington Avenue, 794-2492. Open Monday to Saturday, 10 A.M. to 6:30 P.M. AE, DC, MC, V, checks.
   Other branches: 11 East 10th Street, 505-7666. Open Monday to Friday, 10 A.M. to 6:30 P.M.; Saturday till 6 P.M.

J. MCLAUGHLIN
1343 Third Avenue, 879-9565. See index for main listing.

SAN FRANCISCO

O R I G I N A L L Y, Howard Partman, the owner/designer of this shop, was famous for taking tweediness to a new elegance. Traditional cuts were slightly stylized, updated, and polished in beautiful fabrics. Hallmarks were his tiny wingtip collars and miniature bow ties, along with a superb collection of Fair Isle sweaters, for both men and women. But the trends have changed, and Partman has shifted with the fashion times in his own understated, discreet way.

To begin with, Partman's store is now devoted almost exclusively to women, with only about 10% reserved for men. What's strictly for men are tailored shirts, which now have absolutely normal collars that can be worn on Wall Street. A shirt may be of cream-colored jacquard or of blue-and-white gingham. Prices start at $65.

For women, eclecticism has become the watchword. Women's suits (about $385) are still elegant, but now may recall the 1940s with peplums, or echo Chanel. Casual clothes are old-fashioned funky—polka dot shorts with a Florida sailfish print shirt (shirts start at $38). Standouts are unusual, genteelly extravagant blouses. A pale yellow silk sleeveless shell is intricately hand-embroidered ($225), while a long-sleeved cream silk shirt is hand-beaded across the bodice and along the collar with little pearly sprigs of flowers ($325).

Partman knows how to mine the past and make it modern with elegance.

Sales are held in January and July.   —E.L.

San Francisco, 975 Lexington Avenue, 472-8740. Open Monday to Friday, 10 A.M. to 7 P.M.; Saturday, 11 A.M. to 6 P.M. AE, MC, V.

ASHANTI LARGER SIZES

O N Lexington Avenue between 65th and 66th streets are two shops for large-sized women. The Forgotten Woman (888 Lexington, 535-8848) carries a wide range of sportswear, underwear, business, and evening clothes with commercial labels like Evan Picone. This is a good spot for basics, but most of the merchandise is somewhat drab.

Ashanti, several doors to the south, started out in 1971 selling ethnic gear (hence the store's original name, Ashanti Bazaar). It's gone on to develop several private-label lines that aim at and often achieve true elegance for sizes 14 to 24.

Much of the merchandise is classics in good fabrics: linen shells, silk camp shirts, drapey gabardine coatdresses, and wool cowl-neck sweaters. Nothing's avant-garde here. You won't find size-20 versions of Claude Montana or Rifat Ozbek. But you can buy silk tap pants and camisoles, and jersey tube dresses, trumpet skirts, and double-breasted blazers—the sort of clothes that have traditionally (and maybe mistakenly) been regarded as taboo in large sizes. Ashanti sells a lot of them to eager customers, and the sales staff is adept at helping the occasional doubter overcome trumpet skirt fear and similar prejudices.

The forte here is cocktail dresses with deep V-necks and bias-cut skirts. They're priced from $100 to $800 (for evening velvets). Tops are $60 to $285; jackets, $110 to $300; skirts, $85 to $225; and unconstructed suits, $130 to $375. Handmade kimono coats with collages of precious fabrics are $500.

Sales with steep reductions are held every January and July.

—L.D.

Ashanti Larger Sizes, 872 Lexington Avenue, 535-0740. Open Monday to Saturday, 10 A.M. to 6 P.M.; Thursday till 8 P.M. AE, CB, DC, MC, V, checks.

CHERCHEZ

T H E Anglo-French country ambience—pine hutches, terra-cotta tile floor, and the pervasive scent of fieldflower potpourri—teeters between charming and overkill. It evokes Laura Ashley, though the goods at Cherchez are authentic and of far higher quality.

When it started in 1974, Cherchez carried only handmade Victorian whites surrounded by sachets and potpourris. Over the years, it's branched out into small antiques, European bed linens, fine cotton robes from France and Italy, and its own line of new clothes based on vintage styles.

The antique lingerie and petticoats go from $150 to over $2,000, with most items under $300. Christening gowns seem like bargains at $75 to $150 when the handkerchiefs are over $100. Not cheap, but these wares are in excellent condition, and connoisseurs of Victoriana shop regularly here.

The new clothes are blouses and dresses copied from a man's antique collared nightshirt with yoked back and cuffed sleeves. They cost $125 to $225 and come in wool challis and Liberty cotton prints and lawns, as well as solid-colored linen.

Girls' blouses and pinafores based on Kate Greenaway drawings are extremely adorable in color-coordinated Liberty prints. Sized 6 months to 6 years, they're under $50 each.

Cherchez's most incredibly beautiful commodities are the large silk and wool paisley shawls, circa 1800 to 1870. Originally worn over bustle dresses, they look great today flung over a shoulder or draped on any tattered sofa. But if you can afford their prices, $600 to $1,200, your sofa's undoubtedly in excellent condition.   —L.D.

Cherchez, 862 Lexington Avenue, 737-8215. Open Monday to Friday, 11 A.M. to 6 P.M.; Saturday till 5:15 P.M. AE, MC, V, checks.

PUTUMAYO
857 Lexington Avenue, 734-3111. See index for main listing.

HENRY LEHR

IF you seek the quintessential luxury sportswear—an appliquéd denim jacket or the softest stone-washed jeans—you're sure to find it at Henry Lehr. He offers a unique package—vintage-looking cowboy, jogging, and military looks in new but prewashed luxury fabrics. The hangtags on his clothes say, "washed, wrecked and comfortable," but with his suave sense of style, the clothes come out looking impeccably retro and chic.

Lehr, who was known as the jeans king of 1960s London, brought his notion of luxury casual dressing to New York when

---

he opened his first shop on Third Avenue in 1974. He now has branches on Madison and Columbus avenues, and on West Broadway in Soho. Most of the stores emphasize women's clothes, although the Soho and Columbus Avenue branches tend to stock more menswear.

A lot of the goods, like the Belgian-made cottons, rayons, denims, and cords sold under the Go On and Tomorrow's Surplus labels, are designed by Lehr himself. His latest endeavors are Go Silk, Go Linen, Go Knit, and Go Leather separates, dresses, and especially magnificent big-pocketed jumpsuits in these sumptuous, presoftened fabrics. You'll see them imitated, but only the original Go lines feel unspeakably slithery and sensual, are dyed in lush colors, and have Lehr's assured styling. Their prices range from $100-plus to $1,000-plus (for a full-length leather coat). Most shirts and pants are about $150.

Lehr was also the first to import Katherine Hamnett's sportswear, which has a similar nostalgic, recycled quality and sells for $100 to $400. Also on hand are T-shirts with elegant details—even rhinestones—costing over $150, and the latest in jewel-encrusted and Western belts.

The stores have occasional clearance sales with discounts starting at 50% off, and often more.   —L.D.

Henry Lehr, 1079 Third Avenue, 753-2720. Open Monday and Thursday, 10 A.M. to 7:30 P.M.; Tuesday, Wednesday, and Friday till 7 P.M.; Saturday till 6 P.M.; Sunday, noon to 6 P.M. AE, MC, V, checks.

Other branches: 464 West Broadway, 460-5500. Open Monday to Saturday, 11 A.M. to 7 P.M.; Sunday, noon to 6 P.M. 772 Madison Avenue, 535-1021. Open Monday to Friday, 10 A.M. to 7 P.M.; Saturday till 6 P.M. 410 Columbus Avenue, 580-0533. Open Monday to Saturday, 11 A.M. to 7 P.M.; Sunday, noon to 6 P.M.

CAROL ROLLO/
RIDING HIGH
1147 First Avenue, 832-7927. See index for main listing.

THE UPPER WEST SIDE

INTRODUCTION BY
Elaine Louie

Just ten years ago, the Upper West Side was primarily a residential area peopled by actors, professors, doctors, lawyers, art dealers, socialites—and the elderly poor, living in single-room occupancy apartments or hotels, only a block or two from the neighborhood's grandest apartment buildings.

Among those buildings with endearing and enduring architectural value is the Ansonia Hotel at 2109 Broadway. Built in a Belle Epoque style, it was home to the musicians Enrico Caruso, Arturo Toscanini, and Igor Stravinsky, who favored this place because of its exceptionally thick walls and floors. The Dakota Apartments at 1 West 72nd Street, one of the first luxury apartment houses built in the city, was built in a German Renaissance/Romanesque style topped with Victorian dormers and turrets. This neighborhood landmark was the setting for *Rosemary's Baby* and home to John Lennon and Yoko Ono.

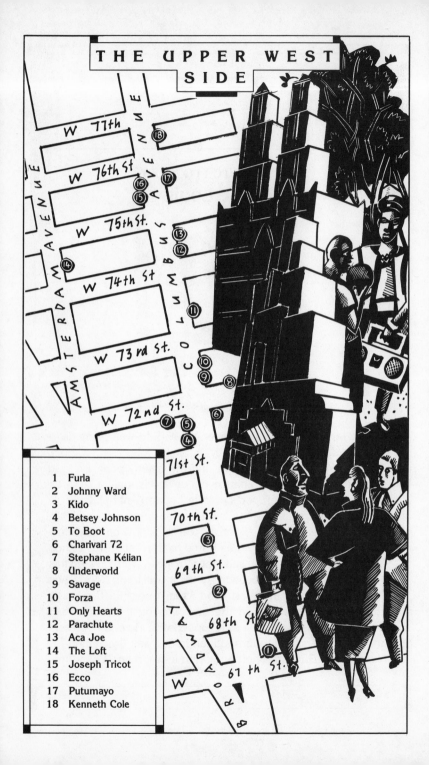

THE UPPER WEST SIDE

1 Furla
2 Johnny Ward
3 Kido
4 Betsey Johnson
5 To Boot
6 Charivari 72
7 Stephane Kélian
8 Underworld
9 Savage
10 Forza
11 Only Hearts
12 Parachute
13 Aca Joe
14 The Loft
15 Joseph Tricot
16 Ecco
17 Putumayo
18 Kenneth Cole

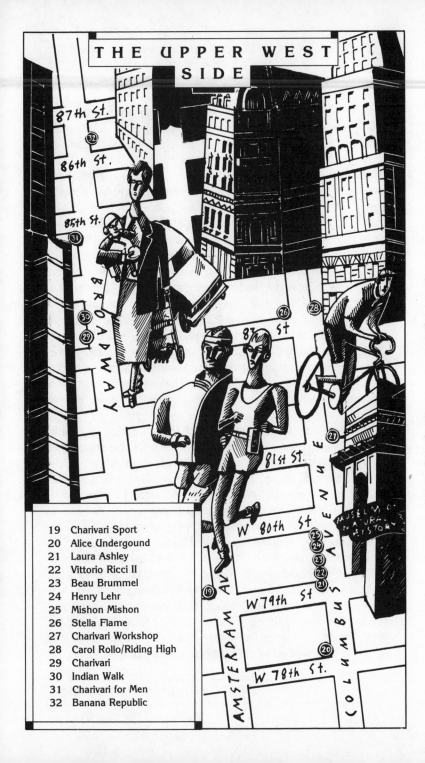

THE UPPER WEST SIDE

19 Charivari Sport
20 Alice Undergound
21 Laura Ashley
22 Vittorio Ricci II
23 Beau Brummel
24 Henry Lehr
25 Mishon Mishon
26 Stella Flame
27 Charivari Workshop
28 Carol Rollo/Riding High
29 Charivari
30 Indian Walk
31 Charivari for Men
32 Banana Republic

And the apartment buildings share space with some of the city's great cultural and educational institutions, such as the Museum of Natural History and, farther north, Columbia University.

But what the Upper West Side had never been until the past few years was a consumer's paradise. Today, this area's tenements are going co-op and its shoe repair shops are turning into trendy, upscale boutiques.

Strolling up and down the three main avenues—first Columbus, then Amsterdam, and finally Broadway—you will actually see gentrification at work, moment by moment. While some of the local residents still maintain their brand of casual dressing, once typified by sweatshirts, jeans, and running shoes for men and women alike, many of the people on the street have become considerably more chic. Where on a winter day you used to see people dressed in down coats, now you see couples clothed in mink, fox, and beaver, hand in hand with fur-coated toddlers, roaming the avenue. (Greenstones et Cie, a children's store at 442 Columbus, actually sells a bunny-fur coat for little girls.) Once you grabbed an ice-cream cone from a drugstore; now you buy gelato from marble-and-poured-concrete palaces lit by neon. To see what gentrification has wrought, begin with Columbus Avenue, which has undergone the most radical change.

Ten years ago, Columbus Avenue had pizza parlors, a couple of plant-filled, blond-wood restaurants, secondhand shops that sold slightly battered oak furniture, Mom and Pop groceries, and drugstores. Today, it's chic. There are limousines double-parked on the avenue, and restaurants catering to the movie star crowd that are so popular that ordinary customers have to line up behind a red velvet rope and pray to get in.

For shopping, it doesn't yet rival Madison Avenue since the haute couture stores—Yves Saint Laurent, Emanuel Ungaro, and Gianni Versace—stay rooted on the East Side. But on Columbus Avenue, in places like the Charivari shops, you will find designs by Versace, Armani, and Jean-Paul Gaultier that are as expensive as those found on the East Side. Don't just go after the major game, however. There are some engaging stores to browse through in between fashion forays.

One of the most whimsical stores in the city is Mythology Unlimited at 370 Columbus. A toy store for adults, it carries antique wind-up toys such as a chef who flips a pancake in his frying pan, odd postcards from the 1950s featuring a mother and daughter baking a cake and beaming unnaturally at each other, and small wind-up Godzillas from Japan. Penny Whistle Toys at 448 is one of the most appealing toy stores in the city because the merchandise is delightfully displayed and includes such classics as Monopoly and Magnetic Fishing, along with silly stuff like hot pink feather boas. Endicott Booksellers at 450 offers a fine selection of quality fiction and nonfiction. For food, Shun Lee West at 43 West 65th Street, right off the avenue, has exceptional Chinese food, including Szechwan dumplings and a curried beef turnover wrapped in a handmade egg crepe fried until golden.

Amsterdam Avenue is also gentrifying. For many years, its chief consumer product was food. Spanish restaurants had (and still have) rich, hearty sopa gallego, full of kale, white beans, potato, and pork, along with cups of rich, aromatic espresso. And for those who like Sundays spent around a platter of smoked fish, Barney Greengrass, at 541, has reigned as the self-proclaimed sturgeon king since 1929. But the buildings were run-down and many shops were boarded up.

Today, Amsterdam Avenue is filled with many of the same fur-coated people who shop Columbus Avenue. Proof that Amsterdam is chic is the fact that Charivari, the group of six stores devoted to elegant and avant-garde clothing for men and women, which began on the Upper West Side, opened its newest branch on the corner of Amsterdam and 79th Street. If Columbus Avenue has more shops to clothe the body, Amsterdam's specialty may be shops with home accessories. Now the old secondhand furniture shops have upgraded their merchandise from scruffy chairs and tired $35 chenille bedspreads to burnished armoires and $400 quilts. Things Antique, at 483 Amsterdam, sells hand-painted wood trunks from England, while Edith's Nostalgia at 469 has hundreds of pieces of Russel Wright china, along with a large collection of authentic turn-of-the-century lighting fixtures.

For noshing, Sarabeth's Kitchen at 423 has expanded from a

nook to a full-blown restaurant offering excellent sandwiches on seven-grain bread, perfect almond croissants, and cup upon cup of freshly brewed coffee. It is one of the few places in town where your cup is automatically refilled.

Of the avenues, Broadway is the least changed. It is basically foodland for the consumer. While there are enormous supermarkets and hamburger joints dotting the street, the great food institution here is Zabar's Gourmet Appetizers & Caterers at 2245 Broadway. It has expanded to include an entire floor of gourmet housewares and household appliances (where it offers the best price in town on the Olympia Cremina espresso machine), and a shop devoted entirely to pastries and espresso. Further north is Murray's Sturgeon Shop at 2429, which is where actor Robert Duvall and food author Craig Claiborne buy their smoked salmon, sable, and sturgeon. The men behind the counter wield their knives with such deftness and dexterity that when they slice salmon, they produce pieces so thin and even that you can see the light through them. Never has fish met with such great respect.

To explore the Upper West Side, assume that Broadway is a route for food, while the other two avenues are for clothing, home furnishings, and upscale restaurants. The entire area is good for people-watching.

To reach the Upper West Side by subway: Take the IRT 1, 2, or 3 to 72nd Street and Broadway, then head east to Columbus Avenue. By bus: Take the M104 up or down Broadway, the M7 or M11 up Amsterdam Avenue or down Columbus to 72nd Street; or take the M29 across 66th Street to Columbus.

■   ■   ■

FURLA

159 Columbus Avenue, 874-6119. See index for main listing.

JOHNNY WARD

"RAYON can be wonderful and so can polyester," says eponymous women's clothier Johnny Ward, who mixes synthetics with luxe cotton, linen, silk, and wool in lustrous, offbeat colors and lean, sophisticated shapes. Johnny Ward caters to the "loose top, tapered bottom silhouette," with innovative designs in stretch fleece. Cotton and vibrant rayon knits are a specialty in crew-, U-, and boatneck sweaters and in above-the-knee and midcalf skirts from $52 to $112; and there's always an ample supply of basic leggings and tank tops.

Ward also works closely with several independent designers to "present an alternative to what department stores do." Look for tailored linen blazers ($175) with matching skirts and bermuda shorts ($90) in vivid linens by Passargada, and slinky silk jersey separates in phosphorescent greens by Anni Kuan.

Though small, this cleverly designed store uses hanging dowel rods and unobtrusive shelving to display garments in a most uncluttered fashion. Ward shops for new items every month with "an open mind to fabric and color," keeping stock in this far-from-the-maddeningly-crowded boutique fresh and exciting. Go-withs include show-stopping belts (to $300 for alligator) and cleverly modish hats by designer Deborah Harper ($120 to $350 for furs), creating a total effect, Johnny Ward surmises, that "is not a revolution, but fills a little niche." And a pretty little niche it is.

End-of-the-season sales here, held in January and July, offer 20% to 50% markdowns. —D.K.

Johnny Ward, 194 Columbus Avenue, 595-7918. Open Monday to Saturday, 11 A.M. to 8 P.M.; Sunday, noon to 6 P.M. AE, MC, V.

KIDO

H E Y, daddy-o! Take your chic child here and dig some jazzy Japanese threads that you'd wear yourself if only they made 'em that big. With clothes produced in Japan exclusively for the American market by a designer known only as Yoko, this is a flagship store for Kidoko, a soon-to-be-major franchise with new stores planned for the East Side and Long Island.

For the past two years, Kido has shown dynamic, high-fashion children's gear—largely unisex for ages six months to seven years—in bright primary colors, geometrics, letter and number prints. It's sportswear, explains one of the ebullient staff "for darling little guys and nursery school innovators" in all-natural fabrics (cotton, cotton flannel, and wool). Prices reflect adult, fashion-conscious styles: shirts are $20 to $40, shorts $20 to $30, pants $25 to $40, jackets and coats $40 and up.

For more conservative parents, there're snazzy accents that will outlast rapid size changes and add flash for a reasonable amount of cash, with or without Kido clothes. Best buys include abstract expressionist socks ($6) and ties ($12), brightly colored patent leather belts and suspenders ($8), belt-, shoulder-, and backpacks in durable nylon ($15 to $20), and straw-brimmed and reversible baseball caps. Totally groovy, baby!

Sales are held in February and August, with 30% markdowns.

—D.K.

Kido, 208 Columbus Avenue, 787-6564. Open Monday to Saturday, 11 A.M. to 8 P.M.; Sunday, noon to 7 P.M. AE, DC, checks.

BETSEY JOHNSON

H E R name and her body-conscious vampwear are legendary. From the shocking pink neon autograph in the window to the eye-popping blend of fluorescent lighting and clothing in the low-ceilinged balcony, this bustling flagship Mod-mart screams Betsey Johnson.

Her gift for the conceptual is everywhere—price tags double as postcards imprinted with her image, crinolines ($65 to $130) hang over the balcony in a claustrophobic chorus line, and fully coordinated ensembles bear fanciful names—like last season's Mary Quantish "Flower Power" collection of tops, bottoms, shoes, and gloves, and the "Hole in One" series with mesh cut-outs that perfectly captures BJ's fun 'n' sexy dress-to-excess ethos. Echoing the impetuous, unpredictable nature of the youthful market she's captured for over twenty years, Betsey Johnson's clothes are jammed onto freewheeling chrome racks that are rearranged according to season or whim.

"It's total nightwear and fashion statements," explains one typically vivacious salesperson, "from Victorian-cut Lycra and bubble lace to cotton sweaters that any woman can wear." Accessories match current fabrics (for example, $20 floral opera gloves) or provide solid-color accents, like her kicky studded belts ($10 to $40) and biker's caps with patent leather bills (from a range of $10 to $30 hats). This is the place to find these accessories and Johnson's full line (which is merchandised here the way God and Betsey intended, unlike the many department stores where she is sold), as well as special store-only items and a constant supply of sale goods. —D.K.

Betsey Johnson, 248 Columbus Avenue, 362-3364. Open Monday to Saturday, noon to 7 P.M.; Sunday, 1 P.M. to 6 P.M. AE, MC, V, checks.
   Other branches: 130 Thompson Street, 420-0169. 251 East 60th Street, 319-7699. Both open the same hours.

TO BOOT

M E N who fancy footwear get their kicks here. From sporty chalk pastel bucks to ostrich cowboy boots that cost megabucks, To Boot has shoes "for work, play, dressing up, and going out." Its made-in-Italia private-label topsiders, saddle shoes, lace ups, loafers (all around $100), and British-influenced "corporate combat boots" are the heart and sole of Bergdorf Goodman's tony shoe department, but this subtly lavish shop also boasts classic boots (from $210 in rough-out suede to a cool grand for alligator), high-fashion designer shoes, and gentlemanly accoutrements.

Linen espadrilles at $35 are a budget-minded option, but the truly well-heeled might plump for Cesare Paciotti's woven slip-ons with driving soles, A. Testoni's hand-pleated silk tuxedo slippers ($425), or To Boot's own crocodile penny loafers ($475). Those in step with fashion's fast lane will discover the fab French designs of Stephane Kélian, whose women's line is housed in its own store around the corner.

A full line of shoe-care products and logo-embossed leather shoehorns ($15) are staples in a handsome array of accessories, including antique stickpins, cuff links, tie pins, and collar bars with interchangeable semiprecious stones, wallets, key cases, cigar cutters, and crocodile manicure sets. There's a large selection of haute hosiery, including cashmeres; suave sunglasses, and silk ties, some with Memphis prints. Gianni Versace and the estimable Briggs, Adeney, and Swaine (whipmakers to the Queen) supply umbrellas from $40 to $170 with a crocodile handle—the final touch for head-to-toe elegance.   —D.K.

To Boot, 256 Columbus Avenue, 724-8249. Open Monday to Friday, noon to 8 P.M.; Saturday, 11 A.M. to 7 P.M.; Sunday, 1 P.M. to 6 P.M. AE, DC, Discover, MC, V.

Other branches: 520 Madison Avenue, 644-5661. Open Monday to Saturday, 10 A.M. to 6 P.M.

CHARIVARI 72

I N Charivari's steady expansion, this store developed for men and women who, as co-owner Barbara Weiser says, "only wanted designer looks"—specifically, European designer looks.

The men's section, which takes up the top level, is a virtual repeat of Charivari for Men on Upper Broadway. There are clothes from Giorgio Armani, Nino Cerutti, and Gianni Versace, along with jackets, sweaters, and coats from Claude Montana, Jean-Paul Gaultier, and Gianfranco Ferré—most of which are elegant variations on classics. For example, one season a refreshing alternative to a Burberry was Ferré's trenchcoat of a lovely, silken, lightweight taupe cotton ($400). A stark and dashing Claude Montana linen sports jacket was striped in black and white ($500), a departure from summer's usual collection of blue-and-white or gray-and-white striped jackets.

The women's section, too, is aimed at the customer who is convinced, even wrongly, that European designer clothing is better than American. For her, Weiser has chosen clothes to be worn to work as well as to cocktail parties, black-tie events, and for pure showing off. The first category might include hand-knit sweaters shaped like cocoons for $150. There have been purple and lavender vertically striped long-sleeved wool tissue chemises that cleverly narrowed as they approached the knees, thereby slenderizing the wearer. For work, you might even choose a jersey shift from Azzedine Alaïa, if it isn't too clingy.

For dressy affairs, there are always beautiful silk blouses and pants, or you might see a Claude Montana satin ballgown with a big-shouldered scarlet long-sleeved bodice with a plunging neckline and a straight black skirt (about $1,500). For pure extravagance, there are beautiful leather jackets that cost thousands of dollars and look it—for example, Valentino's black suede jacket with tiny holes punched around the neckline to create a lacy effect, or a Claude Montana short gray bomber jacket in the supplest smooth leather lavishly studded in chrome ($4,580).

All Charivari stores participate in the twilight sale held from 6:30 P.M. to midnight one day each July, with markdowns up to 80%.   —E.L.

Charivari 72, 257 Columbus Avenue, 787-7272. Open Monday to Friday, 11 A.M. to 8 P.M.; Thursday till 9 P.M.; Saturday till 7 P.M.; Sunday, 1 P.M. to 6 P.M. AE, MC, V, checks.

Other branches: See index for other Charivari stores, each of which carries different merchandise.

STEPHANE KÉLIAN
100 West 72nd Street, 769-3344. See index for main listing.

UNDERWORLD

J O C K E Y shorts look like hell? Check out a real Underworld, Manhattan's haven for "unique intimate apparel for men," where ladies can also find luxurious boxer shorts and sleepwear for themselves. Simply displayed in a neoclassical, tech-gray-and-black interior is a vast selection of fine briefs, thongs, T-shirts, boxers, robes, and pjs from France, Italy, and Switzerland, some of which are sold only here.

Purists will appreciate the world-famous Zimmerli's line of fine cotton basic underwear ($23 to $32); knit T-shirts, tanks and bikinis by Maglificio Biborgomanero ($25 to $55); and cotton boxers in traditional shirt fabrics and primitive prints ($18 to $30). Sleek seekers can choose from genuine Everlast satin boxers trunks (around $18) and a range of silks from $12.50 G-strings to famed lingerie designer Fernando Sanchez's $100 boxer shorts, or choose the engineered designs of Nikos that include a physique-focusing midriff tank top at $45.

Sleepwear nods off toward the luxe. Though there are eighteenth-century-styled nightshirts in fine cottons, the standout jammies are designer numbers in silk, some hand painted. Robes by Cerutti, Lanvin, and Charles Jourdan run from $100 to $200 in all-cotton terry cloth and up to $500 in silk. Dore Dore's comfy none-too-trendy socks pair rather neatly with Adolfo's zip-apart leather travel slippers for the look you've always lounged for. Now if only they sold pipes and newspapers.

—D.K.

Underworld, 49 West 72nd Street, 362-0438. Open Monday to Friday, 11 A.M. to 8 P.M.; Saturday till 7 P.M.; Sunday, 1 P.M. to 6 P.M. AE, MC, V, checks.

SAVAGE

T H E first thing you notice here is an obscenely huge pair of rhinestone-studded horn-rimmed glasses. "They're my signature," gushes Thelma Klein, the spunky woman behind them and this extraordinary collection of tacky-to-tasteful jewelry. Then there's the decor—faux marble walls and a high-camp mural of nude women bathing in a sylvan pond. "Isn't that gorgeous?" Thelma kitschy-coos. Well . . .

Sterling silver is a Savage highlight, from simple finger bands ($20 and up) to a large selection of silver and onyx rings in Victorian and modern settings ($35 to $100) to "one of a kinds in a not-silly price range," including designer pieces from

Glenda Arentzen, Marla Buck, and Steve Rosen. Native American designs in turquoise, wood, and beads are well represented, too. There are also festive, inexpensive baubles in fruit-shaped plastic, porcelain, and anodized metal.

Savage stocks a small range of party-perfect hats, which line the wall next to an impressive display of bolo ties and belts ($12 to $60). Thelma's glittering specs are also on sale and feature holes on the earpieces for dangling extra jewels—Oy! —D.K.

Savage, 267 Columbus Avenue, 724-4662. Open Monday to Friday, noon to 8 P.M.; Saturday, 11 A.M. to 7 P.M.; Sunday, noon to 6 P.M. AE, DC, MC, V, checks.

Other branches: 59 West 8th Street, 473-8171. Open Monday to Saturday, 11 A.M. to 7 P.M.; Sunday, 1 P.M. to 5 P.M.

FORZA

B R A V O! Belissimo! Italian modern doesn't get any fresher than the mostly men's sportswear at Forza, where you're liable to find new looks and lines a year before every other store has them. The secret? Monthly shopping trips to Milan for "very casual stuff, whatever is famous in Italy right now," says proprietor Selin Aykan.

It was Forza that introduced the paisley/brocade conversation-piece shirt and nouveau letter sweater and sweats years ago; last spring they showed Spuma's iridescent floral viscose shirts ($50-to-$100) and cotton "message" pullovers and cardigans in dazzling colors—all New York exclusives.

Striking 1950s mannequins (including a James Dean look-alike) dominate the small, ever-changing display window; inside, the rainbow-colored clothing is neatly organized on blond wood shelves and racks for instant eye appeal. There are terrific zip jackets and some blazer variations, but nary anything as formal as a suit. Designer denim is featured year-round (around $65), and casual, but on-the-expensive-side trousers appear in classic cuts and a variety of fabrics, from khaki to Prince of Wales wovens, according to season.

Though minimal, the accessories are wonderful: glistening silk ties, Dyaguar's mercerized cotton argyle socks (around $10), handmade Italian belts in brilliant colors, and always one or two styles of good-looking and eminently relaxed shoes (around $100). Committed clotheshorses will check in often for constant discoveries and the occasional markdowns between their usual August 15 and January 15 sales.   —D.K.

Forza, 269 Columbus Avenue, 877-2070. Open Monday to Saturday, 11:30 A.M. to 7:30 P.M.; Sunday, 1 P.M. to 6 P.M. AE, MC, V.

ONLY HEARTS

I F you gotta have hearts, all you really need is Only Hearts, a romantic respite from the style wars of trendy Columbus Avenue. The porcelain nameplate on the solid wood door sets a suitably quaint tone; inside, the walls and radiator are pink, the ceiling is mirrored, and the air is sweetly fragrant with potpourri.

Owner Helena Stuart designs virtually all of the heart-festooned clothing—lingerie being particularly close to her heart—and the prices and the selection are better here than at the department stores that carry the Only Hearts line. Boxer shorts and T-shirts are available options for men, but young (and young-at-heart) ladies are the most loyal customers. Baby clothes and underwear sets for little girls ($15) are 100% cotton and 101% cute with tiny pink and red hearts, which also appear on women's T-shirt dresses (around $30) and sleepwear ($30 to $60). Camisoles, teddies, and panty sets (under $30) are both sweet with embroidery appliqués and sexy in stretchy cotton lace.

Knickknacks also conform to the Valentinian philosophy— picture frames, hangers, boxes, Bandaids, lollipops, or egg frying molds. Lolita sunglasses come in plain colors and fancy rhinestones ($9 to $18), and baubles include heart-shaped charms, rhinestone brooches and earbobs, and silver necklaces at prices that are hardly heartbreaking. —D.K.

Only Hearts, 281 Columbus Avenue, 724-5608. Open Monday to Wednesday, 11 A.M. to 7 P.M.; Thursday till 11 P.M.; Friday and Saturday till midnight; Sunday, noon to 5 P.M. AE, MC, V.

PARACHUTE

309 Columbus Avenue, 799-1444. See index for main listing.

ACA JOE

T H E concept developed from the resortwear boutique established by designer Joseph Rank in Acapulco. His vividly colored knit shirts emblazoned with the ACA JOE logo and style number quickly became a cult item for vacationing Americans, and so supplying the demand stateside was the next logical step. This all-cotton clothing operation, franchising faster than you can say McDonald's, offers those famed T-shirts and other seasonless merchandise (including shorts throughout the winter for under $30) in a stacked-to-the-ceiling high-tech milk-crate arrangement. Everything on the shelves is exclusive to Aca Joe stores and so it rarely goes on sale.

Still, these easy-wearing unisex Upper West Side staples like rugby shirts, pullovers, and chambrays achieve distinction through durable construction and a standardized, sober color palette (red, black, gray, medium blue, and always some variation on gold and olive) that minimizes shopping time dramatically. They're clothes that you don't have to think about and that look good on practically everyone, and with the night-owl hours this store keeps, you'll probably drop in just out of curiosity. Mia Farrow buys the wonderfully slouchy fisherman's sweaters here, and, at 68 bucks, who can blame her?   —D.K.

Aca Joe, 313 Columbus Avenue, 362-4370. Open Monday to Thursday, 10 A.M. to 11 P.M.; Friday and Saturday till 1 A.M.; Sunday, 11 A.M. to 11 P.M. AE, DC, MC, V, checks.
   Other branches: Pier 17, South Street Seaport, 406-0770. Open Monday to Thursday, 10 A.M. to 9 P.M.; Friday and Saturday till 10 P.M.; Sunday, 11 A.M. to 9 P.M.

THE LOFT

I F it weren't for the subway-grating-floored balcony featuring workout wear and an all-male video nook, they could easily have called this activewear outlet The Gym. The interior, best described as West Hollywood Nautilus, sports a neon basketball hoop above the entrance (where a giant but friendly German shepherd named Wilson stands guard), lockers line the walls, and the changing booths are toiletless stalls.

Emphasizing knockabout, jockabout separates that are equally attractive to women, and sometimes silly undies and swimwear (dyed jockstraps and suede loin cloths), The Loft's strongest season is spring-summer. That's when they bolster traditionalists like Calvin Klein and Henry Grethel with moderately priced new lines and a huge selection of cotton tank tops, campy printed T-shirts, printed camp shirts, and shorts by New York designers including Village Tailors, Contessa, and the impeccable (if pricey) J.G. White. Cotton sweaters, Speedos, beachworthy pants, and a host of accessories including jolly baseball caps (around $10), Christian Dior polka dot umbrellas ($20), and novelty watches ($25 and up) abound.

Fall and winter merchandise is less dazzling, if sturdy, leaning toward a preppy-cloney mixture of flannel, wool and leather, along with a good supply of athletic apparel. Most notable is The Loft's year-round stock of garment-dyed tanks, tees, and

93%-cotton sweatshirts in vests, extra-extra-large crewnecks, and hooded pullovers ($6 to $24) in more than a dozen dazzling colors. —D.K.

The Loft, 313 Amsterdam Avenue, 580-8430. Open daily, 11 A.M. to midnight. AE, DC, MC, V.
Other branches: 89 Christopher Street, 691-2334. Open the same hours.

JOSEPH TRICOT
320 Columbus Avenue, 787-0036. See index for main listing.

ECCO

I F the shoe fits, and it's fabulous to boot, it's probably at Ecco, purveyor of beautifully built French and Italian footwear in classic and high-fashion shapes and colors for women in sizes 5 to 10. While their Soho store boasts a witty park bench and astroturf decor, this uptown location offers plush Miami modernism with pink tile, moss-green carpeting, and unusually comfy try-on chairs.

From the ridiculous (Thierry Mugler's denim and rhinestone heels) to the sublime (flats that blend canvas and leather with pony polka dots), it's all here in a $50 to $300 spread, but the best buys carry Ecco's own label in timeless styles and a rainbow of colors, made in Italy and styled by owner Fred Marsh. Buckskin moccasins (around $60) are decidedly sporty in Easter egg pastels, and low pumps step lively in bright primaries. Traditional flats get a lift in leather, lamé, and festive patent leather or gain new exposure as in last spring's polka dot cut-out slingbacks ($100 to $125). The pieds-de-résistance, however, are Ecco's best-selling low-heeled, ankle-lacing little granny boots in at least six colors each season, a veritable snip at $160 in luxurious glove leather. —D.K.

PUTUMAYO

P A L M fronds sway gently, and colorful South American tapestries and folk art dot the blond wood walls—the only bit of paradisia missing here is a piña colada dispensary! Putumayo trades in "cool clothing from countries where they know what hot means," offering simple silhouettes in a price range that's just as comfortable as the fit.

Cotton is a year-round priority in knits and exclusively hand-loomed madras from India. Rayon appears in loose fitting "rodeo skirts" and jumpsuits ($30 to $60). Bulky knit cotton sweaters ($40 and up) are seasonless and winter wools are a new addition to the collection. Colors are tropiclassical (white, pink, and sea blue) with a nod toward the fashionable, and the generously cut blouses ($15 to $60) and summery frocks ($40 to $75) in pastel plaids, florals, and Victoriana suggest a Gidget-Goes-to-Laura-Ashley approach to casual dressing.

Accessories, from $6, include indispensable straw hats, voile sashes, and native jewelry. The colorful paintings and weavings decorating the store are also for sale. —D.K.

KENNETH COLE

T H I S is a store for people who think that staidness is a living death. Kenneth Cole has made his mark by designing whimsically inventive shoes in odd materials—he pioneered high-fashion black rubber footgear, for example—and selling them at highly affordable, if not downright cheap, prices.

For women, there recently were fur pumps with inch-and-a-half heels that came in white, brown, or black ($115); and for men, oxfords in olive green or black fur ($140). A pair of short boots for women was pleasantly schizophrenic: One side of each boot was solid-colored leather, and the other a splatter-painted suede ($110).

There are less outré shoes as well, also shockingly cheap. On one visit, the steal of the moment was splatter-painted leather espadrilles for men in black, brown, white, yellow, or turquoise, jazzed up with black squiggles. The soles were rubber, and the price a scant $19. For women, the cheapest shoe was also leather espadrilles, with elasticized rubber sides and black rubber soles, that came in black, white, green, or pink ($35).

Absolutely plain, classic shoes are almost anathema to Kenneth Cole customers, but for their rare sober moments, the designer provides solid-color flats or, for men, black patent leather slippers that can go to the fanciest of events.   — E.L.

Kenneth Cole, 353 Columbus Avenue, 873-2062. Open Monday to Thursday, 11:30 A.M. to 10 P.M.; Friday and Saturday till 11 P.M.; Sunday, noon to 7 P.M. AE, MC, V, checks.

CHARIVARI SPORT

T H E newest of the six stores, Charivari Sport has the lowest average prices, with most items hovering around $150. The emphasis is strictly on play clothes—*sportswear* in a literal sense. Nothing here is suitable for the office, unless your job is being a vee-jay for MTV. These are clothes for hip schlepping—sloppy, bare, and loud. Nearly all are European, and they all scream: *Play. Have fun. Get hip.*

Recent offerings for men included sloppy baseball jerseys with double sleeves ($75), chartreuse ikat shirts ($45), and Paul Smith's raglan-sleeved oversized cotton canvas coats in muted shades of teal or rust. ($175).

Women can find lots of clothes for baring skin or for flaunting a perfectly taut body. There are snug jeans and, last spring, a sexy, floaty collection of separates made of an airy midnight-blue crinkled jersey. The back of one jersey blouse overlapped like two petals, so if you bent over, the petals would separate and the small of your back would be bared. There were also big denim workshirt dresses ($145) that could go to the supermarket but not to the office.

All Charivari stores participate in the twilight sale held from 6:30 P.M. to midnight one day each July.   —E.L.

Charivari Sport, 201 West 79th Street, 799-8650. Open Monday to Friday, 11 A.M. to 8 P.M.; Thursday till 9 P.M.; Saturday till 7 P.M.; Sunday 1 P.M. to 6 P.M. AE, MC, V, checks.

Other branches: See index for other Charivari stores, each of which carries different merchandise.

ALICE UNDERGROUND
380 Columbus Avenue, 724-6682. See index for main listing.

LAURA ASHLEY
398 Columbus Avenue, 496-5151. See index for main listing.

VITTORIO RICCI II

T H I S is the store for the man or woman who likes easygoing, straightforward shoes for work or play that are neither klutzy nor high styled—and at a good, fair price. Its devotees range from teenagers to people in their lighthearted forties.

For women last year, there were red and white polka-dot skimmers for $45, and a plain black suede skimmer for $98. You could have the black ones for work and the polka-dot ones for enlivening summer's white knits. As fall approached, you might find a pair of nicely unadorned boots. An absolutely plain soft suede boot in black, brown, or purple came with a very low, easy-to-walk-in heel and a cuff that rose to just below the knee but could be turned down. It was originally around $175, but was marked down to a highly reasonable $98 at sale time.

For men there are basics like plain loafers in black or brown calfskin or black patent leather ($195); and for after hours, hilarious pointed-toe oxfords in black, red, or gray suede ($135).

Vittorio Ricci's prices are not unreasonable to begin with, so its sales are a bargain-hunter's dream. Recently, a pair of cream-colored low-heeled summer sandals with a wide grosgrain ribbon tied around the ankle was marked down to $25.   —E.L.

Vittorio Ricci II, 404 Columbus Avenue, 874-2830. Open Monday to Friday, 11 A.M. to 10 P.M.; Saturday till 7 P.M.; Sunday, noon to 6 P.M. AE, CB, MC, V, checks.

BEAU BRUMMEL

A C A C T U S plant stands by the door. The floors are bare wood. The customers, says the manager, are "Yuppies, vee-jay Mark Goodman of MTV, and Steve Crispin," the latter a restaurateur known to readers of gossip columns as Mariel Hemingway's husband.

What's popular here are the clothes of Hugo Boss, who may be America's answer to Armani. Boss's silhouette is faintly avant-garde, with jackets cut a little boxy and pants always pleated. Fabrics range from an understated black-and-white subtle tweed linen to a wake-up-and-notice-me muted dark-green-and-purple plaid. Depending on your boss, the clothes can or cannot be worn to work. A suit is $475, a jacket $295.

There are also dress shirts ($60 to $125), sweaters, and a large selection of sports jackets and slacks of linen, silk, and wool. —E.L.

Beau Brummel, 410 Columbus Avenue, 874-6262. Open Monday to Friday, 11 A.M. to 8 P.M.; Saturday till 7 P.M.; Sunday, noon to 6 P.M. AE, CB, DC, MC, V.
    Other branches: 421 West Broadway, 219-2666. Open Monday to Friday, 11 A.M. to 8 P.M.; Saturday till 7 P.M.; Sunday, noon to 7 P.M.

HENRY LEHR
410 Columbus Avenue, 580-0533. See index or main listing.

MISHON MISHON
410 Columbus Avenue, 769-2277. See index for main listing.

STELLA FLAME
476 Columbus Avenue, 874-5262. See index or main listing.

CHARIVARI WORKSHOP

AS the word *workshop* implies, this is the most experimental of all the Charivari shops in the city. While the Charivari 57 and 72 stores *always* carry expensive European designer clothing—you can count on Armani, Ferré, and Alaïa—the Workshop is in endless flux, so you can't expect to find any regular designers. As co-owner Barbara Weiser puts it, "The Workshop changes its identity all the time. It has a lot of clothes from the Japanese and the English, but there are always new rumblings here. We try to be on the cutting edge."

If the Weisers see a brand-new silhouette—say vast, oversized blazers or great, baggy pants—they will tend to bring it to the Workshop rather than to their other stores. If the color of the moment is chartreuse, you will find it here. The customer for this store is one who likes to dress experimentally and to cause heads to turn, probably one who's au courant with fashion, design, and art.

For men, there may be oversized black-and-white-checked ramie (a fabric cousin of linen) shirts from Comme des Garçons, and an oversized white polo shirt of exquisite cotton ($75) from Yohji Yamamoto. There are also double-pleated trousers in cotton/ramie or linen, many featuring intriguing weaves with slightly optical effects. Current jackets, especially from the Japanese designers, tend to be baggy with shoulders that droop a good inch or two beyond the normal shoulder.

For women, there are shirts, skirts, jackets, and dresses from Irie, Matsuda, and Yamamoto, including the latter's large, drapey white overshirts and tricky wraparound skirts that demand that the salesgirl help tuck you in. Katharine Hamnett always has some pieces here, often her signature white cottons that show up as very snug, short white skirts, or sexy sundresses with backs greatly bared. But the emphasis will shift as newer forms and design ideas emerge. This is the store that Barbara Weiser most likes to dress herself from.

Charivari Workshop also has one of the largest sweater collections in town, with prices ranging from $90 for cotton to

$200 for wool. In the back of the store to the left, there are moderately priced items. One summer, it was the season's basic designer T-shirts. An oversized short-sleeved tee in chrome yellow, chartreuse, black, or white was $40, and a skimpy halter was $15.

All Charivari stores participate in the twilight sale held from 6:30 P.M. to midnight one day each July, with markdowns up to 80%. —E.L.

Charivari Workshop, 441 Columbus Avenue, 496-8700. Open Monday to Friday, 11 A.M. to 8 P.M.; Thursday till 9 P.M.; Saturday till 7 P.M.; Sunday, 1:30 P.M. to 5:30 P.M. AE, MC, V.

Other branches: See index for other Charivari stores, each of which carries different merchandise.

CAROL ROLLO/ RIDING HIGH

MOST of the clothes here are for rich sexpots, both male and female.

A Thierry Mugler cream-colored rayon dress has strips of fabric for sleeves and for the bottom two-thirds of the skirt, so that each time a limb moves, it is entirely exposed ($935). For men, there are swim trunks and underwear by Nikos, who is to men what Azzedine Alaïa is to women. Nikos makes swimsuits and briefs that barely cover the crotch, just hide the buttocks, and are cut straight up the thighs to the waist ($85 for the swim trunks). The most curious thing, says the manager, is that the straightest-looking men in pin-striped suits buy these briefs ($50 to $85) by the gross.

There are also handsome ribbed sweaters by Jean-Paul Gaultier for Fuzzi (pronounced fooot-sy), cotton shirts and pants by Paul Smith, and in the winter, sports jackets and suits from Romeo Gigli.

For women, there recently were funny knockoffs of serious

Chanel suits, such as one where the classic cardigan top was paired with a miniskirt and the fabric was a turquoise-and-black abstract print ($325).

Sales are held in late January and late June, with markdowns at 30% to 50%.
—E.L.

Carol Rollo/Riding High, 483 Columbus Avenue, 496-7600. Open Monday to Saturday, 11 A.M. to 7 P.M.; Sunday, noon to 7 P.M.; Thursday during the summer till 8 P.M. AE, MC, V, checks.

Other branches: 1147 First Avenue, 832-7927; exclusively for women, with a wider range of merchandise. Open Monday to Saturday, 10:30 A.M. to 8 P.M.

CHARIVARI

TWENTY years ago, Selma Weiser opened this, the first Charivari, which at that time was the first and only store in the neighborhood devoted to stylish clothing for women. Prior to 1966, the chic Upper West Side woman had to trudge downtown to Bendel's and Bergdorf Goodman whenever she needed to shop, even for such common luxuries as a silk shirt or a cashmere sweater. Weiser gambled that she would find a clientele and soon she was proved right. In two decades, she and her daughter Barbara and son Jon have opened five more Charivaris, each store a little different.

This is the only Charivari devoted strictly to women and, according to Barbara Weiser, the "straightest" store. "It's geared to the working woman, who is our most traditional customer." Nothing is outré. Shirts are not see-through. Sweaters aren't skin-tight. Suits don't have miniskirts. Everything can go to the office without eliciting chauvinist hoots and whistles. Even if there is a piece of designer clothing, such as an Issey Miyake wool jacket, it is a simple kimono style that hangs loose and easy, not one that twists and fastens in mysterious, secret ways.

The store is aimed specifically at the woman who likes fashionable clothing but refuses to pay $400 for a linen dress or

$900 for a wool suit. Here, Weiser has cleverly interspersed clothes by Rebecca Moses, Adrienne Vittadini, and Cathy Hardwick (whose sweater-and-skirt outfits might cost $250) with the occasional jacket or coat by Miyake or Kenzo. The preeminent label is Max Mara, the Italian company, along with its less expensive Sport Max line. A recent Sport Max poplin dress that looked like an elongated shirt with deep pockets and big shoulder pads was offered in olive or chrome yellow khaki for $150. A black linen sleeveless blouse was also nicely priced at $40.

While this Charivari doesn't have the razzle-dazzle of the other five, it is an absolute institution for the local working woman. Whether she's a secretary or a top-notch lawyer, she can shop here and breeze through her work week.

All Charivari stores participate in the twilight sale held from 6:30 P.M. to midnight one day each July, with markdowns up to 80%. —E.L.

Charivari, 2307 Broadway, 873-1424. Open Monday, Tuesday, Wednesday, Friday, 10:30 AM. to 7 P.M.; Thursday, 10:30 A.M. to 8 P.M.; Saturday, 10 A.M. to 6:30 P.M.; Sunday, 1 P.M. to 6 P.M. AE, MC, V, checks.

Other branches: See index for other Charivari stores, each of which carries different merchandise.

INDIAN WALK
2315 Broadway, 877-5260. See index for main listing.

CHARIVARI FOR MEN

THIS is the store for the Upper West Side man who cannot tolerate the conservativeness of a Brooks Brothers or an

Oxxford pin-striped suit, and hates a pair of pants without pleats. He should also have lots of money to spend and have the aplomb to wear a slightly wrinkled linen sports jacket to a business appointment.

Not that the clothes are outré—the suits here are primarily by Giorgio Armani, Nino Cerutti, and Gianni Versace—but what distinguishes them are the fabrics. From any one of the three designers, you may find a black-and-white wool tweed sports jacket with the subtlest, faintest optical art effect that remarkably never jars. Or there may be a suit made of charcoal or teal wool with tiny rust-colored horizontal flecks woven throughout. Suits range in price from $500 to $700.

There are also sports shirts in odd shades of chartreuse, or iridescent gray, along with more discreet dress shirts. Sports jackets and slacks round out the store's stock. Come summer, many of the jackets and slacks are in linen, which wrinkles at the first sigh. These clothes are for men who can get away with the rumpled Don Johnson look without being fired by their bosses for looking sloppy and unprofessional.

All Charivari stores participate in the twilight sale held from 6:30 P.M. to midnight one day each July, with markdowns up to 80%. —E.L.

Charivari for Men, 2339 Broadway, 873-7242. Open Monday to Friday, 10:30 A.M. to 7 P.M.; Thursday till 8 P.M.; Saturday till 6:30 P.M.; Sunday, 1 P.M. to 6 P.M. AE, MC, V, checks.

Other branches: See index for other Charivari stores, each of which carries different merchandise.

BANANA REPUBLIC
2376 Broadway, 874-3500. See index for main listing.

ABOUT THE
CONTRIBUTORS

INDEX

ABOUT THE
CONTRIBUTORS

MARY PEACOCK (editor) is Style Editor of the *Village Voice*. She created and edits "V," its weekly section on fashion and downtown life, including the shopping column, "Getting & Spending," that inspired this book.

Peacock began her publishing career in the late 1960s as associate editor for *Harper's Bazaar*. In 1970 she cofounded and edited *Rags*, the seminal style magazine bridging the underground press and the regular fashion periodicals of the time. Two years later she helped launch *Ms.* magazine and became its first features editor. She joined the *Village Voice* in 1980 to develop "V" and, in 1986, the experimental color monthly, "Vue."

She has also written articles for a number of national magazines, including *Ms.*, *Redbook*, *Savvy*, and *Working Woman.*

STEPHANIE CHERNIKOWSKI (S.C.), from the wide open spaces of Texas, now roams downtown Manhattan snapping pix, spinning tall tales, and listening to longin' songs. She has published around, most faithfully in the *Village Voice.* Her photographs have appeared in publications ranging from the *New York Times* to *New York Rocker*, and have been exhibited internationally. She is a founding member of the exclusive equestrian society, the All-Girl Betting Team.

LINDA DYETT (L.D.), formerly taught English and American literature at the college level. Now she writes mainly about fashion and is trying to reconcile the shopping urge with the mercantilist experience of Joseph Conrad. Her articles are regularly published in the *Village Voice* and *New York* magazine. They have also appeared in *Family Circle, Travel & Leisure, American Craft, Vogue Knitting, Savvy,* and *Mode.* She is a contributing editor for *Threads* and style columnist for *Eastern Review.*

SUSAN FLINKER (S.F.) is the author of *Hip Hair,* a history and how-to guide on hairstyles with a rock & roll slant (Dell, 1985). She also was a contributor to *Fresh: Hip Hop Don't Stop,* a history of graffiti culture (Vintage, 1985). Her specialties are underground style/fashion and entertainment, and her work has appeared in the *Village Voice,* the *New York Daily News,* the *New York Post, Soho News, Trouser Press, Music/Sound Output, Rockbill, New York Paper,* and other publications. Currently she is writing about fashion for cable and network television shows, including the NBC prime-time newsmagazine *Fast Copy.*

DAVID KEEPS (D.K.) was born and raised in Detroit, where he wore an awful lot of plaid. He is currently living in New York, editing *Star Hits* magazine, contributing to the *Village Voice, Harper's Bazaar, Company,* and *IN Fashion,* while shopping his guts out. The three little words he longs to hear are "showroom sample sale."

ELAINE LOUIE (E.L.) writes about fashion, home furnishings, and food. She is the author of *The Manhattan Clothes Shopping Guide* (1978) and *The Manhattan Home Furnishings Shopping Guide* (1979), both published by Macmillan, and the shopping editor of *New York Access* (1983), published by Access Press. She is the "Home Beat" columnist for the *New York Times* and has also written for *New York* magazine and the *Village Voice.*

LYNN YAEGER (L.Y.) has lived in New York City for thirteen years. A lifelong trade unionist and compulsive shopper, she writes about clothes for the *Village Voice.*

INDEX

MAIN BRANCHES OF STORES*

* Main entries have store descriptions as well as listings of other branches.
Other branches also appear on neighborhood maps.

STORES BY MERCHANDISE CATEGORY*

Department stores and large specialty stores, with departments devoted to most of these merchandise categories, are listed separately to avoid repetition.

■ ■ ■

Department and Large Specialty Stores

Barneys New York,
176 – 177
Barneys Women's Store,
177 – 178
Bergdorf Goodman,
226 – 228
Bloomingdale's, 265 – 266
Henri Bendel, 223 – 225
Macy's Herald Square,
204 – 206
Saks Fifth Avenue,
237 – 238

■ ■ ■

Accessories

Agiba, 24 – 25
Amalgamated, 34
Antique Boutique, 82 – 83
Army Navy Stores, 257
Batislavia, 58 – 59
Bernard Krieger & Son, 135
Betsey Bunky Nini,
281 – 282
Betsey Johnson, 323 – 324
Canal Jean Co., 85 – 86
Capezio in the Village,
10 – 11
Chameleon, 23 – 24
Chanel Boutique, 230
Clear Metals, 63 – 64
The Dress, 146
Enz, 48
Fil à Fil, 282

* In category indexes, stores are listed alphabetically by first word of name.

■ ■ ■

Children's Clothes

Opium, 139–140
R. C. Sultan Ltd., 134–135
S & W Stores, 200–201
Syms, 163–164

■　■　■

Handbags

Fine & Klein, 143–144
Furla, 276–277
Jacomo, 270–271
La Bagagerie, 278–279
Lace Up Shoe Shop,
　141–142
S & W Stores, 200–201

■　■　■

Hats

Bernard Krieger & Son, 135
Clear Metals, 63–64
Dorothy's Closet, 26–27
Jay Lord Hatters, 213–214
Josephine Tripoli, 256
Modiste Fur Chapeau,
　203–204
Susanne Bartsch, 97–98
Victoria DiNardo, 125–126

■　■　■

Hosiery

Fogal, 272–273

Lismore Hosiery Co.,
　135–136
R. C. Sultan Ltd., 134–135

■　■　■

Jewelry

Agiba, 24–25
Back in Black, 101
Bumbleberry's, 185–186
Clear Metals, 63–64
Design East, 73–74
Detail, 124
Einstein's, 65–66
Eleven Saint Marks Place,
　48–49
FDR Drive, 119–120
Fiorucci, 268
Graffiti Design Studio,
　33–34
The Great Salt Marsh,
　298–299
Harriet Love, 112–113
Ibiza, 8
Ilene Chazanof, 293–294
Jenny B. Goode, 309–310
Jóia, 261–262
Lee Cheong Corporation,
　153–154
Le Grand Hotel, 96
Linda Dresner, 269–270
Malvina Solomon, 304
Maripolitan, 84–85
Massab Brothers, 263–264
Mishon Mishon, 266–267
Modern Girls, 14
Mood Indigo, 116–117

■   ■   ■

Larger Sizes

■   ■   ■

Lingerie

■   ■   ■

Men's Clothes

■   ■   ■

Pet Clothes

■   ■   ■

Men's Shoes

■   ■   ■

Trimmings

■   ■   ■

Vintage

■   ■   ■

Watches

■   ■   ■

Women's Clothes

■   ■   ■

Women's Shoes